AND THEN THERE WAS ONE

A Nurse's Memories of
A. G. Holley State Tuberculosis Hospital

AND THEN THERE WAS ONE

A Nurse's Memories of
A. G. Holley State Tuberculosis Hospital

A Memoir

Peggy Butler, RN, BSW

The New Atlantian Library

The New Atlantian Library
is an imprint of
ABSOLUTELY AMAZING eBOOKS

Published by Whiz Bang LLC, 926 Truman Avenue, Key West, Florida 33040, USA.

And Then There Was One, A Nurse's Memories of A. G. Holley State Tuberculosis Hospital copyright © 2012, 2015 by Peggy Butler. Electronic compilation / paperback edition copyright © 2015 by Whiz Bang LLC. Second edition.

Originally published by SeaStory Press.
Library of Congress Cataloging-in-Publication Data
Butler, Peggy, 1937- And then there was one : a nurse's memories of A.G. Holley State
Tuberculosis Hospital : a memoir / Peggy Butler. p. ; cm.
ISBN 978-1-936818-12-9 (perfect bound) -- ISBN 978-1-936818-13-6 (e-pub) --ISBN 978-1-936818-14-3 (e-pdf) 1. Butler, Peggy, 1937- 2. Nurses--Florida--Biography. 3. A.G. Holley State Hospital. 4. Tuberculosis--Patients--Florida. I. Title. [DNLM: 1. Butler, Peggy, 1937- 2. A.G. Holley State Hospital. 3. Nurses--Florida--Autobiography. 4. History, 20th Century--Florida--Autobiography. 5.Hospitals, Chronic Disease--Florida--Autobiography. 6. Tuberculosis,Pulmonary--Florida--Autobiography. WZ 100] RT37.B87A3 2011 610.73092--dc23 [B] 2011022520

All rights reserved. No part of this book may be reproduced, scanned, or transmitted in any form or by any means, electronic or mechanical, including photocopying, recording, or any information storage and retrieval system, without permission in writing from the publisher. Please do not participate in or encourage piracy of copyrighted materials in violation of the author's rights. Purchase only authorized ebook editions.

This work is based on factual events. While the author has made every effort to provide accurate information at the time of publication, neither the publisher nor the author assumes any responsibility for errors, or for changes that occur after publication. Further, the publisher does not have any control over and does not assume any responsibility for author or third-party websites or their contents. How the ebook displays on a given reader is beyond the publisher's control.
For information contact
Publisher@AbsolutelyAmazingEbooks.com
ISBN: 978-0692416280 (New Atlantian Library, The)
ISBN:10 0692416285

AND THEN THERE WAS ONE

Contents

FORWARD i

TUBERCULOSIS 1

   From a Historical Perspective 1

SIGNIFICANCE OF THE BOOK 13

Dedicated To Some Special People 17

PART ONE: 19

   A Nurse in Training 19

PREFACE 21

1937 21

ONE 43

TWO 57

THREE 67

FOUR 81

FIVE 95

SIX 111

SEVEN 123

EIGHT 139

NINE 169

PART TWO: 187

TEN	189
ELEVEN	201
TWELVE	211
THIRTEEN	223
FOURTEEN	237
FIFTEEN	249
SIXTEEN	259
SEVENTEEN	271
EIGHTEEN	283
NINETEEN	293
TWENTY	305
TWENTY-ONE	313
TWENTY-TWO	323
TWENTY-THREE	333
TWENTY-FOUR	341
TWENTY-FIVE	351
Postscript	365
Acknowledgements	367
Glossary	375
SUGGESTED READING:	383

FORWARD

In her memoir, *And Then There Was One*, Peggy Butler captures the spirit of A.G. Holley State Tuberculosis Hospital, the last freestanding TB hospital still functioning as such in the United States today. She gives us a true glimpse of it, its staff and changes in tuberculosis medications and treatment over three decades of her involvement with it.

She has also taken us back in time to nursing school as it was in the fifties when three-year diploma schools at large city hospitals were prevalent, and student nurses worked eight hour shifts and attended classes another eight hours five days a week. Her candid portrait of this type of nurses training bears little resemblance to the nursing schools of today, which are more academically than clinically based. The diploma schools trained their students to go directly from graduation and passing state boards to being in charge of floors or departments in hospitals. Their students did not need externships before taking this responsibility, because they had been in charge of entire floors of patients for the better part of three years in their training school hospitals, as well as on rotations in psychiatric, pediatric and tuberculosis hospitals.

This retired RN admits she never thought, during her days on rotation in a Cincinnati tuberculosis hospital in 1958, she would fall in love with tuberculosis nursing. She credits this love for it to coming to work as a young nurse at what was then Southeast Florida State Tuberculosis Hospital, in Lantana, Florida, in 1961.

All of us, who have had the privilege of being a part of this great hospital in beautiful southeast Florida, feel the same way about it. For those of us who work in tuberculosis, it is not unusual that, at one time or another, we have been told we are crazy to work with such a dangerous disease; one that puts all of us at risk for our own lives. However, tuberculosis care hooks a medical person and caregiver so deeply, it is difficult to turn away. To see patients from all walks of life come into treatment in such debilitating conditions it seems they will never recover, leave the hospital cured, healthy and productive in their communities again, is a blessing to those of us who have had a part in their recovery. Thank you, Peggy, for sharing and portraying this passion to others.

I highly recommend this book to all medical and nursing students and anyone else who has never worked extensively with tuberculosis patients. It is an interesting read for lay people, as well, especially those who have lived in southeast Florida and witnessed the large sprawling building which houses A. G. Holley State Tuberculosis Hospital on the beautifully landscaped grounds in Lantana, east of I-95, change from a 500 bed tuberculosis hospital to a 50 bed tuberculosis hospital within a multipurpose facility. I have had the honor of serving as its medical director since 1992.

David Ashkin, M.D.
Medical Director,
A. G. Holley State Tuberculosis Hospital

TUBERCULOSIS
From a Historical Perspective

Around 400 B.C, Hippocrates, often called 'the father of medicine', diagnosed a disease he named phthisis, derived from a Greek word meaning "to waste" or "dry up."

Before the nineteenth century, this same disease was commonly called consumption, from the Latin *consumare* meaning "waste" or "to take".

This disease is known to all of us, presently living on earth, as tuberculosis. At the beginning of the twentieth century, it was the leading cause of death in the United States.

Unfortunately, because the cause of tuberculosis and how it could spread so quickly from person to person was not known, there was no way to treat or prevent it. The only thing that could be done for the person so afflicted was to isolate him in a hospital called a sanatorium, derived from the Latin *sanare* which means "to cure".

These sanatoria originated in Scotland and came to the United States in 1885. This was due, in large part, to a man by the name of Edward Livingston Trudeau.

Trudeau, in his autobiography, tells of watching his brother die three months after being diagnosed with what was then called consumption, in 1871. As a result of taking care of him, he also was diagnosed with it in 1873, in his late twenties, the same year he became a medical doctor. He was determined to live out his life to the fullest and not let the disease destroy him as it had his brother.

With his wife, Charlotte, by his side, he set up camp in the Adirondacks in what he called Adirondack Cottage Sanatorium. He hunted and fished for hours every day in this brisk mountain air. It so revived him that despite his physicians pronouncing his TB hopeless, Charlotte and he started their family in those mountains of upstate New York.

Of their four children, three lost their lives to TB; Charlotte died in her teens, Henry, in infancy, and Edward, Jr., also a physician, in his twenties. That left his remaining son, another physician, Francis, to take over as director of the sanatorium when his father died.

In an amazing contradiction to the doctor's prognosis of a few months, not only did Edward live, he lived a positive and productive life for thirty-three more years. He did what he wanted during this amazing life, including writing about what was happening to him and the other TB patients who'd come to be cared for in Saranac at the sanatorium. For a man to live that long after he was given a death sentence, especially from TB, was unheard of, or there was no record of it until Edward Trudeau contracted it and created that record.

He died in 1915 at the age of 67. Known for his optimism, Trudeau believed it was within man's power to eliminate all infectious diseases, including TB. He devoted his life to that cause. After his death, the sanatorium he established was renamed Trudeau Sanatorium.

Americans living today are familiar with the work of his great-grandson, cartoonist Garry Trudeau, the author of the popular comic strip, "Doonesbury." Trudeau is the husband of former "Today Show" co-anchor, journalist Jane Pauley and the son of Francis Trudeau, Jr., whose father, Francis Sr., took over the sanatorium for Edward.

Besides isolating the patient in a sanatorium to prevent his spreading the disease to others, the only treatment given to him during those early times was doing what Trudeau did: getting him into the fresh air, regardless of the weather, assuring he ate nutritious foods and placing him on bed rest. Since there was no known causative agent, there were no medications to make him well.

Patients died in great numbers and most of those who did not, lived in the sanatorium for several years, often for decades, as had Edward Trudeau before them. Rarely did a patient's own natural body defenses 'cure' him and allow him to return to his home and loved ones. This pattern of living or dying went on until the late 1960s, when several things occurred to change it.

However, the cause of the disease was discovered long before then, in 1882, after many years of research by German scientist Robert Koch. His discovery was the tubercle bacillus, also called mycobacterium tuberculosis. Eight years later he discovered an extract could be made from killed tubercle bacilli. This led to the tuberculin skin test, still an important TB diagnostic screening tool.

Koch's paper was called "The Etiology of Tuberculosis" (the cause of tuberculosis). In his autobiography, Edward Trudeau credited it with being "one of the most, if not the most, important medical papers ever written." It was the inspiration for his own research on tuberculosis, which confirmed, not only Koch's bacterial discovery, but proved isolating TB patients in sanatoriums for open-air treatment was the best way to treat it in that day before the discovery of TB medications, and to assure the public health of those not infected.

A few years later, in 1895, a physicist by the name of William Roentgen discovered a type of radiation he called x-ray because he did not know what type of ray it was. This discovery led to the process of visualizing the lungs and the disease within them. From the 1930s to the 1960s, mass chest x-ray programs were conducted on adults in the United States, but because they yielded so few positive results, they were discontinued. However, the chest x-ray remains one of the most important diagnostic tools for tuberculosis.

A live attenuated, or weakened, vaccine, called the BCG, was developed early in the twentieth century. The Bacillus Calmette-Guerin was named after the two French molecular biologists, Leon Charles Albert Calmette and Jean Marie Camille Guerin, who developed it, not from the mycobacterium tuberculosis, but from a related mycobacterium called mycobacterium bovis. Bovine lactoferrin is a natural protein used to enhance the effect of the BCG. Contrary to what its name implies, it does not come from cow tissue. BCG, however, is also used as a vaccine against bovine (cattle) tuberculosis, which humans cannot contract.

The BCG was first administered to humans in 1921. Its widespread use in the United States was discontinued after tuberculosis medication regimes were discovered, because it (the vaccine) was not very effective. However, it is still administered in under-developed countries and, especially, to those infants and young children living within those countries where antituberculosis medications are rarely available.

Florence B. Seibert, born in Pennsylvania in the late 1800s, contracted polio at the age of three. Despite a permanent disability, she was able to walk. In her teens, she developed an interest in science. Whether it was a result of the polio and the disability is not known. One can only assume it was related.

Seibert planned to become a doctor, but working in a chemistry lab while in school changed the future for her. She became a scientist in the early 1900s, after earning her doctorate in biochemistry from Yale University. During graduate school, she was credited with discovering a way to remove bacteria from distilled water given intravenously to patients.

In Chicago in the 1930s, Seibert was working under a grant from the National Association for the Study and Prevention of Tuberculosis, founded in 1902, and known today as The American Lung Association. During this time, she improved a method for purifying the protein from tuberculin bacteria. She had isolated the protein while in Sweden on a Guggenheim Fellowship at Uppsala University. After several more years of research on this purified protein derivative (PPD), she perfected the PPD method of skin testing for the tubercle bacillus, also known as MTB, which became the standard TB skin test used in the United States. This PPD, or Mantoux, test remains the most reliable tuberculin skin test used in screening for TB exposure (infection).

Another important discovery, Streptomycin, was isolated from the soil in 1944 by soil scientist Selman Abraham Waksman, American professor of biochemistry and microbiology. Streptomycin, the first drug effective against the causative agent of tuberculosis, is an injectable antibiotic. Waksman was awarded the Nobel Prize for Physiology and Medicine for this discovery.

Surgery was often the only way to try to cure tuberculosis in many patients before medications to fight the disease were discovered. These surgeries were often disfiguring because during many of them, not only was a lung or large segments of a lung removed, but ribs, as well. This left the affected side of the body without the structural skeletal support it had prior to the surgery.

Even into the 1960s, after the advent of anti-tuberculosis drugs, surgery was sometimes necessary for a cure, but by then, the more drastic surgeries were rarely performed. Lung surgery for tuberculosis in the sixties usually was lobectomy or partial lobectomy, which saved most of the lung.

Within six years of its discovery by Waksman, several pharmaceutical companies were manufacturing Streptomycin and it was being administered to all tuberculosis patients. This was cause for hope until it was discovered many of the patients, who had initially improved after being treated with it, became resistant to the drug and grew progressively worse.

The breakthrough came in the early 1950s when multiple drug therapy was introduced in the form of three other drugs, paraaminosalicylic acid (PAS), Pyrazinamide (PZA) and Isoniazid (INH). Streptomycin was still given but no longer alone. It was the multiple drug therapy that caused tuberculosis to become a curable disease. Ethambutol and Rifampin were introduced in the 1960s and added to the anti-tuberculosis chemotherapy regimens.

By this time, most patients were treated as outpatients by the county health departments, although some still required hospitalization. The same is true today, although today's hospitalizations are for much shorter periods than in the 1960s.

This outpatient treatment has proven to result in no further spread of the disease to contacts of the diseased patient, because the patient remains on the medication as long as his disease process warrants. The key then, as now, was for the patient to take the anti-tuberculosis medications, as prescribed, on a regular basis, so he will not risk becoming resistant to the drugs. This is, and always has been, the only way a cure can be affected, and transmission to others can be avoided.

In 1958, INH was given to PPD positive (infected) persons on a daily basis for a period of one year. By the end of the

1960s, the United States Public Health Service had demonstrated, after studying nearly 70,000 of those on INH, there was a great reduction in the number of tuberculosis cases among this population.

INH remains the only drug used as preventive

treatment against tuberculosis in PPD positive persons. It is given with pyridoxine (vitamin B6), which prevents the side effect of peripheral neuritis, a condition that presents as numbness and tingling in the extremities.

Despite all these advances in the treatment and prevention of tuberculosis, although it no longer is the death threat it was at the turn of the 20th Century, it continues to be a serious public health problem, especially in the male population, the nonwhite population, the elderly, immigrants and those who reside in crowded cities. Those particularly at risk are persons recently exposed (infected) to the TB bacillus, alcoholics, intravenous drug users, the homeless and immunosuppressed persons, especially those with HIV infection.

In 1988, there were 10,000,000 persons in the United States who had been infected with the tubercle bacilli at sometime in their past, which made them among the higher priority risk groups since most cases of tuberculosis come from this group if preventive measures are not taken with them. Often there is a medical or age barrier to their participating in a preventive program of INH therapy, also known as TB chemoprophylaxis. (A history of hepatitis, any type, is an example of a medical barrier. Chemoprophylaxis usually is not given after age 35.)

This decision is made on a case-by-case basis, especially if the individual is a close contact to a patient with active tuberculosis.

Most AIDS patients are not given INH

chemoprophylaxis; however, they must be treated for their tuberculosis, if their TB infection becomes active as a result of their HIV virus. If they are not treated, it is possible the disease might escalate their AIDS to the extent they might die early. Today, because of the improved HIV medications, AIDS patients are living for decades with their disease. They are advised it would be foolish to risk not treating their TB, which can be cured with the proper regime of tuberculosis medications. With this TB treatment, sound medical follow-up and their HIV medications, they still could live for decades.

In 1987, the Advisory Committee for Elimination of Tuberculosis (ACET) was established by the Department of Health and Human Services. Its purpose was to make recommendations for the elimination of tuberculosis as a public health threat. This committee developed a plan, urging a national goal of TB elimination or a TB case rate of only 0.1/100,000 population by the year 2010. This was from a case rate of 9.3/100,000 population in 1987.

The three steps by which the ACET planned to achieve this goal were: 1) to make more effective use of the prevention and control methods already established, especially in the abovementioned high risk groups, 2) the development and evaluation of new technologies for diagnosis, treatment and prevention and 3) the rapid assessment and transfer of newly-developed technologies into clinical and public health practice.

By 2006, the national TB case rate was down to 4.6/100,000 population, well on the way to this goal.

On March 19, 2010, the Centers for Disease Control (CDC) reported in its "Morbidity & Mortality Weekly

Report (MMWR)": 3.8 cases/100, 000 population.

This is not yet the 0.1/100,000 population goal by 2010, but it certainly is cause for celebration since TB cases have been in a steady decline since 1987.

This writer was privileged to witness some of the technological advancements in TB diagnosis prior to leaving Tuberculosis Control in 1988. For example, a rapid method, MAT (Micro TB Direct), was developed in the laboratory for growing sputum cultures for definitive diagnosis in a matter of days rather than weeks, and the test was performed directly upon the specimen.

Patients had to wait up to two to three months for the specimen to grow out positive or be negative, prior to the laboratory's use of the MAT technique, before they knew whether they had or still had the TB bacillus in their sputum. This was discouraging because, if they were hospitalized, without three negative sputum cultures, they could not be discharged from the hospital.

The MAT technique is performed exclusively at the State Laboratory in Jacksonville, Florida, so all specimens, including those from A. G. Holley State TB Hospital in Lantana, are sent there where MATs are run on a daily basis during the week. Afterward, the results are faxed to the particular laboratory where the specimens originated.

Director of the State Lab at A.G. Holley, Dr. Roberta Lopez, has been associated with laboratory techniques on tuberculosis since she was a medical technologist in TB in the State Lab in 1969. As Director, she has been responsible for the lab's advanced techniques, following the guidelines set by the Committee in 1987.

On February 26, 2009, Science Daily reported there

might be "improvements in the efficacy of the BCG. Specifically, a team of Italian researchers discovered a new role for type 1 interferon in which it improves the ability of dendritic cells to stimulate an immune response against the bacteria" that causes tuberculosis. They believe it might give the vaccine a boost, which would make it more effective against the disease.

This is exciting news for the medical community, especially those who work in tuberculosis care and control. Although a bit of caution is always exercised along with hope in any new discovery, if the scientists are correct in their assumption, it could be one of the most important discoveries of the 21st Century and certainly could help in achieving the goals of the Advisory committee for Eliminating Tuberculosis, as outlined in 1987.

In the course of speaking about the tuberculosis hospital on the following pages, I incorporate discussions of TB Control at the county health department. The reader who has knowledge of neither, will come to realize how closely related these two entities are with regard to tuberculosis teaching and the care of the patient with tuberculosis.

An important note: Despite this historical perspective and the medical information contained in and throughout this book, it is not a medical or nursing textbook and should never be classified as such by any library or bookstore, even though medical and nursing students will find it informative.

It is important, also, to note that my personal involvement with A.G. Holley State TB Hospital ended in

1988. With that said, I will concede, without a doubt, there have been changes in tuberculosis treatment that might make some of my observations obsolete; however, they are for someone who has been in the field since 1988 to write. I look forward to reading that book one day.

SIGNIFICANCE OF THE BOOK

And Then There Was One is as much the story of the people who worked in both the hospital and the health department as it is about tuberculosis. I attempted to portray them as they truly were, including, at times, amusing anecdotes to give the reader a glimpse into their personalities outside their professional roles. In any serious field such as medicine and law enforcement, humor is often used to relieve work-related stress, but it in no way subtracts from the serious work these dedicated people do every day.

As in any true story, there are those who shy from the spotlight and do not wish to be named. I have honored this by giving them fictitious names. In other instances, some are named whom I was unable to locate for permission. It is my hope they will not mind the use of their real names in my story. At other times, especially in my earlier years before becoming a nurse, I used some fictitious names because I could not remember those of some persons, but I wanted to include these individuals because of their importance to the story and to me.

Since *And Then There Was One* is not a sensationalist type of memoir, every effort has been made to show respect and consideration to everyone mentioned in this book. No harm is intended to anyone referenced on these pages. Rather, I wanted to illustrate his or her importance to the hospital, the health department, the patients and, lastly, to me, within the years of my tenure until I left state service in 1988.

The practice of nursing is a shared adventure, so all those who have taken this journey with me, whether they be patients, other nursing and ancillary staff members or medical staff members, are important to this story, even if it was not feasible to name them all.

A few patients were mentioned who were in hospitals in which I trained and in the Southeast Florida State TB Hospital, but other than a celebrity whose illness was a matter of public record, having been covered by local and national media and the press at the time, full names of patients were not used in this book.

There were thousands of whom I could have written, including a beautiful princess from a South Pacific island who was writing her own interesting memoir, but I chose to limit examples to unusual cases. Suffice it to say there were countless other TB patients, too ill to sit up when they came to the hospital, who became so strong after their course of treatment, it seemed miracles had been wrought.

There were also patients who never seemed able to stay healthy because of their lifestyles; they had the same old problems that had always hindered them, waiting for them to get better and come back to them. Two primary examples of this were, and still are, the buddies with the bottle and the dealers with the illegal drugs. As sad as we were about them, we rejoiced over the ones who got completely well and went on to live happy productive lives as though their battle with tuberculosis had never existed.

For the lay reader or the professional who has not worked in tuberculosis care, there is a glossary at the end of this book to define any medical terms with which you might not be familiar.

Because this book is in great part, a memoir, I gave the reader a glimpse of the personal me; not always a flattering portrayal since I'm the first to admit my decisions and choices sometimes were not the wisest I could have made.

I thought it important, also, to first describe nursing school as it was in the 1950s when I became a nurse. Because I enrolled in a three-year diploma school, that depiction covers training in different hospitals besides my home hospital during those years. Much of it reads as fiction, but I assure you it all happened to my classmates and me during that significant period of our lives.

Finally, it is my hope and desire that all who read this book will realize how imperative it is to keep this last freestanding tuberculosis hospital in the United States functioning as a TB hospital. I want them to realize what a mistake it was to throw out the baby with the bath water decades ago when the states began to cut corners and closed the other TB hospitals, erroneously believing TB was no longer a serious public health threat.

Patients from all parts of the United States have come to A. G. Holley State TB Hospital for treatment over the years since the other hospitals closed, and yet the threat of closing A.G. Holley to tuberculosis patients is always looming on the horizon. This should never happen, and after reading the book, I hope the reader can understand why and will try to influence elected officials to keep it open indefinitely for the public health of the country.

Dedicated To Some Special People

Writing this book has been a labor of love, not just for the memories it evoked of a great hospital and those who shared in its history, but of a profession whose active membership I was proud to claim for five decades of my life.

Certainly the book is autobiographical because the memories are mine, but it is so much more than that. It is the story of ordinary people who faced extraordinary tasks in their struggle to make life better for those entrusted to their care, even though I did not go into much detail of this.

Instead, I wanted to show how dedicated they were to the seemingly tedious tasks they had to carry out and what caring professionals they were to understand why these tasks had to be performed with daily repetition for the welfare of the TB patients and all those with whom they came in contact. All of them, from the nursing assistants to the medical directors were, and always have been, patient educators.

Tuberculosis professionals, sub-professionals and volunteers are a rare class of people, even those who work behind the scenes rather than having much or any contact with the patients with whose cases they are involved. Not everyone wants to work in this field of healthcare nor is everyone suited to do so. Therefore, to all of you who have worked in TB in the past or currently work in TB, I applaud your efforts because the patients need individuals like you who truly care and understand. This book is dedicated to you, with my love and respect.

PART ONE:

A Nurse in Training

And Then There Was One

Below, clockwise from front:
Bebe, 3; Don, 8; Jean, 9;
Mother (Norma Gardner)
Peg, 12; Ron, 8. 1949
Left: Peg, age 6 months

Left: Larry, 9; Mother, 26;
Ron & Don, 2
1943
Right: Peg, age 11 years

PREFACE

1937

On January 25, 1937, while the raging waters of the Ohio River were overflowing its banks in southern Ohio, leaving 5000 to 7000 people homeless in Portsmouth, Ohio, my father, Floyd Edward Puckett, moved with my pregnant mother, Norma Juanita Gardner Puckett, from their home there in the foothills of the Appalachian Mountains to higher ground in Adams County, some thirty miles from the swollen river.

It was in Adams County our Gardner ancestors settled in the late 1800s, because it reminded them of their home in the English hills. My great-great-great-great grandfather, Adam Gardner, did not make it all the way to Adams County. It was Adam, a seventeen-year-old eager to make his way in life during the early 1800s, who braved the seas from Scotland, after boarding a ship leaving Edinburgh docks to set sail to America. A Native American tribe murdered him as he made his way down from the northeast, years after he married and had children. Adam reached southern Ohio, but not nearly far enough before the tribe ambushed him. His children left Adams County years later to settle in Rarden, in Scioto County, a few miles from their first Ohio home. Grandma Gardner's family (Williams) came to this country from France and the Netherlands. One of her distant grandfathers later married a Cherokee Indian.

On February 5th, ten days after my parents left Portsmouth, I was born in my paternal grandparents' home in Adams County around the bend from Serpent Mound, a well-known state park and burial ground of Native Americans from another era. It is called Serpent Mound because throughout the large park, what are believed to be the graves of these souls form the curving shape of a single gigantic serpent.

My paternal grandmother's family (Colvin) came to this country from Germany and Switzerland and my paternal grandfather's ancestors were German, Swiss and Welsh. To our collective surprise, through ancestry.com, my niece recently traced six Welsh kings in his family, dating back to the 700s. One abdicated the throne but later reclaimed it. She also learned another member of the family was one of the original Knights Templar.

My mother named me Peggy Anne, after the young movie actress, Peggy Ann Gardner, who later played a memorable young Jane Eyre in the 1944 movie of the classic tale by Charlotte Bronte, when I was 7 years old. This became my favorite Gothic book and movie.

Mother almost lost me at the age of one month, after they moved back to Portsmouth, because of what a doctor said was pneumonia in both lungs. From that time on, I suffered every year with multiple bouts of chest afflictions.

We moved often, but except for a few years spent within the suburbs of Cincinnati, we were always in the more depressed regions of the Appalachian foothills. After my parents had several children, as was more customary than not in that day, it was all my father could do to put food on the table and a roof over the heads of this growing family. Dad had a high school diploma and always had work, often as a foreman in such factories as Trailmobile in Cincinnati and the Atomic Energy Plant in Pike County, near Waverly, yet, there never was enough money left over for doctors, so it was up to Mother to bring me through each illness.

Even though she married at sixteen and did not get to finish her last year of high school, Mother, instinctively, knew what to do for me. This included forcing me to drink hot fluids, including a nasty tasting concoction she made from boiling onions in water, percussing my upper back to get the secretions in my lungs to move and massaging my chest with the old standby of that day, Vicks Vaporub, while a flannel cloth heated on the oven door. When she applied the flannel, it was such a soothing thing to absorb its heat and smell the aroma of the salve. Only then could I sleep. She did this over and over throughout every day, long after my fever broke, until I no longer coughed.

I had to smile years later, when my children's pediatrician said using Vicks Vaporub was not good for children. It certainly helped to bring me through respiratory illness more times than I can remember, and in addition to the antibiotics he prescribed and vaporizers, sometimes I resorted to my mother's remedy and it eased my daughters into slumber, as it did me all those years before.

I continued to suffer from bronchitis and pneumonia until I received the pneumonia vaccine in 1992. My mother is no longer on this earth, because of metastatic breast cancer, but I will never forget her loving care and soothing hands during those early years. If I close my eyes, I can still feel those hands massaging that healing balm into my chest before the heated flannel was applied to it. From middle age to her seventies, she was a certified nursing assistant, beloved by her patients. From firsthand experience, I could understand why.

The year before I was born, my parents lost a son in infancy, from what the doctor said must have been blue baby syndrome. In those days of little or no medical care, unlike today, autopsies were not performed routinely for deaths not witnessed by medical personnel, because most people, including children, died at home. Even without the benefit of this diagnostic tool, the doctor believed the baby had a defect in his heart called tetralogy of Fallot or what was more commonly known as blue baby syndrome.

Despite this, my mother asserted that right before he took his last breath, his skin was as pink as any other baby's, not blue or gray tinged as in most babies with this condition. This always made me wonder whether his illness might have been misdiagnosed. Or, perhaps fever brightened his skin. In any case, it was a difficult thing for my nineteen-year-old mother to go through, with only my older brother, Larry, age two, by her side. It happened so fast, even had she realized the end was so near, my father would not have had time to get home before their second son, Jimmy, died, at the age of one month.

I think, because of his death, my mother was determined to do whatever it took to assure my survival from each battle with bronchitis and pneumonia. She once told me she did not know what closure meant because "you never get over losing a child." It made me sad when she talked about the brother I never knew. I wanted to take away her pain, but no one could do that. I never heard my father speak of the child they lost, but then, it was rare for him to express his deepest feelings about anything.

The only health problems my siblings, Larry, Jean, Don and Ron had when we were young, except for Larry who had his appendix out, were the so-called childhood diseases measles, rubella, mumps and chickenpox. We all had them at the same time, so Mother had her hands full when this happened. None of us suffered complications and the illnesses were soon forgotten. They had occasional sore throats and colds, also, but seemed to fight them off in short order, so being such a thin, sickly child did not make me popular within this household of four other robust children. Two more, Lela and Kathi, would arrive in later years before my mother's childbearing was finished.

The year I was six, Jean was three and the twins were two. Mother used to say it was like having triplets, as the three of them were always into something together.

Because I didn't need so much care, when Mother was busy with any or all of the three, I was sneaking her romance magazines out of the trash can in the kitchen, wiping the coffee grounds and egg shells off them, and taking them upstairs in the big house we rented in

Cincinnati. (I have no idea how much Dad paid for that house, but judging by today's rent standards, it was probably something like $50-$100 a month, for a large three-story house in 1943.) I could read well at six, but no one knew it. I would read the stories, stuff the magazine in between the coiled springs and the mattress, and then take my used school script pad and write my own romance stories. They all contained a lot of kissing and heaving bosoms. I had no idea what a bosom was or how it heaved, but since all the stories seemed to have at least one heaving bosom in them, especially during all that kissing, I figured it must be important, so included it in my stories. Not wanting to get into trouble for reading her magazines, I tore my compositions into tiny pieces and flushed them down the commode in the hall bathroom. No one ever learned my secret, despite my bedroom smelling like a used bookstore from all the old magazines stuffed under the mattress.

That same year, on a bright sunny day, we noticed several of the neighbors standing outside across the street and looking up. When we went outside, Mother screamed, and it's a wonder she did not faint onto the sidewalk. On the roof of that three-story house were two-year-old Donnie and Ronnie having a great time, chasing each other. Dad was at work, but someone must have called the police and fire department, because a police car and fire truck came barreling down the street and firemen rushed inside the house to the third floor, as one went up a ladder to the roof.

They brought the twins in through the window they'd gone out, without harm to them. Those boys and usually,

Jeanie was with them never seemed to have any fear of anything, but rarely got a scrape from any of their escapades.

What their punishment was for cavorting on the roof, I don't recall. Did they ever do anything like it again? Sure! Like the time, my brother, Larry, and I were taken out of class and driven home, because all the siren-screeching fire trucks we heard were speeding to our rented house in Montpelier, Indiana. Our barn was on fire, and our twin brothers, then five, were in it! Donnie and Ronnie were all right, but the barn burned to the ground. When confronted, they swore to the firemen, "a guy in a plane threw out a lighted cigarette, when he flew over the barn." Of course, the firemen found the box of matches and the discarded ones they'd thrown into the dry haystacks after lighting them.

I'll never forget their punishment for that stunt. Like something stolen from a Stephen King novel, had there been Stephen King novels in the fall of 1947, Mother stripped them and made all of us watch what was about to happen, apparently to curtail any fantasies we might have harbored to imitate their deed. To our horror, she held lighted matches to their arms and legs, not close enough to burn them, but close enough for them to feel the heat and scream that it was burning them. To my surprise, when I looked at her face, tears were falling down her cheeks, and I realized how frightened that burning barn had made her. She never left a mark on them, not even a sunburn pink, but it was enough to scare them and put a rapid end to their only trek into pyromania. No doubt, if that had happened today, she would have been arrested for major child abuse, and I would be one of those screaming for her conviction, but it accomplished her goal of stopping this dangerous behavior in its tracks before the twins or someone else got hurt. To our knowledge, they never touched another lightened match for the remainder of their childhood together.

Since Ron usually was the instigator in most of their misadventures, we always believed it was he who thought of that one. To our collective surprise, when several of us were gathered around Mother's bed in the inpatient center of Hospice of Palm Beach County in March of 1998, tearfully remembering one thing after another of our life with her, as that life was ebbing out of her, Don admitted, with a sly grin, it was he who'd persuaded Ron to join him in playing with the box of matches in that old barn in Indiana when they were five.

At the age of nine, a few months before Dad took the job in Montpelier, Indiana and we moved there for a year, I contracted rheumatic fever with chest and joint pain. My knees would be so swollen and the pain so pronounced, I could barely walk down the long lane from our house to catch the school bus, especially with snow piled high the entire length of the lane.

Everyone told my mother the pain in my legs was just growing pain. Strange; none of my brothers or sisters had leg pains and they were also growing. Finally, it got so bad she had to take me to a doctor who ran blood tests and listened to my heart which, he said, had developed a murmur. He told her he was certain I had been suffering from the affects of rheumatic fever for several weeks. He prescribed medication and vitamins to protect my heart, as well as that could be done in the late 1940s. Before we left his office, he told Mother I could not run, climb, or play anything but quiet board games and such for a whole year.

This was the worst news I could have received. From the time I can remember being in school and living in the country, after we left the suburbs of Cincinnati when I was seven, I loved to walk alone into the hills behind the house to read or wander along the creek beds, looking at the butterflies, birds and other creatures of nature in the spring and summer time. I was terrified of snakes and occasionally saw a copperhead or blacksnake. When I came upon one, I could not move from the spot, as though they had hypnotized me. I did not know standing still was exactly what I should have done. In any event, they went about their business and did not come near me.

There was one exception to this, not in the hills but along a dirt road, years later when I was seventeen and riding the only bike we had in the family. A long copperhead snake was lying in the road when I happened upon it. I had no way of knowing whether it felt threatened by me, since I ran off the road and almost crashed the bike, to avoid hitting it. Regardless, it chased me for a long way before it slithered off into the bushes, leaving me breathless with terror. That was the first time I ever saw how fast something without visible legs could move. I hope it was also my last.

After the rheumatic fever diagnosis, no longer could I climb the hill and walk in the woods. I had to sit in the shade during recess at school, watching the other students running and playing games. It made me feel like an outcast and so lonely I could have cried. I never told anyone about these feelings, but they lasted for many years beyond this period in my life.

There was another reason my siblings teased me besides my being so puny. No one out of the family ever knew it because it made me so ashamed. Until my adolescence, I was a bed wetter. Had this problem occurred in my own children, I would have been sought medical help for them. My parents, with good reason, ignored it: There was still no extra money for visits to doctors and dentists, except in emergencies like Larry's nearly ruptured appendix. And, too, people in those times did not believe it was something that had to be treated to correct. As with so many other things, they believed children simply outgrew it, or the child was just too lazy to go to the bathroom or outhouse and would get tired of it as she grew older.

My favorite great-aunt was Pauline Bush, my mother's maternal aunt. A retired schoolteacher, she was the only member of either side of the family to attend and graduate from college or university before our generation grew up. She and my great-uncle Harry owned a general store in the small village of Clarksville, Ohio, an hour or two away from us. They used to take me to their home for a few weeks every summer and later to Wilmington, eight miles from where they lived in Clarksville, after they moved there. Sometimes they'd take Jean, three years younger than I, but never the two of us at the same time, which made us feel special.

It was at her house I first started trying to play the

piano because we had none until I was nine. Although it was in the living room, she didn't care how often I played it or how loud it was. She just encouraged me to keep trying.

They had one son, whose name was Charles, but everyone in the family called him Bushy. He was several years older than Larry. He is in his 80s today but is still Bushy to me. I did feel special while in their home. He was seventeen or eighteen when I was kindergarten age and he loved to carry me around the house on his shoulders, with me giggling all the while.

Bushy was laughing not too long ago and told me he was amazed I "can remember all that stuff," when I told him I still remember how the toast tasted at breakfast in their house and how Aunt Pauline always made fruit and vegetable Jell-O, which I'd never had before and loved. We had no toaster and Mother always fixed our toast, usually with sugar and cinnamon, in the oven. I loved her cinnamon toast, but that was probably why my first taste of toast from a stand-alone electric toaster made such an impression upon me.

Uncle Harry and Aunt Pauline sat on the couch and clapped their hands, laughing with me when Bushy gave me those shoulder rides. I loved being there and having so much fun with this family who took the time to give me this kind of attention I'd never had from my own family. There were always smaller children who needed the attention more than I did at home. As the oldest daughter, I was considered old enough to fend for myself, except when I was ill.

I used to think, while I was taking psychology courses in

nursing school, this was the reason for the respiratory illnesses, but since they started when I was the youngest child just a month old, I suspect that was not true. Persons of any age, with repeated bouts of any lung disease are vulnerable to it over a lifetime unless vaccinated, which was what stopped it in my case in 1992, as I said earlier, with my first dose of the pneumonia vaccine. Within the past five years, I have had a couple episodes of atypical bronchitis and pneumonia, but no vaccine prevents them.

When I was this young, Aunt Pauline would put my hair up in rags at night and then brush the curls out in the morning, twirling them around her fingers. I was a kid with straight and stringy hair, but she could always make it shine and coax the curl into it. Even as young as I was, I found this to be amazing.

Then, she would dress me in a pretty dress she brought home from their general store. After she had me all dressed up with a bright satin bow in my hair, I would ride with them to the store, and she would give me small projects to do like sorting buttons or ribbons or just coloring in a coloring book she'd give me.

Sometimes, she even let me sit on the counter beside the cash register while she worked. I remember one time, one of her customers told her, "Oh my, what a pretty little girl you have." I was stunned. I had been told by my siblings and young cousins, how skinny I was and how ugly I was, but never had anyone said I was pretty until that moment.

There was an even more important thing my great-aunt did for me one summer when I was close to my teens.

At her house, and because of her, I stopped wetting the bed. She was astute enough to realize how much this bothered me. One day she asked whether I would like to try something to correct it. This was after she took me to a doctor who said I had a small bladder, but I "would grow out of the bed-wetting." Of course, I told her yes, I'd do anything to stop it.

Statistically, even today, only 15% of children grow out of bed-wetting (enuresis). The other 85% require the intervention of their parents and/or pediatrician. Of course, I fell into the latter group.

Even though she had to be up early, Aunt Pauline started setting her alarm for three in the morning. When it went off, she slipped into my bedroom and awakened me, telling me it was time to go to the bathroom. After only a week of that, my nocturnal accidents never returned, even at home, because I would awaken and go to the bathroom. I felt like a normal young girl for the first time in my life, just in time for my teenage years.

Aunt Pauline had Alzheimer's disease and metastatic breast cancer at the end of her life. The last time Mother and I visited her in a home for patients, she smiled the same and said she was glad to see me, but she had no idea who I was. Although this saddened me, I smiled and told her how grateful I'd always been for everything she did for me as a child.

She smiled again and said, "Well, thank you," in that polite educated voice I had always admired and can still hear when I think of her. Then, she asked me again what my name was. To see this frail little woman with no memory of someone who loved her, sitting there in place of the vivacious, confident and generous woman I'd always known, was one of the saddest days of my life.

It was because of her influence, I taught myself to play the piano when I was nine years old in Montpelier. My father loaded an old forty-year-old piano he had paid as many dollars for onto a truck and surprised me with it. He claimed, to the week before he died, the minute he and his boss set it down in the house I started playing boogie-woogie on it. I still laugh at that, but he swore it was true.

I did not know how to read music but within a few months, during which time I locked myself in the cold unused parlor for six or eight hours at a time with that piano, I had taught myself to play. It became the most important thing in the world to me; I wouldn't come out to eat, if I were still practicing. If I heard a song, whether country, popular, standard or classical, I could play it. And, the best part about that was people would recognize it.

My best friend at school that year in Montpelier, Barbara Gray, loved the piano, too, but she got to take lessons. My mother was pregnant with my sister, Bebe, although none of us children knew that was what was wrong with her, and my dad never went to church, so Barbara's dad always picked me up on their way to church every Sunday morning.

Barbara and I always dressed in similar-looking flowered dresses and wore our hair in two braids fastened up in round Os, so they came about to the bottom of our ears. After church we'd have dinner at their house and then Barbara and I would play the piano. I was fascinated by her ability to play the little songs in her lesson books and wished I knew how. I could imitate her and play them by ear but not the perfect way in which she played them. She thought it was great I still could play them, though, and we had great fun while we were sitting at that piano.

Barbara and I were inseparable that year. When summer came, Mother let me go to the United Brethren Church camp where her church took all the children from their Sunday school. Barbara had been baptized in White River (also the name of the camp) the year before and talked to me about her experience. She encouraged me to be baptized, also, when I went with her. Along with her stories, I'd also been told the horror stories about some people almost being swept out of the minister's arms when he ducked them under the water and apparently, from what one of the camp counselors told us, one woman was swept away a few years before and was never seen again.

I was caught up in all the crafts, teaching and baptizing that went on that week. The day before the Sunday we were to come home, I was also baptized in White River. I was scared to death the minister was going to drop me and let me drown in the rapidly moving waters, but I came up, unscathed, but feeling different, as though God really had filled me with the spirit. It was a very impressionable period in my life. I didn't say much about it but I could tell Barbara was happy I was baptized as she was. She told me we'd both go to heaven to be with God someday now that we were baptized. I had no idea how prophetic that statement was.

We were such good friends and truly loved each other. Everywhere you saw one of us, the other was right there beside her. Someone once said we were like two peas in a pod. We just looked at each other and laughed, then ran off holding hands and giggling. We expected to be friends forever, go to the big high school together and go away to college together.

One day Barbara didn't come to school. The teacher said she had tonsillitis, was in the hospital, and the doctor was going to take out her tonsils. I didn't have any idea what tonsils were except they were somewhere in the throat. I remember getting on a chair in the bathroom when I got home, trying to see my own tonsils. If they were in there, I hoped I wouldn't get tonsillitis and have to go to the hospital, even if I did miss being with Barbara at school. Her dad didn't come to take me to Sunday school while she was in there. I supposed he, her mother and big brother were at the hospital so she wouldn't be lonely. I couldn't wait for her to get well and come back to school.

A few days later the teacher was called out into the hall and when she came back in, she stood quietly before us for what seemed a very long time to me. There were tears in her eyes. My third grade class was very quiet, also, as though we knew something had happened. Finally, she cleared her throat and I've never forgotten her words: "Class, I'm afraid I have bad news. Barbara Gray just died of uremic poisoning."

I could hear sniffles around me but instead of crying over my best friend's death, I started giggling, softly at first, but then it became louder until it was hysterical and uncontrollable laughter. The other students glared at me, unable to understand why I'd laugh so hard because my friend was dead. I was embarrassed and I couldn't understand it, either. We had an astute teacher, though, who knew I was near tears and she was right. She came to stand beside my desk, not saying a word at first, and then when my laughter turned into loud sobbing, she told me she was sorry. She gently urged me out of my seat and took me into the hall.

She walked with me to the principal's office where it was arranged for me to be taken home. When I got to my house, I ran past my shocked mother and upstairs to the room I shared with my six-year-old sister, Jean. I fell onto the bed weeping. After a while, Mother came upstairs and sat on the bed, not speaking a word but gently massaging my back. Finally, she said, "Peggy, I'm really sorry about Barbara. I know you loved her and it hurts you that she's gone."

I turned to her and screamed, "Why? Why did God have to take her away like that? I hate him! I hate him!" I sobbed again, uncontrollably, and when my crying subsided, I told my mother, "It isn't fair, Mother. I hate God for doing that!" I wailed again, as I denounced the God I'd loved when I was baptized just a few months before. The God my best friend Barbara talked about so much to me.

Mother didn't lay a guilt trip on me by telling me I shouldn't say things like that about God or recite a meaningless platitude like, "God needed another angel in heaven." Instead, she agreed with me. "No, Peggy, it isn't fair," she said, "but, you'll learn as you go through life, sometimes that's just how things are. You won't always understand why, but there's nothing you can do about it. It's just a part of living."

With her 11th grade education, my mother could be the

wisest person on earth at times like that. She didn't sugarcoat anything, but told it just as it was. She didn't make excuses for how life was, and although she didn't always accept things in an easy way and could be mighty emotional when things went wrong, she also was quick to shrug hardship off and just get back to what needed doing.

"But I want Barbara here. I don't want her to be in heaven with God. I want to see her again," I cried.

"You can't see her right now, Peggy, but you'll never forget her, will you?"

"No," I sobbed. Then, I threw myself against her and cried until there were no more tears. She held me to her until I was so tired I went to sleep. That was the only day I remember my mother's arms around me like that until we all got into our late teens, and hugged her every time we came into the house. It was exactly what I needed to get me through that heart-breaking day and I was grateful for it.

As Christmas neared, Mother told us we were getting a very special gift and it would be for all of us. We must have guessed everything from a pony to a new house, but Christmas came and went without a special gift we could all share. I remember being so disappointed and wondered why she would have promised us something special, but then not given it to us.

The following day, we found out what it was she gave us a beautiful new baby sister, Lela Ruth. We were all excited and happy over this great event and it no longer mattered we didn't have her on Christmas Day. The twins, Donnie and Ronnie, were in awe of this tiny baby and the fact they were no longer the babies of the family. They couldn't pronounce Lela Ruth and called her Bebe Boo. The Bebe stuck and that's all anyone in the family called her from that time on, except for an aunt and our maternal grandmother.

(When she got older, Bebe called herself Lela, and that's the name most of her friends and co-workers called her after she was married and went to the post office to work when she was still in her teens. She stayed at the post office all her life until she retired in her early fifties as postmaster of the main Boca Raton Post Office, the one involved with the anthrax scare in the '90s.)

Before I went into the 4th grade, we moved back to southern Ohio, and I was playing piano for the church congregation and singing solos. I was also singing and playing at local songfests and once, at a tri-state singing convention to which my father took me. The Stamps Quartet and The Blackwood Brothers were featured performers on the program. We amateurs played before this part of the program commenced.

The amazing J. D. Sumner, with his beautiful bass voice, sang first with the Blackwood Brothers and later with the Stamps Quartet. Years later, Sumner and the Stamps Quartet sang backup for Elvis (Presley). This was heavenly music to my ears at the age of ten. I couldn't believe I was there listening to it, much less walking up when my name was called, before that part of the program began, to play and sing my solo. When I was through, even more amazing, people were clapping and shouting just as they'd do after the professionals sang later in the evening.

I never understood this until just a few years ago, and then I realized whenever I heard a small child sing, play piano or other instrument on TV, U-Tube or anywhere else, I was as moved and thrilled they were able to do this, as people were who heard and saw me. I believe it is because we don't expect strong voices or quality instrument playing to come from one so young. I was moved to tears a few months ago when I first heard the voice of ten-year-old Jackie Evancho, the young opera singer on "America's Got Talent." No one expected that strong and pure angelic voice to come from that diminutive child, either.

Being able to express myself through music gave me a confidence I'd never had before. I even began to believe I would go to college and learn to play the piano the correct way. I played slow songs with emotion and fast songs in the style of Jerry Lee Lewis in those country churches. People shouted, clapped and cried when I sang and played, so I knew my music was appreciated.

However, I wanted to know how to read music and play classical music as it was written. I knew I did not come close to doing that. I never felt proud of the way I played, despite the new confidence it gave me, because I knew, even if others did not know or care, I lacked the rudiments of music by not knowing what it was I was playing.

A music teacher once told me I was un-teachable because my playing was "too sophisticated." He said I was playing the correct notes and chords, but that did not help me to read a piece of music. I could not understand why he wouldn't even give me a chance to try to learn how to do it.

How I longed to sit down, look at a piece of classical music and play every note without adding anything else. I would fantasize about playing Chopin on a grand piano in a large venue, such as Carnegie Hall. Conversely, I thought I'd like to perform on the Grand Ol' Opry since I loved singing country music, too. In those days until around 1989, female country singers belonged to a very small club, unlike today when there might be nearly as many female country singers as male, so I might have had a better chance at that than the concert hall.

I did not know which direction in music I wanted to go, as I loved it all. I just knew I wanted to be a performer. As it turned out, fate intervened. I continued to play in church, accompanied Jean and myself on a Sunday morning radio show when she was eighteen and I, twenty-one, and later in life in small clubs and on cruise ships just for fun. Occasionally, I got paying gigs and even had my own three-piece band at one time, but music was not to become my chosen profession.

ONE

From Viral Hepatitis to Nursing School

At the age of fifteen, I became ill with viral hepatitis. I was in my freshman year of high school and my homeroom was on the third floor of the school in the current small country town in which we lived, Amelia, Ohio. I had been sick with what we thought was the flu. I was weak and light hurt my eyes, so Mother kept my bedroom darkened.

When I was feeling better and my symptoms were gone, I was allowed to return to school. I got to the third floor landing and fainted before I made it to my homeroom. When I was awakening, I heard another classmate say, "She's got the yeller jandice."

I had no idea what that was, but the teacher took one look at me and called my brother Larry, a senior, to take me home so my parents could get me to the doctor. She told him I had yellow jaundice. Apparently, being in the darkened room most of the time I was ill, it was not noticeable my skin and eyes had a yellow tinge to them. Of course, jaundice means a disease that turns the skin and whites of the eyes (sclera) yellow, but most country people put the two words together.

My mother berated herself not to have noticed this and got me to the doctor right away. He concurred I had infectious hepatitis, known today as hepatitis A. My father had recently installed an indoor bathroom, and the doctor said there must have been some cross-contamination during the process; perhaps the bacteria had transferred to the well where we got our drinking water, and that's how I contracted the disease. He told my mother there was nothing she could have done to prevent my contracting the virus under those circumstances, but she could prevent everyone else in the family from getting it.

As he instructed, she brought everyone else into his office. Blood tests confirmed no one else had the disease, so his nurse gave all my family members a dose of gamma globulin to prevent it by boosting their own immunity against it. The injections did their job as none of them contracted hepatitis. I think this made my mother feel better and she stopped blaming herself.

The doctor told Mother when the active symptoms left, it did not mean I no longer was sick. He told her I was still very ill and my liver was enlarged. He ordered me to stay home at least another six weeks, maybe longer, to give myself a chance to heal and my liver to go back to normal.

This was my first year of high school. I was taking courses like algebra, which were not easy for me. I was afraid I would fail everything and have to repeat the grade. I was always a good student and had never gotten below a

B in anything, so the thought of failing the ninth grade was distressing to me.

The teacher assured my parents I would be able to make up the course material, and when I was stronger, she would give my homework to Larry. That relieved my mind and I concentrated upon getting well, though it was no easy task. By then, I had lost considerable weight and my weakness persisted; it was difficult to stand without help.

The doctor told my mother I needed lots of carbohydrates and protein. He instructed her to feed me steak or lean hamburgers at almost every meal. He even told her to let me drink all the Pepsi I wanted because my body needed the high sugar content.

In our family, steak was unheard of and except for when my father drove a Dr. Pepper semi-truck as a distributor when I was a few years younger, we rarely had soft drinks, either. It was the same with hamburgers, as in those days, even ground beef was too expensive. Our protein came from the chickens and rabbits we raised on occasion, and fish when Dad or the boys went fishing. And, beans; always beans of one kind or another at every meal.

We had restaurant hamburgers only on those rare occasions we went to the White Castle drive-in restaurants in Cincinnati. We never went to an indoor restaurant. My, were those burgers worth the trip. Dad could get something like a dozen White Castle hamburgers, loaded with soft onion pieces, sitting on soft warm square buns, for a dollar. He would always get two or three dozen of them so we would all get our fill. We thought those were the best tasting things we had ever had and eating them put smiles on our faces.

A few years ago, returning to Florida from visiting relatives in Ohio and feeling nostalgic when I saw a White Castle off the highway, I pulled up to its drive-thru window to get one of the burgers. It was a disappointment to bite into it and to find it was not the same at all. The onions were sparse and hard, as was the cold bun.

Mother insisted while I had hepatitis, my father had to get the kind of food the doctor ordered and she made sure I ate it, even when I did not feel like eating anything, much less a large high protein meal.

I felt sorry for my siblings because even though I was eating steak, there was not enough of it for them. Despite my being the recipient of their frequent teasing and pranks, because I had never been rowdy and robust like they when we were younger, I loved my siblings fiercely and did not like to see them hurt or deprived of something I had.

During this lengthy recuperation, I had plenty of time for reading and reflection. I began to think in earnest of what I wanted to do with my life. It had always been a given it would be performing music, after I started playing and singing in church and other public places. Somehow, this ambition was pushed aside after I became ill. Music would always be a part of my life as it had been since I was nine years old.

However, I was so inspired by the care I received from the doctor, his nurse and my mother after I contracted hepatitis, I knew at the age of fifteen, I was put on this earth to be a nurse; to serve others during their illnesses. I could serve God in that way as well as by singing and playing in church, although I knew I would never stop doing that. Because of this new goal, I studied harder than ever after I got well and returned to school. I passed the ninth grade, with relief, as despite studying so hard on my make-up work at home, I still was fearful I would fail and have to repeat the year.

The next year, 1953, when I was a sophomore, we moved back to the small town where my mother was born and grew up, Rarden, Ohio, twenty-five miles from Portsmouth and the Ohio River. It was a beautiful tree-filled town in the Scioto Valley, surrounded by the foothills of the Appalachians, where most of my maternal relatives still lived, and where I spent much of my childhood. Everywhere I walked through the little town, I inhaled the aroma of the wild honeysuckle bushes or abundant lilac trees. Maples and majestic oaks lined the streets, providing canopies of shade from the bright sunlight, and weeping willow trees were everywhere.

Each course I elected to take after that experience was because the nursing schools I wrote to required it. One of these courses was Latin. I'd always loved school and excelled in almost everything, but, oh, how I hated that class.

Despite being a good student otherwise, it was disconcerting to realize I had a learning disability when it came to conquering Latin and other subsequent foreign languages when I went to college and the university after I had my own children. Rosetta Stone is on my bucket list, as I do want to prove to myself I am capable of learning a foreign language. I barely made the required B in the Latin course. My graduating class was only fifteen students and I'll always believe the teacher, knowing I could not go to nursing school without it, gave me every possible shove to learn enough Latin to make that grade.

When I was a junior, Mother was pregnant again. When she was ready to deliver, Dad drove her to the hospital in the next town, Peebles. She was told the baby wasn't ready, so she was sent home. They almost got to the house, when she told him the baby was coming, so they turned around and got as far as the doctor's office. Our youngest sister, Kathleen Jo, came shortly after she said those words, on March 10, 1954.

Dodie, the nickname the boys gave her, did not look like any of the rest of us, with our fair complexions and light hair. She looked exotic to me, like a beautiful baby Indian princess. Her hair was so dark, it was almost black, and her eyes were like little dark brown marbles. Kathi, as she later came to be called, favored our paternal grandmother, the one who was the granddaughter of the Cherokee chief. (Both our grandmothers had Cherokee ancestry.) It was special to have another baby sister and we doted on her whenever we were home from school. Larry, in the Marines now, was stationed in California when she was born, so she was very special to him. He could hardly wait to get home to see little Dodie.

I did qualify to enter nursing school in 1955. And in 1958, when I was twenty-one years old and a senior nursing student in Cincinnati, Ohio, I was beginning what I did not know, then, would become a love affair with tuberculosis nursing. And, had anyone told me this at the time, I would have wondered what was wrong with him. What an absurd idea loving TB nursing!

My training school was in a seven-story teaching hospital in the heart of Cincinnati. In 1886, seven German Methodist Deaconesses started a makeshift miniature hospital in a small cottage in the city, devoting their lives to caring for the sick and poor. Two years later, because they'd outgrown the cottage, the Association purchased what became Bethesda Hospital at the corner of Oak Street and Reading Road. That's where the school of nursing was located after it was started shortly thereafter by the deaconesses. I lived in Draher Hall, the student nurses residence, across the street from the hospital.

Today, there is no more Bethesda Hospital at Oak Street and Reading Road. It closed its doors on February 4, 2000. Since the 1990s, it had been part of a merger with the newer Bethesda North and rival hospital, Good Samaritan, and became known as Tri Health. Today, what I knew as Bethesda Hospital at Oak Street and Reading Road is occupied by the offices of Children's Hospital, plus a same-day surgery suite and emergency room/urgent care center.

In 1989, Bethesda Hospital School of Nursing graduated the last diploma class and the first associate degree class from the Cincinnati State Nursing Degree Program. In 1992, the school moved to Cincinnati State campus and in 2002, my former residence, Draher Hall, was demolished. Today it is a parking lot. It brought tears to my eyes to learn of all these changes, but it does reflect the changing face of nursing education throughout the country.

I almost did not get to go to nursing school. Deaconess and Director of Bethesda Hospital School of Nursing, Geneva Rubins, RN, of whom it has been said, "her heart was in nursing," ran the school. She earned a Master's in Education during the time she was the Assistant Director of Nurses for the hospital and Director of the School of Nursing. She became Director of Nurses in 1960. Later, she served as Director of Nurses at Miami Valley School of Nursing in Dayton until her retirement in 1983. She returned to Cincinnati in 1986 and volunteered at Bethesda for the next ten years. She served on the board for American Nursing Care, Inc., was advisor to Student Nurse Association of Ohio, consultant on National League for Nursing Board of Review of Accreditation of Diploma Programs and Site visitor for the U. S. Public Health Service Division of Nursing. She died at the age of 86, the last of the Deaconesses. I wish I could have seen her again.

Looking over my transcripts when I went for my interview in 1955, after a long period in which I don't believe I took a breath, Miss Rubins told me, "Miss Puckett, although you were at the head of your small class in high school, you'll be competing against as many as 100 freshman students here at Bethesda. Do you still think you want to do this?"

"Oh yes," I told her, "more than anything. I know I'll have to study very hard, but I love school and I'm a good student. I know I can do it."

With what seemed a begrudging smile, she said, "All right then, we'll be in touch with you after we've received the release from your dentist."

Because there was no dentist in our small town and no money for preventive dental or medical care, anyway, I had never seen a dentist in my eighteen years of life, until the dentist in Cincinnati examined me during my pre-entry check-up. Of course, having had no preventive care, I knew, despite how vigorously I brushed my teeth after meals, I had cavities. That was obvious. One cavity even showed in my upper bicuspid when I smiled. Still, it was a shock to learn I had 33 of them!

I had no money for the required dental work, but I did not tell this to Miss Rubins. Instead, one morning, shortly after my return from Bethesda and the interview, I dressed in the only suit I had beige plaid wool, totally unsuitable for a spring day, beige pumps and white gloves. I took a Greyhound bus to Dayton, Ohio, 80 miles northwest, where I had learned of a job opening at Standard Publishing Company.

I was self-conscious about my appearance as I sat in the outer office among several other applicants, all flawless-faced young women, dressed in lovely spring dresses or suits, waiting to be called into the interview. Well, I told myself, I have good typing and shorthand skills so I will just make the best of it.

I did not really want to get the job and was certain I would not get it, after seeing how many other applicants were there to be interviewed. On the other hand, since it would pay more than baby-sitting or waitressing, I knew it was the best option for me, if it were offered to me. My objectives for how to accomplish my dental work were incongruous, to say the least.

The receptionist told me I was twenty-sixth in line to be interviewed. I had a long wait. Smiling, I thanked her and took a seat. It was nerve-wracking to sit there, feeling so out of place among the other applicants who were clearly from the city. Dayton was not a large city compared to Cincinnati, but it was not a small town like Rarden, either.

After two uncomfortable hours of waiting, the receptionist called my name, opened the door and led me into a small cubicle where a tall, stocky man in his forties was standing. "Please, sit down, Miss Puckett," he said, pointing to a straight back chair. I thanked him and tried to sit straight but felt I was slouching.

"My name is Del Nims and I'm the one who needs a new secretary."

"How do you do," I said, still feeling about as ill at ease as a girl could feel.

I suppose it showed since his next words were, "Are you afraid of me?" That startled me and he laughed aloud, a laugh so hearty, it calmed me and I felt a bit better.

"Oh, no sir, of course not," I lied. I smiled and tried to sit even straighter. I felt my hands perspiring under the cotton gloves, but I didn't know whether it would be proper to remove them. Such a hick, I silently chided myself, again. Until that day, I'd never referred to myself in that way, but that little negative voice inside me had grown to enormous proportions as I awaited that interview. There was so much I did not know about city ways and etiquette, in general.

"Tell me, Miss Puckett," he said in a more serious tone this time, "how old are you?"

"I'm eighteen, sir," I replied, trying my best to sound sophisticated. I'm sure he could see my attitude was a charade, but if so, pretended not to notice.

"I see by your application you just graduated from high school two weeks ago."

"Yes, that's correct but I had excellent commercial training. Our typing teacher was a perfectionist. He would sit in the outer classroom and if he so much as heard a break in rhythm from a typewriter, he somehow knew who had done it and the guilty student was in for a good rap on the fingers with his ruler." It was the truth, but after I revealed it to him, I felt foolish and was certain it was proving even more what a country girl I was.

"He sounds like a man dedicated to his teaching rare these days, I might add. And, did you have bookkeeping and shorthand, also, Miss Puckett?"

"Well, no sir, not bookkeeping. I never thought I'd need it in . . ." I caught myself before I blurted out "nursing" and said, "in a secretarial position. I did have shorthand, though, and Mr. Fouch had me take his private dictation my last six months in school. My average typing speed was 110 words a minute."

"Well, let's see if you can do half as well for me this morning. There's a typewriter in the other room, but first grab that pad and pencil. Let me see how well you can transcribe my dictation."

He started dictating almost before I got my gloves off. "Now, please read that back to me."

I read every word back to him without fumbling, just

as he'd dictated it. "Why, that was excellent, young lady. Now," he said, indicating the chair before the typewriting table in the small alcove behind us, "sit there and when I indicate for you to begin, start typing from that test paper."

I sat down and placed a sheet of typing paper into the manual typewriter. Now, I was in familiar territory and began to relax. He told me to begin. He left the alcove, but did not close the door. I typed the article he had placed before me on the small table. When he heard the bell go off, he came back into the room. I had finished typing minutes before it sounded.

He looked over the paper and then looked up at me. "Are you always this perfect?"

"Excuse me?"

"Peggy, there's not a single mistake on this piece of paper. It's a duplicate of what I gave you to type. I've never had anyone do that before."

I smiled and told him, "If they'd been in Gilbert Fouch's class, they would type without mistakes, too. It was a matter of self-preservation. If he saw mistakes on any of our papers, we had to do the whole thing over again, so I quickly learned to concentrate and do it right the first time."

He smiled and said, "And your speed was incredible. I timed you from my desk and you typed 120 words a minute." He stood and reached across the desk to shake my hand. "Report to Personnel at 8 sharp on Monday morning, Peggy. Consider yourself hired. You're my new secretary."

I tried to react with aplomb, but I'm afraid my shocked

expression gave me away. He laughed again and said, "I interviewed twenty-five young women this morning before you walked in, but none came close to being what I need in a secretary. I like your professionalism and, certainly, your shorthand and typing skills. You're exactly what I want in a secretary."

"I thank you, Mr. Nims. I will do a good job for you."

I know you will." He opened the door after telling me to take a seat again in front of his in the larger cubicle. I heard him telling the receptionist he'd found a new secretary, and I fought an urge to laugh aloud. I could not believe, instead of one of those chic sophisticated applicants, he had chosen me. I could hear unpleasant mumbling as the receptionist dismissed the applicants still waiting to be interviewed.

Closing the door again, he said, "Well, now, before I let you go, let's get a couple of things straight. Number one nobody in the department calls me Mr. Nims and that definitely includes my secretary. I'm the Chief of Industrial Engineering, by the way, and everyone calls me Del. So, young lady, don't you dare show up Monday, calling me Mr. Nims. Understand?" He was smiling despite how gruff he sounded.

"Yes, Mr. Nims, er, I mean, yes sir."

"What?"

"Yes, Del," I managed to blurt out, even though saying it sounded downright disrespectful to me.

"That's better," he said with a smile. "Number two your duties will include being Girl Friday to a couple of engineers. Hope you won't mind that."

"Not at all," I assured him, having not the slightest

notion what a Girl Friday was, much less what an engineer did in an office. The only engineers I'd ever heard of drove the trains that sped through Rarden at all hours of the day or night. Did I ever have a lot to learn!

"My secretary is always called by her first name, as well. We're happily married men all of us so don't worry about the familiarity. It's just much quicker to yell, 'Hey, Peg.' So get used to being yelled at, too." Then, he laughed.

I laughed, too, at that point. He continued talking while he walked back and forth with his hands behind his back, reminding me of the posters of Smokey, the Bear, saying, "Only you can prevent forest fires," prompting me to suppress another giggle. "Another part of your job, silly as it might seem, will be to put together our department's newsletter every month. The plant puts out a fine little newspaper for its employees once a month and each secretary is responsible for putting all the news marriages, babies, new hires, promotions that sort of thing, into it. It's time-consuming, but necessary, if we're to remain a happy family type place to work."

"I can appreciate that. It sounds nice." I was beginning to feel very at ease with this large gruff-sounding gentleman.

"Now, go have one last fling, Peggy, and I'll see you Monday at 8 sharp."

"Goodbye, Del. And thank you. Thank you very much," I added, as I walked through the door. I was sure I must have left him grinning, but I didn't turn around to see it.

TWO

Working Girl

Monday came before I realized it and I felt lost in the crowd of employees clocking into the large firm as I made my way to Personnel. By 8:30, I had signed all the necessary papers and was escorted to the Department of Industrial Engineering.

"Welcome aboard, Peggy," Del Nims told me as I walked through the glass door of the department. "Come on, I'll introduce you around."

I followed him into his large private office, where a slightly overweight, but pretty blonde in her early twenties, was pouring coffee. She whirled around when she heard us. "Boy, am I glad to see you, Peggy!

"I thought Del would never find a replacement for me. Oh I'm Susie, his former secretary." She smiled and held out her hand. She had a lovely relaxed smile and I liked her right away.

"I'm happy to know you, Susie. I'm sure they must be sorry to see you go." At that moment, I wished there were a way we could both work there, so she wouldn't leave.

"You can say that again. It took us five years to make a secretary of her, then she decides to get married and the heck with us," Del said.

Susie made a face at him and handed him his coffee. "This is the first thing you have to do every morning, Peggy, to take the bark out of the old crab," she said, with a laugh. "It's drudge duty, but it works to your advantage. After about two cups of this, he's almost human."

Laughing also, Del told her, "Show her where to park herself, Suz, then let her meet the others."

"Okay, Chief," she answered, and we went through the door. She closed it behind us. "Always close Del's door when you go out. He likes to work in a quiet office and we can get a little rowdy out here. Here's your desk. I'll be clearing out Wednesday so most of my things are out already. Here's where I keep my purse and compact." I placed my own purse in the large bottom drawer and moved along with her.

Across from her desk was one belonging to one of the engineers, a younger man than Del Nims, with a fiery red crew cut. "Peggy, meet Andy. Andy, Peggy."

He smiled in a pleasant way and took my hand. "Hi Peggy, hope you like us."

He kept my hand in his until Susie interrupted with, "I said meet her, not court her!" Everyone laughed, including me, but I knew I was blushing. I was not used to people interacting in such a friendly relaxed manner with one another.

"And, this is another of our friendly crew, Jack."

This one, with dark brown hair, stood and bowed. "My pleasure, madam," he said, kissing my hand.

"See why I hate to leave this crazy place." She steered me to the next desk, that of a tall, attractive brunette of around forty.

"Grace, I'd like you to meet Peggy, my replacement. Grace is the vice-president's right arm and has been my lifesaver on many an occasion, as well," she explained. I was to learn, in the coming days, exactly what she meant by that.

"How do you do, Grace," I replied, noticing the difference between the two women. Grace, though older and more reserved, was the more attractive of the two and the essence of chic, yet something told me they were great friends despite this.

"Welcome to Standard Publishing, Peggy. I know we'll become good friends," she said, with a warm smile. Just then her boss buzzed and she took her pad, waving goodbye with her little finger as she disappeared into the office of the vice-president.

Moments later, my own boss buzzed. I started and looked panicky at Susie. She grinned and tossed the steno pad to me. "Good luck, kid. You're on your own, now." I picked up a pencil and walked into Del's office.

My easy and pleasant first day was drawing to a close when a call came for me to go through the mill to pick up the daily report for Industrial Engineering. "The where?" I asked, looking at Susie.

"The mill. We do produce paper forms here and publish magazines, you know. Not everything is a big shiny office. Come on, don't want to keep the boss waiting. Don't worry, you'll enjoy it." She winked at the others. The two engineers laughed and Grace smiled, but no one shared the joke with me. It did not take long to realize what it was.

She led me through several other offices, much like ours, and then, opened a wide door and we stepped into another world. It was a vast noisy room, smelling of sawdust, with what seemed to be thousands of machines, all running at the same time. Beside each machine was a man and each man's eyes were on us. Several whistled, some yelled, but we continued walking past them.

"That's not meant for me, Peggy. No one's whistled at me in here for years!" She laughed, and again I felt my face color. "Well, don't be embarrassed. Don't you know it's a compliment for men to whistle at you, girl?"

"Why no, I I mean, I never thought it was. I always thought it meant you were a loose woman or something like that," I stammered, sounding again like the country girl I was.

Walking on and looking ahead, she said, "Oh boy, do you have a lot to learn. Honey, you'll grow up in a hurry here, believe me. No, the men aren't whistling because you look like a loose woman, as you put it. They're just doing it because they think you're pretty and because of your hourglass figure."

She looked at me then, and I knew my face was scarlet. "Oh, for heaven's sakes, girl, don't tell me you didn't know you had a nice shape." This conversation was getting more and more embarrassing by the minute.

"I never thought anything about it, I suppose. My clothes always fit nice, but I never got particularly excited about it," I told her. I didn't share with her that, when I first started developing, I avoided standing with erect posture; I was fearful someone would say something about my strange new shape. My siblings and boys at school said things despite my trying to hide it, so I stopped trying.

"Well, believe me, if I had what you have instead of what I've got, it would sure make me excited. I can't even look at a candy bar without gaining inches in my waistline and believe me, honey; men don't exactly get excited over extra inches on the waistline." She laughed again and I laughed with her.

I had never met anyone as worldly as Susie. She was downright outrageous, but so much fun to be around, I loved being in her company. I would be sorry to see her leave on Wednesday and knew everyone else would, too. I had to face the fact that as a conversationalist, I was no match for her.

As an aside to this new venture of mine, in 1969, I had my first short story, "A Chance in Winter," a fictionalized account of an Ohio patient, who was dying of cancer, published in The Lookout, a magazine published for Christian Churches by the same Standard Publishing Company in Cincinnati, for whom I'd worked fifteen years earlier in Dayton. After our congregation built the new sanctuary in Palm Springs a few years later, we were surprised to see my small family and I, at the dedication service of the new building, on the cover of the same magazine. My husband Ron, the music director, was at the podium, I, at the piano, our eight-year-old Karen was in the front row, looking back at our three-year-old Suzy, cavorting in the aisle.

Wednesday did come and many more Wednesdays after it. I fell in love with my new job and felt like the luckiest eighteen year old in the country. Del was a dream boss, never raising his voice and always thanking me when I typed a letter or transcribed something. The two engineers were fun, but treated me with respect, and when they asked me to do anything for them, they were almost apologetic about it, although I never minded doing what they asked of me. The men in the large plant got used to my presence and stopped whistling as I walked through the mill every week, for which I was grateful. I had received the occasional whistle from a boy in high school, but never from a group of men, so despite what Susie said about its being a compliment, it had felt degrading to me. I wanted to be respected as Del's secretary, not admired for any other reason.

The nicest person in the office besides Del was the secretary to the vice-president. Grace, at a little urging from me, taught me how to dress for the job, and I took a small portion of the good salary I was paid every week and acquired a new and suitable wardrobe, after I paid the rent, bought groceries and paid my dental bills. Nothing fancy, but certainly more appropriate than a woolen suit in springtime. I ditched the hat and gloves when I dressed for work.

One day, Del called me into the office to take a letter to the union. I had never had to do that before. He'd given me a brief run-down of his involvement with the union and had several large manuals on it for me to become familiar with during my first week as his secretary. It was not a lengthy letter but I was not that familiar with the union language yet. Therefore, later, when I was trying to transcribe my shorthand, I could not, to my dismay, read what I'd written in more than a couple of places. I hated to admit that to him, despite knowing he would not have chided me for it.

The other secretary came to my rescue, as Susie'd assured me she would. Del and the other two engineers had left for the day and we were alone in the office. Between Grace and me, we figured out what my shorthand symbols meant. I successfully transcribed the letter and left it on Del's desk for his signature. We must have guessed correctly since he perused it and signed it right away, without asking me to redo any portion of it.

Another quiet day, when all three men were out of the office, I was staring at my desk blotter, when Grace called to me. In fact, she said she'd called three times before I looked up.

"What? Oh, I'm sorry, Grace. Guess I was day dreaming."

"Yes," she said, with a laugh, "that was obvious. Got a picture?"

"Oh no, did I forget to take a picture of someone?" I picked up the Polaroid camera and stood, ready to rush out. It was not unusual for Del to send me to the mill to snap a photograph of someone or something.

Laughing, she asked, "Have you a picture of your young man, Peggy? I'm sure you must have been thinking of a young man."

I smiled then and put down the camera. "Yes, I was," I admitted. I reached into my drawer and pulled out a miniatureframed photograph of Buck, my boyfriend who was in the Air Force. He had on his dress uniform. I walked over and sat down in front of Grace.

She held the photograph out at arm's length and said, "No wonder you're so lost without this guy! Don't hide his picture away in a drawer. Why aren't you married to him? Or hasn't he asked?"

"Oh, he's asked all right. I just have to wait a few years before that can happen," I told her, feeling sad all of a sudden. Buck and I met after my senior play practice one night and fell for each other right away. When I went to Dayton to work, we'd been dating for several months. He asked me to marry him before I left. He couldn't understand why I wouldn't marry him before he reported to his next base in Newfoundland, Canada, so we could stay together. After all, I'd already received my diploma. When I told him I couldn't marry him for three years, he looked like I'd shot him with his own rifle or whatever type of weapon he carried when on duty. After I explained the reason, he was as furious as he'd been disappointed. It was obvious he did not want me to become a nurse.

Shaking her head, Grace said, "My, I just can't understand you young people these days. I can see saying you have to wait for a few months. But years? No, I can't see that not if you're in love. You are in love, aren't you?"

I had never admitted this to anyone, but we'd become good friends as she'd predicted. "Yes, Grace, I am. I ache to be with him more every day," I told her, on the verge of tears.

"Then, honey, for goodness sakes, get on a phone tonight and tell him you've changed your mind. Nothing's more important than being together when you both feel like that," she advised.

"I can't. I just can't. And, I'm sorry but I can't tell you why. Something else has to be done first, that's all." I hurried back to my desk, set Buck's photo down and dabbed powder on my nose, red from being so close to tears.

The other secretary shook her head, put her glasses on and went back to transcribing. We did not discuss it again.

THREE

Ominous Phone Call

That night, I received a call from Mother, telling me I had a letter from Bethesda. "Do you want me to open it while I've got you on the phone?"

"Yes, please." I was trembling, fearful my Alumni Foundation loan application had been rejected. There was no money to send me to school, so it was my only hope. All the money I'd made that summer, besides the small amount I spent on food, rent and the wardrobe, was going to the dentist, who had been sending his reports to Bethesda, as he completed each piece of work.

"It's from Miss Rubins, Peg. She wants you to come back for another interview Saturday. She said it has to do with your loan application. Will you come home Friday night?"

"Yes, of course. I'll catch the first bus out after work. Thanks for calling to let me know, Mother. Goodbye now. I love you." We disconnected, after she told me the same.

The one hundred mile bus ride to Cincinnati, Saturday morning, did nothing to calm my anxiety. When I arrived, the receptionist led me to Miss Rubins' office. Geneva Rubins was attractive when she smiled, which, as I'd noticed the first time, was not often. Maybe that's why I'd missed the small gaps between her teeth. She had an unlined face, framed with short, wavy gray hair. She wore no wedding band, which puzzled me, because she looked pregnant. I could not reconcile this with her being a Deaconess.

"Come in, Miss Puckett. Please, sit down," she invited.

"Thank you, Miss Rubins." I sat in the same chair as before, in front of the large desk.

Without preamble, she said, "I understand you're working as a private secretary at the present time. Is this correct?"

"Yes, I'm employed by Standard Publishing Company in Dayton, as secretary to the Chief of Industrial Engineering," I answered, curious to know why she'd asked, but of course, I knew better than to question her motives.

"From what I understand, it's a very good position for a young girl to have. Your next step up would be secretary to the vice-president."

It was a rhetorical question, and I wondered how she knew. At once, I felt panicky, believing she might have called the company. If so, Del must know I might be leaving. As quickly as it came, I dismissed that idea. He was too open and out-spoken; he would have said something. She'd called my house and spoken with Mother once when I was in Dayton. Perhaps she said something after I shared with her what Grace told me about the possibility of replacing her, when she retired.

She seemed to want me to address that, so I said, "Yes, Miss Rubins, but I really am not that interested in furthering a secretarial career."

"What do you want then, Miss Puckett?" Her look was so stern and I thought the question absurd, considering the fact I was in her office to make sure I could get a student loan to become a nurse. It took all my self-control not to react.

"Miss Rubins, I've wanted to be a registered nurse since I was fifteen. I still want it more than anything," I told her with determination.

"Fine. I had to be sure nothing had changed in that respect. The alumni foundation needs to know its money is not tossed down the drain." She almost smiled then, but did not quite make it.

"I understand."

"Just remember, as I told you at our first interview, even though you were at the top of your graduating class, which is something we're always glad to learn, you were competing with only fourteen other students." She stopped and cleared her throat. "Miss Puckett, it bears repeating; here, you'd be in competition with as many as one hundred other top students from much larger schools. Many students are weeded out every year because they can't keep up academically. Even though your overall average in high school was an A, you will find it difficult to maintain even a C average in nurses training. We tolerate nothing less than that from any of our students and we expect more from them."

She was making me feel intimidated again and I wondered whether she was trying to tell me it would not matter whether I did or did not get the student loan I was not coming to Bethesda. But, because she seemed not to want to be interrupted, I remained silent.

"Remember, you did not have chemistry in high school – through no fault of your own, of course. We take into consideration small rural schools do not have the funds for laboratory equipment. And, you had very little science. The way I see it, you'd be playing constant catch-up in the nursing classroom."

I felt myself swallow several times and was embarrassed by the reflex. She said nothing further, so I stated, "I realize my limitations in that area, Miss Rubins. I knew it was required, but my school only offered basic science and biology, which of course, I took. I would have liked to attend night school in Portsmouth to fulfill the chemistry requirement, but I just didn't have the money or a car to commute back and forth. I . . ."

"Of course, I understand all that," she assured me. "What I'm trying to get across to you is that it won't be easy for you here. Are you one hundred percent certain you still want to come to nursing school?"

I smiled with relief, then, and told her I wanted to, very much. "I'll work so hard if I'm accepted," I assured her.

She stood and so did I. Still without smiling, she shook my hand and said, "Thank you for coming in on your day off, Miss Puckett. You'll be hearing from the foundation within the next week."

"Thank you, Miss Rubins. Goodbye," I told her and walked out into the sun-brightened lobby. As I walked down the many steps after reaching the outside, I glanced back over my shoulder at the towering, seven-story, dark brick building. I'll be back, I told myself.

When I got home that night, I wrote to my boyfriend: "The hospital's just as beautiful as I'd remembered. It was so exciting to be there, today, Buck. I'll be living in the dorm across the street. I say will, because I refuse to believe I won't be accepted. A whole new life is waiting there for me. I just know it!"

I left on the nine o'clock bus the following night, after church services. I'd longed to stay home until I entered training, but I needed money more than I needed more time with my family. I had not finished all the dental work, so I had no choice but to return to Dayton. I had scheduled appointments on Saturdays and even on the 4th of July, my only holiday from the office.

Four days later, a letter from Buck was waiting under the door when I got home from the office. I picked it up and hurried inside my small studio apartment, happy, as always, to have a letter from him. After tossing my purse onto the bed and my shoes across the room, I tore open the envelope. My elation faded as I read his letter:

"I know somebody has to take care of sick people but it doesn't have to be my girl, my wife! Peggy, can't you see? Nursing once you get into it, will change you and make you hard. You'll see men when they're naked and have to bathe them. To put it bluntly, as much as I hate saying it, it will make you easy. "Sweetheart, I fell in love with a sweet, innocent and loyal girl. I couldn't love you if you weren't the girl I left behind. Can't you understand that? And, don't tell me nurses aren't like I'm insinuating they are. Remember, I'm in the Air Force and spent four years in the Marines. I know nurses. Do I ever know nurses! Ask any guy in the service, sweetheart. They all say the same thing. If you're looking for a wife, pick a nice homebody secretary, teacher, even a store cashier. But, if you're looking for sex, just pick up a nurse."

Infuriated, I threw the letter on the table and fell onto the bed. How dare he try to degrade the profession I want to be a part of? That I feel called into? What's his hang-up about my having to bathe a man's body, anyway? I doubt every man in the service has such blatant disrespect for nurses. The wounded soldiers probably thank God they're there to help them.

I cried myself to sleep that night, despite fighting against it. I fixed a light supper, but could not eat a bite of it before going to bed. After a sleepless night, I was able to put the memory of his stinging words aside and burst into the office, greeting everyone with my usual pleasant words and cheerful morning smile. There would be plenty of time to deal with my personal life later. I refused to let it interfere with my work.

Word came to my temporary address from the hospital's alumni foundation the following week. I had been accepted into nurses training, commencing August 1st. "Yes!" I yelled to noone and hurried to the public phone on the corner to tell my family the wonderful news. Mother was overjoyed to hear it because she knew how badly I wanted it. She said I was going to be living her dream. My mother had always wanted to be a nurse, too, but her dream went unfulfilled, even though Aunt Pauline offered to put her through training if she finished high school.

Though I'd shouted it to my walls and told my family,

telling Del Nims was going to be another matter, I told myself as I walked into his office the next morning. "Here's your coffee, Del," I told him with my usual smile.

"Ah just right, Peggy. Thank you. You know, you've certainly fit right into things here. I sure haven't had any reason to regret hiring you. I know I'm a big boob to work for, but I'm glad you've been enjoying it," he said, with his big happy smile. "Yes, Del, I have enjoyed it, so much." Now, I knew I couldn't tell him the news right away. It would be so hard to tell him at all. He was the greatest boss anyone could ever hope to have.

The next afternoon as I was going through the accounts on the large worktable in his office, I decided, easy or not, he had to be told I was leaving. It was the end of June and it wouldn't be fair not to give him ample time to replace me. "Del?"

He looked up and smiled. "Yes?"

"I have to tell you something, and you're not going to like it," I said, about as nervous as it was possible to be.

"Oh boy, what have you done—put us over budget?" He wrinkled his brow and looked at me, obviously puzzled but still smiling.

"Del, I wish it were something that minor," I told him. Reaching into my skirt pocket, I removed the letter from Bethesda and handed it to him.

He read it and his rugged face pinkened. I had seen this happen before, not in anger, because he never seemed to get angry over anything. However, when he was disappointed about something in our office or the mill, it always happened. He held the letter in his hands and said nothing; he just looked at me. It seemed so long before he said a word and I found it difficult to breathe.

I stood up, walked to the other side of the room and took a deep breath. Turning back to him, I started to open my mouth, but no words came. I sat back down, put my head in my hands and tears ran down my face. He handed me a tissue.

"Peggy, how long have you been planning a career in nursing?" he asked, finally, with a calmness I hadn't expected.

"Since I was fifteen, I've wanted it. But, since we had no money for it, I never really expected to get into a school. It wasn't until last weekend I really felt any reason to hope it might happen. I couldn't go at all, if it hadn't been for getting the loan." I looked at him, not knowing what to expect after that.

"Well," he said, after clearing his throat and standing to face the window, "I guess you'll have to hurry and break in a replacement. Call Personnel and tell them I'll have to have a new secretary within two weeks. I want you to spend at least half a week with her, if you can stay that long, Peg." He was being so kind and I could not detect a trace of anger or resentment in his voice.

"I can give a three week notice, if it will help you, Del. I I'm so sorry it's turned out this way, really I am. Despite how much I've wanted to become an RN, I've loved working for you."

"Yes, I know you have and all of us have loved having you. I knew the moment I met you, you'd be the perfect fit. I know the boys and Grace will be just as upset as I over your leaving. Three weeks will help me a great deal, Peg. Thank you for that. Better go now and call Personnel." He looked like he was going to cry all of a sudden, which shocked me.

"Yes, I'll do it right away." I hurried from the room and closed the door behind me. I couldn't look at anyone in the room before I picked up the phone. Since the outer office desks were not spaced that far apart, the two engineers and Grace could not help overhearing my request to Personnel.

After I disconnected, Jack came over and put his hand on my shoulder. "Come on, kid, what happened in there to make you want to quit Standard?"

I looked at him and then at the other two who were staring at me. "I don't want to quit," I managed to say. I felt a tear on my cheek and brushed it aside. He handed me a tissue from the box on the desk. I thanked him and handed him the letter Del had just read. He read it and just shook his head, saying nothing, but handed it to Andy who, in turn, gave it to Grace.

"Well, for goodness sakes, boys, this is a great opportunity for Peggy." Despite the two engineers being grown men in their thirties or early forties, she and Del always referred to them as boys. "I thought she'd be replacing me when I leave here in a few years, but she can go anywhere she wants as a registered nurse."

I smiled at her and said, "Yes, it is a wonderful opportunity, Grace. Actually, it's what I've wanted since I was fifteen, but I love it here and hate to leave all of you. You've been swell to me."

Finally, Andy said, with a big smile, "Guess we idiots should congratulate her, eh, Jack?"

"Yes, you're right. Congratulations, Peggy." He kissed

my forehead. "I hope you'll be a happy little nurse." The others laughed and the room filled with its usual pleasant voices.

Before the end of my last working day, Del called everyone, except the new secretary I'd been training, downstairs into the large conference room that doubled as a party room. They'd surprised me with gifts and sat around the table, toasting me, as I fought back tears. Finally, Del stood.

"Oh no," Jack said, "I was afraid of that. The boss is going to make a speech." They all laughed but Del ignored them and started talking.

"Well, men and Grace it's pretty obvious we've been had. I don't mean that as an insult to Peggy, but let's face it; we were just a means to an end for her."

I felt my face go hot and red. I also felt awkward and traitorous. That man I'd come to love and respect continued talking. "But, knowing now how much becoming a registered nurse means to her, I can't say I blame her for trying to land the best possible job after graduation. And, let's face it, guys and Grace, working for me is the best of all possible jobs!"

He grinned and they all clapped their hands. He raised a hand for silence and went on. "Peggy, I have a daughter, Carol, who's a year older than you. Believe it or not, she's a student nurse at Christ Hospital, in Cincinnati. Right around the corner from where you're going to be soon."

My mouth flew open. He had not said a word about that when he realized I wanted to go to school.

"So, you can be sure I understand what's causing you to leave," he continued. "I won't try to talk you out of it, as much as I'd like to. We tried for two years to talk Carol out of it because we wanted something easier for her, but nothing doing." He swallowed and cleared his throat. "Well, I guess there's nothing left to do, but wish you all the success and happiness in the world." He sat down and took my hands for a moment.

"Thank you, Del," I said, as I swallowed my tears. "Thank all of you. You've been wonderful to work with and I mean that from the bottom of my heart."

Grace had already told me, weeks before, she was retiring within ten or fifteen more years and her job would be mine, if I wanted it. She said her boss had lunch with Del once every week or so, and they'd already discussed how well I was doing for someone still in her teens.

It would be an honor to be the private secretary to the vice-president. At that moment, I regretted what I was doing, not just for the security such a position would offer, but because I was leaving a wonderful job and the nicest co-workers anyone could ever want. My regret was only for a moment, as I did want to be an RN, despite the difficult road ahead. I knew I was doing the right thing.

They all told me how much they would miss me and I told them, with sincerity, the same thing. I'd loved being a private secretary in that office and, after all, it was what Gilbert Fouch trained me for. I knew, in my heart of hearts, I might never find that kind of camaraderie and respect again, even in nursing.

I was to remember that thought many times over the years when being a nurse became difficult in so many ways. Even though I earned the respect of most of my peers and doctors, as much as nurses could in those early

And Then There Was One

days, it was never quite the same as it was in that first wonderful job as a private secretary. Still, my heart told me nursing was what I was supposed to do, so I turned the corner and headed in that direction.

Draher Hall, Peg's home during training, 1955-58.

Bethesda Hospital, 1920s.
Maternity at left; main hospital at right, before 6th and 7th floors added.

FOUR

Private Secretary to Probie

It was a hot summer day when my parents and I arrived at Draher Hall, the student nurses residence at Bethesda Hospital School of Nursing. It was three stories high and, like the hospital across the street, on the corner of Oak Street and Reading Road.

Draher Hall was named in honor of Minnie L. Draher, who graduated from the Bethesda Hospital School of Nursing in 1901. Ms. Draher, a deaconess, became Superintendent of the school in 1905, after she completed graduate studies at Johns Hopkins. She served in this capacity until 1946 when she became the superintendent emeritus until she died in 1954, one year before I came to live in her namesake home.

I had dreamed of this bright Sunday for three uncertain years. The next morning, August 1, 1955, was the beginning of my academic life at Bethesda Hospital School of Nursing. Words can't express how excited I felt to be there, knowing it was where I belonged; knowing it was my first day as a student nurse.

The first person we encountered, when we walked through the front door, was the Dean of Women, Suzy Kreutziger. She was six feet tall, towering over every student who crossed that threshold. How intimidating that was to those of us who had no idea how prominent this woman's role would be in our lives from that day forward. She introduced herself, as we did to her, and then asked me to sign in before she pointed us in the direction of the stairway to our right. This was the first of over one thousand times I would sign in at the front desk of Draher Hall over the next three years of my life.

"I doubt we'll ever make it up there with all this luggage!" My huffing father made that skeptical remark. There was no elevator and the stairs led to the second floor before curving to the third floor where upperclassmen lived.

"Oh don't you worry, Dad. If I made it to Cincinnati, I can guarantee you I'll make it to my room," I told him with a laugh. My father and I never had much to say to each other. He'd always been a quiet man around his children, unless they did something he didn't like and then they'd know it. He seemed in an especially good mood that day, which pleased me. Maybe it meant he was proud of me, though he never would have said that. He never did say it, or even that he loved me, until the week before he died, almost fifty years later, and it was a priceless gift to me.

All the way up the stairs, we kept bumping into members of other families who looked like they were feeling just as hopeless about going back and forth to their own daughters' dormitory rooms. Girls, fresh from high schools from many different states, entered training that day in Bethesda Hospital School of Nursing. It appeared all had picked the same hour to arrive on the scene.

Finally, we arrived at room 209. "Peggy, this is really nice. A big corner room, too. Look at this nice furniture, Ed," Mother said to Dad. In between twin beds was a large bedside table with double compartments. All the furniture was made of limed oak, giving it that patina look of antiques. Across from each bed was a pull down desk connected to bureaus filling three-fourths of the wall space.

Large double closets took up the rest of the space. A mirror ran five feet across the top of the bureaus. Each bed had a lovely bedspread to match the draperies on the two large windows. One of them faced the hospital across the street. I knew I'd spend a lot of time staring out that window in the coming weeks, wondering what mysteries that hospital would reveal to me during the next three years.

My dad went back to wait in the car for my mother, while I started to unpack and hang my clothes in the closet. Right after he left, my roommate and her family approached. They all seemed shy.

"Hi," the quiet girl told me, "I'm Mary Ann Mann. Are you Peggy Puckett?"

"Yes, aren't you lucky!" That broke the ice and everyone laughed. It was obvious their daughters were going to get along just fine.

"Peggy Puckett?" Another voice appeared from nowhere, startling all of us in the room.

"Yes," I answered, "I'm Peggy."

"Hi," the stranger said. She wore a student nurse's uniform and starched white cap, with two short, pale-blue velvet ribbons, one above the other, at the top corner of one side. "My name is Henrietta Bresch. Just call me Henri."

She sounded French or like someone of French ancestry whose family had raised her to speak the language. "I'm a junior and your Big Sister," she continued. "You each have one. It's our job to take you under our protective little wings and help you adjust to training. We're also the ones you come to in the middle of the night when you need a shoulder to cry on you know, when you've had a fight with the boyfriend or the Great White Lady has chewed you out. That sort of thing. Anyway, I hope you'll love it here. I'm in 316. Come by later tonight. I'm off at seven. See you," she called as she scurried out, leaving us wondering, who's the Great White Lady?

We learned soon enough she was Ms. Drysdale, our primary medical service instructor. She was on my case often throughout my years at Bethesda, and I was scared to death of her. She once ordered me to make an entire bed over, because she came by right after the patient had poked her foot out, messing up my perfectly mitered corner!

Poking her head back through the door for a moment, Henri laughed and said, "After the initiation, that is!" That sounded ominous.

Mary Ann was putting a few of her own things away when she came to a picture among them. She held it close to her ample chest and then put it on her bureau.

"Who's he your brother?" We both giggled. "Yeah

some brother, eh?"

Soon our parents told us they had to leave and start the drive back home, a one hundred mile drive for my parents, but right across the city limits into Indiana for Mary Ann's family.

"Well, honey, be sure to write. I know you'll have plenty to write about." Mother laughed and gave me a long hug, before kissing me goodbye.

After all the goodbyes were over and they had all left the dorm, we looked at each other. "Whew! Glad that's over. I can't stand goodbyes. Parents get all sloppy and bawl well, you know, Peggy. Your mom was just as bad as mine. Another minute and we'd be mopping the floors of their tears."

"You're right about that, roommate," I answered, as she removed some more things from a suitcase. After having four adults to relate to in the office all summer, it seemed strange to be relating to another teenager again, for although I'd been treated as a responsible young woman and had felt like one all summer, I was still a teenager.

"Hey, I like that! Roommate; makes it all sound so official. Yesterday, a nobody; today, a roommate."

I laughed at her and picked up an 8 x 10 of Buck. I set it on the bureau across from my bed.

"Your brother?" She giggled and I had to laugh, too. "Mary Ann, Buck. Buck, Mary Ann. I hope you'll be good friends. On second thought, not too good, though. You're prettier than I am."

"Yeah, fatter, too, by twenty or thirty pounds," she said with another hearty laugh. She was a very pretty girl with long, wavy, dark brown hair with a widow's peak at the center of her forehead and enviable thick, gently-curved dark brown eyebrows over deep-set dark brown eyes and a straight patrician nose. She never had to use eyebrow pencil on her brows and she had the ability to lift one brow instead of both when she was teasing. She was plump, weighting 135 to my 100, but she was two inches taller, also, so I did not think it looked bad on her at all. She was just curvaceous, in my opinion, and I told her so.

We never did finish unpacking, but then nobody else in the dorm did, either, that first night. There was too much getting acquainted and girls bursting into other girls' rooms to learn all they could about each other. It felt like being back in high school on our senior trip to New York where this went on almost all night. There was laughter and gaiety all evening and noise. Mostly noise!

At 7:30, we probies were asked to assemble downstairs in the lounge. It was a large pretty room, and I remember the strong aroma of lemon furniture polish as we walked in. Everything was shiny and spotless. Once there, we learned what the "initiation" was all about. We sat on the floor, surrounded by upperclassmen.

"Okay, gang," a junior student shouted, above the din. Suddenly, all the upperclassmen, with linked arms, were singing, "Getting to Know You," swaying gently to the music. Some had tears in their eyes, remembering their first night in Draher Hall, no doubt.

After this was over, the spokesperson told all probies to stand. All of us did. We were a wide-eyed bunch, not having the least idea what to expect next.

"The beanies," she said, holding out her hand as a

surgeon for the knife. Another stood by her side with a stack of blue and white beanie caps in her arms. They went down the rows of probies and handed a beanie to each big sister standing in back of each of us. The big sister, in turn, placed the little caps upon the heads of her dubious-looking little sister.

"Consider yourselves officially capped, little sisters." "This cap is the Bethesda Beanie. Treat it with respect. Do not I repeat do not remove it from your head until your big sister tells you it may be removed. This will not be for several weeks, I can assure you. If you are caught without the Bethesda Beanie at any time, be it in the classroom or in the shower, you must joyfully, and I do mean with joy, polish the duty shoes all of them of the upperclassman who caught you." Snickers were heard all over the room from other big sisters.

"And, in case you aren't sure what an upperclassman is," she continued, in a faux pious tone, "an upperclassman is any student nurse, in or out of uniform, above the level of probie." Of course, since we were probies for only six months and sophomores at the end of that time until our second year when we became juniors, that wasn't exactly an accurate statement. There would be no probies when we were sophomores. But, we knew what she meant.

She stopped and looked around the room. Her cohorts were grinning with sheer pleasure. We figured they were all glad their time in our spot had already passed. She managed to keep the straight-faced drill sergeant look, as she said, "Is that clear?" Looking both bewildered and excited, we said a collective.

"Yes, ma'am!"

"Okay, Probies, you're dismissed for now. Be back here at exactly 8:30 tonight, dressed for walking," the older girl commanded.

We looked from one to the other, and then all at once, we tore from the room. We were laughing and shouting so loudly, we'd disturbed the dean of women. We soon learned not to disturb her, if at all possible.

Suzy Kreutziger stood in the center of the hallway, blocking our path across from the switchboard and front desk. Her hands were on her hips and her snake eyes dared anyone to move. Her lips were tightly pursed.

"If you young ladies think you're going to behave like wild animals in Draher Hall, you've got another thought coming!" Her voice could be so loud and reprimanding that it was described by most students who'd ever lived in the hall as being "able to break up a cyclone."

"Now," she continued, "certainly we want you to make this your home away from home, but you have a responsibility to this home. You must not give it the name of being a zoo or something worse. Some student nurses have night duty tonight. I'm sure they must be trying to sleep. You will also have your share of night duty and will appreciate the quiet so you, too, can sleep. Now, you may proceed to wherever you were going, but let's see if we can be a little quieter on our way. Thank you," she said, still unsmiling.

One by one, we filed past her and up the stairs, where we once more started running to our rooms, as un-quietly as before. I noticed, even though she was standing right beside Ms. Kreutziger with a smile on her sweet face, Mrs. Weed, the tiny housekeeper/housemother, whose disposition seemed the direct opposite of hers, never said a word the entire time the dean of women was speaking.

We loved Mrs. Weed as soon as we met her. All the upperclassmen did, too. I suppose that was the problem. If she'd been more of a disciplinarian, Suzy's job might have been easier. But, she did not seem to have it in her to be bossy or strict, which endeared her to all of us. It was easy to see she loved every student who ever enrolled in the school. Beneath her rigid and austere nature, Suzy might have, also, but she probably figured some one had to keep order in the hall, so we never knew this if it were true. Mrs. Weed was supposed to keep a close eye on us when the dean of women was not around, but needless to say, she was lax in that respect, also.

Upstairs, our class of 1958 was rushing about, getting into Bermuda shorts, tee shirts and saddle shoes or penny loafers, while trying to keep the beanie on our heads.

"Well so, that's the famous Suzy Kreutziger," Anita Brate said. "I've heard about her for years." Anita was a pretty brunette, who said she hated to smile because her teeth protruded, but she was fun to be with and we liked her instantly. I didn't think her teeth looked bad at all.

Her roommate, Mary Beth Brackemyre, herself a pretty brunette, was an enjoyable girl, too. She also had an imperfection which embarrassed her, but one which she poked fun at quite a lot. She was terribly thin and was what she called, "flat chested." She shared with us that when she came during the summer for her interview, she was almost rejected for being so thin. But, she was such a good student in high school they had second thoughts. They allowed her to enter training, believing they could put weight on her, no doubt. She never gained a pound in three years.

We made quite a foursome, they with their quirks, Mary Ann with what she perceived as being overweight and I had a bad case of acne; so bad, one of my patients asked to speak with the assistant director of the school, unbeknownst to me. She convinced her to get help for me. Geneva Rubins called me to her office, handed me a slip of paper with a doctor's name and address and told me I was to go to the dermatologist's office the very next week. After three months of painful and intense treatment, I was cured of a five-year case of acne vulgaris and left with small scars on my face. I much preferred that to the pustules Clearasil only camouflaged.

"Hey, Mary Beth," Anita said," look at him. Wow!" They examined the photograph of Buck in his full dress uniform.

"Gee, some girls have all the luck! Are you engaged to this flyboy, Peggy?"

"Yes, I hope so," I answered, as I, too, stared at the image.

"What do you mean you hope so? Either you are or you aren't!"

"Well, Anita, Buck wanted me to marry him, but he didn't want me to come into training, so right now, your guess is as good as mine whether we'll be married or not," I explained.

"Do you have a ring?"

"No, he told me in his last letter, he's getting it in the PX."

"Ditch him!" Her roommate said, emphatically. "A

friend of mine says training's hard enough without man trouble."

"No, I love him too much to give him up."

"Are you sure, Peg? After all, you did choose nurses' training," Anita said, with a small smirk.

"That's not true. It wasn't a matter of choosing it over him." I thought that was true, but of course, it wasn't. Against his wishes, I'd entered training.

"Hey, will you two knock it off. Stop being drags. Tonight, guys, except for any strangers we might meet on our little mysterious outing after while, are strictly off limits," Mary Ann said, with a twinkle in her eyes.

I laughed and told her, "Okay, you win. Hey, look at the time!" It was 8:20, so we all ran for the stairs and reached the lounge at exactly 8:25, puffing as we caught our breaths, Suzy glaring in our wake.

"Okay, you probies," the same junior, who spoke before, said. "Follow us. Oh, by the way, my name is Marilyn Gaskins. This is Ella Watkins."

They filed out, with us on their heels, trying to stay within hearing distance. They stopped at the switchboard. "Before any student leaves these sacred halls, slide the marker out beside your name on the Logbook, write in the time and where you're going (or fake it)," she said, under her breath, "then you're free to go."

Outside, we paused, some sitting on the high steps until all of us had logged out and were together. The upperclassmen started walking. "Oh girls, another thing; on weeknights, you must be in the dorm by 10 pm and on Saturday and Sunday, by midnight."

"Oh, that's just ducky," someone, we later learned was

fellow probie Andy Andrews, groaned.

"Don't worry," Marilyn said quickly, "you'll find a curfew only adds a little more spice to your life here at Bethesda. The smoker has a ground-level door." The two of them exchanged smiles. Most of us shrugged, not getting that one. Soon, we all learned that door was the one the students who smoked and hung out in the room constantly, even while studying, unlocked when a student was late for curfew, so she could get in. She could always say she forgot to sign in, if they noticed she was still signed out the following morning.

"In case you're wondering where we're going," she added, "we're your official escorts to The Cellar, as we call it, which is going to become your home away from home over these next three years."

The owners of the little restaurant and bar were husband and wife. They got to know all of us by name and treated us as their surrogate children, giving us more than we asked for if we had little or, as was often the case, no money to pay for a good meal away from the hospital. Of course, The Cellar, as most other places we frequented, was off-limits to us, because of its bar, but that didn't stop any of us from enjoying it and its proprietors.

And Then There Was One

Capping Ceremony, February 1956

FIVE

Reality Check

We had a great time that night and countless other nights, but learned, sooner than we wanted to, being a student nurse was not all fun and games. And it surely started early in the morning!

Every morning before we reported for work at 6:45, we had to have breakfast in the large sunny cafeteria eaten by 6:30, so we could listen to devotions. If we had class at eight but were not on day duty, we still had to eat breakfast and listen to devotions. We could always grab a quick nap between devotions and class, which most of us became adept at doing. We were excused only if we were on evening or night duty and had no 8 am class.

I was never a morning person, so just waking up by 5:30 or 6 was a chore for me. I began to hate my alarm clock, as did Mary Ann. Even after breakfast and coffee, until I started my day of work or in the classroom, I was not alert enough to absorb what Ms. Goetz, a Deaconess, was trying to tell us at that hour.

She was also our religious education instructor and Andy hated having to memorize Bible verses in her class. Her family took her to the Unitarian Universalist Church and she'd never been exposed to the kind of Sunday school some of us Baptist and Methodists had. In their Sunday school, the UU exposed their children to all the religions of the world and encouraged them to use their minds about their beliefs rather than to blindly accept the strict dogma preached in our churches. Even though I'd grown up in the Baptist Church and Sunday school, I couldn't understand why we had to do it, either, at our age and in nursing school!

Although she forbade us to touch our forks or spoons as she was bringing us the inspirational lesson of the day, some of us, who always seemed to arrive late for breakfast, tried to sneak our food into our mouths as she was speaking.

More than once she caught us with our scrambled eggs almost to our lips and called us on it. Once when she caught Andy and told her to put down her fork, Andy said, "Oh, hell." "What did you say, young lady?" Ms. Goetz was livid and her voice, shaky.

"Me?" Andy, dripping with innocence, goaded her. "Yes, you. What did you say?"

"Gee, I don't remember now, but it was probably, 'yes, ma'am'."

The rest of us suppressed our giggles. As soon as our shaken religious instructor went back to her lesson, our classmate went right back to eating, as though nothing unusual had occurred.

An admitted tomboy, Andy was always pushing the bar and more than once got into trouble for it. She never seemed interested or concerned about towing the mark, as we were supposed to, as genteel and proper student nurses. I have to admit, as much as I disapproved of being disrespectful to one's elders and never would have dared the things she did, there were few dull moments with Andy in the room.

Bethesda's training school was a three-year program of hard work, classes and study. And, if you worked hard enough, studied hard enough, performed everything exactly as you were taught and passed all your senior comprehensive exams, you graduated with a diploma in nursing. This made you eligible to take your state board examinations and to wear the coveted black stripe on your Pfleuger cap, named after the hospital's motherly Director of Nurses, Martha Pflueger, RN.

She could afford to be loving and kind toward us, since it was Geneva Rubins, RN, Assistant Director of Nurses and Director of the School of Nursing, who ran it with an iron fist. Most of our academic instructors were professors from the University of Cincinnati, who taught the courses on our hospital campus, but most of our clinical instructors, although affiliated with the university, were employees of Bethesda Hospital School of Nursing.

Although Miss Rubins did know how to smile, she was grudging with them when it came to us, her students. Except for the day after she was admitted to the surgical ward when I was on my first surgical rotation. Although she was not married, she'd had a large abdomen and looked eight or nine months pregnant from the day we met her, something we'd all speculated about from our first day as students. It turned out it was not a baby she was having out of wedlock by a secret lover, as many of us romanticized about this Deaconess; it was a nine-pound uterine tumor the surgeon was going to remove in the morning. I was the unlucky student, or so I believed, assigned to get her ready for surgery. I was determined to do everything to perfection and I did almost.

Ethics was the only class Geneva Rubins taught and in it, we learned a nurse never says "good luck" to a patient going into the operating room, since the connotation was the success of the surgery depended more upon luck than the skill of the surgeon.

Yet, despite knowing this, as the orderlies wheeled her out of the room to take her to the operating room, I looked at her and said over a lump in my throat, "Good luck, Miss Rubins."

Then, realizing I had spoken the forbidden words, I closed my eyes for a moment and waited for the lecture. It never came. I opened them, just as with a broad smile she'd never had for me before, she said, "Thank you, Peggy."

She had never used my first name before, either, so both were a shock to me. I almost cried, because I was so happy to see her smile and hear her say that. We were all relieved to learn her tumor was benign. She was back to her former stern self within the month.

One of my favorite classes, though it was so difficult for me, and I had to attend extra autopsies just to learn enough to get a low C in it, was anatomy class. A tall lanky professor from the University of Cincinnati, by the name of Dr. Ingersoll, taught it. He had seven children and when the last was born, he was so engrossed in a baseball game on TV, the nurse did not tell him the baby was born until the game was over, even though the baby came during the 2nd inning. Joking about his large number of children, he told us, "OJ's the best contraceptive. Don't drink it before and don't drink it after. Drink it instead of." All of us enjoyed his class.

After the first six months of training, our probie days were over and we had our capping ceremony. We were now sophomore students. One of the proudest moments of my young life was when that white starched Pfleuger cap was placed upon my head and I recited the Nightingale Pledge with the rest of my class. I had just turned nineteen and unlike my high school classmates, who had gone into other schools, occupations and the armed services after graduation, my focus was on helping to heal the sick and minimize the anxiety and pain of the dying.

One of the first assignments I had as a sophomore was to get a woman, recovering from a heart attack, out of bed. She told me she was "feeling wonderful" when I first introduced myself and helped her with her bath. These were the days before there was such a thing as anti-embolus stockings to prevent blood clots after surgery, heart attacks and strokes.

"Okay, let's let you dangle your feet a little first," I instructed as I helped her to swing her feet off the bed. "That will get the blood circulating again."

She smiled and said, "That feels good."

I returned the smile, let her take her time, and said, "Tell me when you're ready to stand." After she indicated she was ready to take those first steps, I helped her step down to the floor. And, then, she slumped over in my arms.

"Help!" I called, pressing the emergency call bell. "I need help in here!"

Other students, the head nurse and instructor hurried into the room, an intern on their heels soon after. "My God," the head nurse said, and they helped me get her back onto the bed. It was then we realized she was dead. And, I had killed her.

I certainly needed the support of my roommate and big sis when I got off duty at three that afternoon. Henri told me, "Peggy, she probably threw a clot. It happens just that quickly if there's a clot in the leg or groin. You couldn't have done anything to stop it from happening. She said she was fine before she dangled and stood up, so how were you supposed to know there was a clot? You did nothing wrong. You followed proper procedure before letting her stand."

Those were almost the exact words the intern and my instructor told me right after it happened. I was so shaken by her sudden death, that I could not even help another student take her to the morgue. I knew it was my fault; that I'd done something wrong despite what the three of them told me. I had killed my patient.

Lois Montgomery, my astute instructor, arranged for me to attend her post-mortem examination. On the day the post was scheduled, I went to the autopsy room, always thick with the aroma of formaldehyde. During the autopsy, Dr. Hans Gerth, the resident pathologist I had a secret crush on, found a large blood clot that had caused the death of my sweet elderly patient. "See, Miss Puckett," he told me in his thick German accent, his crooked smile reassuring me, as his blonde hair fell over one eye, "this pulmonary embolism was what killed her. It probably was lodged somewhere in her upper thigh or groin. When she put her legs down, the deep vein thrombosis broke loose and started traveling to her lung. When she stood, the clot was already moving, cut off the blood supply and she died. Patients don't always die from pulmonary emboli, but this one was so large and caused so much damage, she didn't have a chance. There was nothing you or anyone else could have done to prevent it, since there had been no indication it existed before you were told to get her out of bed."

"Then, I really didn't kill her?"

He smiled again and said, "You really didn't kill her."

I could have hugged the man at that moment, but I contained myself. It would not have been too prudent for someone to walk through the autopsy room doors to see a student nurse with her arms around the pathologist.

It was a relief to know I'd done nothing wrong and could not have done anything to prevent her from dying. Perhaps had we learned about CPR in the mid-fifties or even if we'd had crash carts with all the right cardiac emergency drugs and equipment on each floor, we might have been able to do something, but since we did not have any of that, yet, her death could not have been prevented.

I was too busy working eight hours on the floor and eight hours in the classroom, and then studying after dinner every night, to dwell on my first patient death, and it certainly was not my last.

I was beginning to understand why Del Nims tried to talk his daughter out of nursing school. There was nothing easy about it. But, I loved being a student nurse and still did not regret my decision to become one.

One evening, in my junior year, which was my second year of training, I was the medication nurse for the evening shift and was checking a post-op patient on the surgical floor who had just undergone a hysterectomy. This was before the days of the intensive care unit (ICU) or continuous care unit (CCU), so all the patients came straight to the surgical floor from Recovery Room, when they were stable and not vomiting, just as the cardiac patients came straight to the medical floor straight from the emergency room, if they survived the first hours of a heart attack.

On the evening shift there was one student charge nurse and one student medication nurse, but no registered nurses on the floor and no instructor. There was an RN supervisor over the hospital in the evening and one on night duty until the morning shift arrived.

This young mother, in her early thirties had a cancerous tumor removed with her uterus. She was in a great deal of pain but seemed to be doing well, otherwise. Because she was a fresh post-op patient, besides medicating her for pain every three to four hours, as she needed it, I checked her vitals and dressings every hour as I went about my rounds. Suddenly, things turned for the worse.

"Please, come right away," I told the resident surgeon on the phone, after I explained what measures I'd taken during the past few hours. "She's bleeding and going into shock."

I went back to the patient, in the room to the right of

the nurses' station and packed more heavy dressings over her fresh one, which was bright red with blood. I knew not to remove the original dressing. Keeping one hand on her abdomen, I checked her carotid pulse with the other. Her heart rate was even higher, 118. When I re-checked her blood pressure, it was down to 80 over 40 from 100 over 60 just five minutes before.

When the resident got there, he removed the dressing. Blood poured from the wound. I already had plenty of sterile 4 x 4s and ABD (abdominal) pads, plus a suture set beside the bed, in case he needed it. Also, I'd asked the supervisor to alert the OR team in case he had to take her back to the operating room.

The resident looked at me and said, "I can't do any more here except pack more dressing on her, as you did. The bleeder's too deep. Can you have the supervisor get the OR ready? I'll have to go back in right now."

"I've already done that, Doctor."

He looked surprised, but left right away to scrub for surgery. The patient looked at me with tears running down her chalky face. "What's happening to me?" I knew she feared she was going to die, but that question remained unspoken, despite the terror in her eyes and voice.

I squeezed her hand and told her, "You have a bleeding problem. It happens sometimes after surgery, but the doctor will take care of it. We just have to take you back to the operating room where the lights are brighter, so he can see the bleeding area better." That was all true insofar as it went. I saw no point in adding to her state of anxiety and fear by telling her how serious the problem was, and if the bleeder was not stopped right away, she might die from the loss of blood.

She mumbled a faint "Okay," and then passed out. She was in and out of consciousness as an orderly and I wheeled her to the elevator and into the OR on the 7th floor. She lived, thanks to the quick work of the young resident, but I was scared for a while. I knew she had a young husband and small children and did not want them to lose her. She was also my patient, and I did not want to lose her, either.

Before I write more about my own days in nursing school, I want something to be clear to the reader. I know in my heart I could never have become a good nurse had I not gone to a diploma school of nursing, where actual practice of nursing eight hours a day, combined with academic studies, was the norm.

However, there are young men and women who attend nursing school in colleges and universities, throughout the United States, where this rote practice of nursing skills for entire shifts five days a week, throughout the training program, is not as important as the academic end of the nursing spectrum. It is not part of their nursing education except in smaller clinical doses toward the end of their academic program. After graduation, most of them have what are called externships, working under RNs in hospitals for a certain length of time before they're deemed ready to work alone in a hospital after they pass their boards and receive their RN. Yet, I know these schools produce excellent nurses, like my youngest daughter, Susan Herne, who maintained a 4.0 average throughout the years of her college nursing program and excelled on her nursing boards.

Suzy (not named after Suzy Kreutziger, the dean of women in Draher Hall) is a practicing certified hospice RN. She graduated in 2004 and within a year after passing her boards, started working the same area on a hospice outpatient team I worked before I finished my nursing career in telephone triage for the same company, Hospice of Palm Beach County. Today, she is a team supervisor. I did not sit for my certification because I was within a year of retiring when approached about it, but she has been a nurse for just a few years, so it was good for her to become certified in hospice nursing.

I would recommend certification for any young nurse, or even an older nurse who is going to continue working at least five more years, regardless of the type of nursing in which she works. The reason is two-fold: The extra credential recognizes the nurse as having expertise in that particular field of nursing and also qualifies her for a substantial and immediate higher pay grade.

So, student nurses reading this book, keep that in mind when you begin your RN career and do it as soon as possible after your first year of employment, which is the earliest you can sit for the certification exam in most areas of nursing. Even if you change your nursing specialty after you are certified in another area, do the same in your new field when you're eligible. The more credentialed you are, the better for your future in nursing.

I know, from having overheard my daughter on the phone when the team physician or another team member called her after she finished her workday, how adept, ethical and knowledgeable she is about the practice of her profession. She speaks with total confidence to each person with whom she is in contact. On occasion when I was visiting her, she confided in me about some of the things she encountered in her daily nursing walk. Always mindful not to divulge the name of any of her patients to me, she discussed what happened and how she handled it. Every time, she was right on the money and I could not have performed better. Or as well, I'm certain, in some instances.

So, the type of nursing education one has, does not equate, necessarily, to its superiority over another way of becoming a nurse. I am grateful three-year diploma schools were the norm when I was learning my profession, because as difficult as it could be, I am convinced it was still the best, and probably the only, way for me to become a nurse. Years later, I went to college for my degree in nursing, but I could not have become a good nurse without all the practical experience combined, equally, with the academic.

Years after graduation, when I was already married (not to Buck, as we called off our engagement during my first year in school) and a mother living in West Palm Beach, Florida, I was taking a continuous education course to fulfill my required quota of 24 continuing education units (CEUs) within every two year period. There on the screen, the presenter flashed a photograph, unlabeled, of my probie class taken the day we were capped, just six months after we began nurses training. Tears sprang to my eyes. Still in our teens, we looked too young to shoulder the responsibility we were soon to be handed.

Most of the participants in the course were laughing at the way we were dressed: blue chambray, short-sleeved dresses with convertible collars and white pinafores, almost down to our ankles, and the white starched Pflueger caps atop our heads.

White nursing caps went the way of the Nightingale Pledge. I am not so sure that is a good thing. Once the movement to ban caps started, I thought it would never change, but the cardiac floor of JFK Memorial Hospital in Lake Worth, Florida, recently began an experimental phase of having all their nurses wear white nurses uniforms and white nurses caps.

For years, patients have complained, as have I when a patient in a hospital, because there is no way to distinguish the nurses from the nursing assistants or other ancillary personnel since nearly all wear colorful scrub suits, white scrub suits and no caps. I've always believed the real reason hospitals stopped requiring their nurses to wear caps was because so many young men were going into the profession, a good thing. However, if a male nurse did not wear a cap, it would still help if he wore a white uniform different from a scrub suit to distinguish himself from other personnel.

I know today there are some hospitals that require their nursing assistants or associates, as some call them, to wear a certain color of scrub suit, while the nurses wear all white, even if it is a scrub suit. Even this is preferable to everyone dressing any way they wish, regardless of which category of employee they are. Of course, OR and Labor and Delivery nurses need to wear scrubs because of the nature of their work.

The nurses at JFK told reporters covering the story, they enjoy wearing all white, and especially, wearing the nurses cap. For most of them, it was their first experience wearing caps or uniforms. They'd always worn scrubs. They are getting positive feedback from the rest of the staff on other floors who want to wear them, and from the patients who say, finally, they know who is the nurse and who is not. The nurses, unanimously, agreed they're going to continue to wear white uniforms and white caps even though it was supposed to be just an experiment.

I was happy to hear that. The old argument that the nurses cap is loaded with bacteria is not valid, as far as I'm concerned. A good nurse launders it frequently and it almost never comes into contact with the blood and other contamination from the patients that her uniform can during a shift of duty. She never touches it while it's on her head, so her hands do not contaminate it during her shift. She, also, does not wear it out of the hospital, but carries it to work and home in a sealed plastic container for that purpose.

I did not say anything when I saw the photograph on the screen but after the class was over, I walked up to the gentleman teaching the nursing history course and asked where he got it. He asked why and I told him. He was delighted to know its history and thanked me for telling him where it originated, so he could label it for future classes. He said he found the photograph in a dumpster somewhere in Florida.

I knew I was not the only Bethesda graduate who

ended up in Florida, Andy among them, but I never asked any of the others who might have thrown away the photograph. I had a good idea who might have tossed it, anyway; someone who never enjoyed much about our nurses training and wanted no momentos of what she described as "the most horrible three years" of her life. Because the hospital could not have functioned without the (unpaid) work of the student nurses, she called us "indentured servants."

I suppose she had a point, but I looked at it as the only way I could have become a nurse. I've always learned everything in life by doing it over and over, so, for me it was a fair trade-off. Besides, my student loan for the entire three years was only $365, and that included my tuition, books, uniforms, laundry service and room and board! What kind of three-year professional education could one get today for that amount of money, that included all of the above? I dare say, none. Sure, getting a little paycheck for all the work we were doing would have been a nice thing, but no one paid student nurses in those days.

Despite the hilarity with which it was met by most of the other class participants, it was a shock to see our class photograph on a screen in West Palm Beach, Florida, over a thousand miles from our training school in Cincinnati, Ohio!

Unlike many other young women of our age, the focus for student nurses wasn't on parties and dates after school or a day at the office. Our days were focused on how much pain medication to give a suffering young mother or helping the doctor in his futile efforts to stop a thirty-year-old man with cancer of the neck from bleeding-out onto the walls of his room, as he lay dying. Even the student assigned to him that morning was covered in his blood. It was an image none of us ever could get out of our heads, even those of us who were not there. To this day I remember his room number to the left of the nurses' station 315.

    We student nurses enjoyed our hours off duty. We had dates and fun in the beautiful sprawling city of hills, but for the most part, life was somber. High school seemed light years away.

SIX

Student Nurses Revolt

Mary Ann met the love of her life in our junior year. She, too, had broken up with the handsome boyfriend in the photograph. Victor Farrell was much older than she, but a hard working, ruggedly handsome man. Like her, he had dark brown hair, thick dark eyebrows and a big smile for everyone. I'd never seen two people so much in love. I adored Vic and he treated me like a sister. I thought they were a perfect couple in every way. And, he never thought she weighed too much. He loved her curves, he told her.

One day she came to me and said, "We're getting married."

"Hey, roommate, that's wonderful news. I'm happy for you. Vic's a great guy."

"Thanks, Peggy, but I mean we're going to get married —tonight!"

"Oh my goodness, Mary Ann. What are you going to do about school?"

"I'll stay right here. We'll live together on weekends."

"But, you know they won't let you do that."

"They won't know. We're not going to tell them. I'll just

sign out for home every weekend I'm off and go to my new home. They won't suspect I'm not in Aurora."

I stood up for her during the small ceremony and she came back to the dorm after spending her weekend with Vic in their little love nest not far from the hospital. Their secret life remained a secret, until one day she announced, "I'm pregnant. We're gonna have a baby!"

"Oh my gosh, Mary Ann! That's wonderful and I'm thrilled for you, but you can't hide a growing baby like you do your wedding ring. We've got too long to go before graduation. I think it's time we have a meeting with our big sisters. Now! This can't wait."

We did have that meeting with them, and then, because the school would not change the marriage rules, we had a bigger meeting, in the upstairs lounge with our all our classmates. Andy's roommate, June, wanted to marry her boyfriend, Clayton, also, so the meeting was as much for her as Mary Ann. We told them the problem, and Barbara Lumpkin who was as short as I, a little overweight during training, and went by the nickname, Lump, came up with a solution. "Well, we'll threaten to go on strike until they get the rule changed that says a student can't be married until her last six months of training."

"But, that won't help Mary Ann now. She's going to have a baby," one of the other students protested.

"I'm getting to that," Barbara said. "When she starts to show, we'll get the pregnancy rule changed." Barbara Lumpkin never lacked a confidence gene.

One student, Patty Barnes, the sweet, but timid niece of our nutrition instructor, said she was going to work. Andy and a few others threatened to tie her to the chair, if she so much as moved a muscle or even looked like she was going to go over to the hospital the day of our threatened strike. She stayed where she was, although she looked as frightened as the proverbial deer caught in the headlights, to have joined our revolution.

The threat to strike seemed so simple, but would it work? Our big sisters thought so. Thanks to Barbara, a born negotiator, and Geneva Rubins, who relented to meeting with us since it was obvious no one was going on duty unless she did, the rule was changed to allow students to marry after their first six months of training instead of the last six months, and they could remain in school unless they became pregnant.

A few words here about Barbara Lumpkin. She moved back to Florida after graduation; in fact, at one time, she lived a few blocks from me in Palm Springs, west of Lake Worth, until going to Central Florida. She also became quite a bit thinner than she'd been in training and it would have been ludicrous to address her by that ridiculous nickname, so no one did. All nurses in the state of Florida get higher pay and benefits because of her continued nursing activism. Patient care was not her forte; negotiation for the betterment of nurses was. Nurses had no union, so Barbara started a movement to improve conditions and salaries, as a member of the Florida Nurses Association Board, shortly after we graduated and never stopped working for nurses her entire career. She caused state legislators to take notice when she made her frequent trips to the state capitol in Tallahassee. Barbara is retired now, but remains a consultant to the FNA board. She is widely respected, especially among the nursing community in Florida. The FNA still is the only state nursing association that advocates for all nurses, regardless of their specialty or area of nursing and regardless of whether they are members of the association.

When Mary Ann (Farrell, now, not Mann) began to show, Barbara, true to her word, called another meeting and before we knew it, she had worked her magic again. The rule was changed to allow pregnant nursing students to take maternity leave at seven months instead of drop out of school.

So, Mary Ann had her sweet, beautiful baby girl, Beth, and came back to school to finish training and graduate a little later than the rest of us, although her graduation portrait is represented with the rest of our class of 1958. She and Victor still live in Aurora, Indiana where she grew up. She worked for more than thirty years in a hospital near Aurora. They had a houseful of other children, in addition to that precious little girl who became the reason our rebellious class got the rules changed twice at Bethesda Hospital School of Nursing.

We students still had much more work to do and sometimes, as when the young man bled out that day, our shifts could become sad ones in the blink of an eye. We had to be taught to turn off that sadness and stress in order to relax when we were out of uniform. That was as essential as any other lesson we had to master. Our well-being and ability to function effectively depended upon how well we could do this.

We each had our own way of cooling down after our shift was finished. We had no counselors to talk with in those days; there was no professional to de-brief us. Our instructors, if something happened when they were on duty, helped us through it but we were on our own after we walked out of the hospital at the end of the shift.

When I experienced a particularly sad or difficult day on duty, if I could speak of it at all, I talked about it with my roommate (at different times, depending upon which hospital we were in at the time, Mary Ann, Andy, or Phyllis Ryle). If it was not something I could discuss with her, I could walk up to the third floor of the dorm and talk it over with Henri, before she graduated, if she was not on a tour of duty at one of the other three hospitals in which we were required to train, which I'll discuss later.

If I could not talk about my day, at all, I went down to the lounge in the student residence, closed the door and played the baby grand piano for hours. By my senior year, I'd become adept at turning off my workday as soon as I was off duty, without consciously trying, as had my peers.

Sometimes, Andy and I went to Mecklenburg's, a little beer garden near the hospital, where I'll never forget dancing with a handsome guy we all knew, to the lilting tune, Twilight Time. We never dated, but for some reason, that scene with him walking up to the booth where I sat on the end, taking my hand and leading me to the dance floor when that tune came on the juke box, stayed forever etched in this brain of mine. Yeah, I've always been a romantic. Sometimes at another little place called Melbourne's, I played piano and Andy, drums. That was a good way to cool down, as well. Of course, like all the others, including Mecklenburg's, it was off-limit to us student nurses.

Other times, when I was dating a nice young man by the name of Tom, in his senior year at the Cincinnati School of Embalming, formerly the Cincinnati College of Mortuary Science, I picked up free tickets at the switchboard of Draher Hall, for the symphony or a hockey game. The two of us would enjoy a wonderful night of music or sitting close to ringside and watching the hockey game.

I loved the symphony, especially, as I had never been to one in my life until I started to see him, and of course, I'd always loved music. It was exciting to watch dozens of excellent professional musicians playing so many different instruments and listening to the vast variations in sound blending to make those wonderful pieces of music come alive before my eyes.

I can see us now, all in black, him in his black suit, overcoat and Homburg atop his head. I had one slim black dress I would wear with a dress-length faille coat and opera pumps on my feet. We made a debonair-looking couple, leaving Draher Hall to walk to his car.

We were great pals; just two friends keeping each other company for a little while, never wanting it to be more than it was. Neither of us felt romantic about the other, despite his being very handsome and one of the nicest men I'd ever met. We were both centered upon our respective careers and what it took to make it to those careers.

At dinner one night, while we were talking about where our futures were leading us, Tom, who knew he was returning to his hometown to work in the family business, encouraged me to become a stewardess (now called flight attendant) after I graduated. I'll never forget his words. "Peggy, when you have that RN after your name, you can be anything you want to be and do anything you want to do."

I laughed and protested that, at five feet, I hardly was tall enough for a stewardess, but he sloughed that off, repeating if I wanted something badly enough I could pursue it with my new credentials behind me.

I never pursued that avenue, even though I'd had a fleeting moment when I thought perhaps being a stewardess would be a great career; I certainly had a natural wanderlust and would love to have seen the world. However, I had never flown before and harbored a secret fear of flying I didn't share with my friend. This fear never left me, even after I began to fly in later years.

After Tom's graduation, we said goodbye, and he returned to the family funeral home business in Warren, Ohio, while I continued to push ahead to that day I could leave Cincinnati for my career in nursing.

Not long after Tom graduated, I dated a Mennonite graduate student for several months, who was an instructor at the University of Cincinnati. He picked me up on Saturday and Sunday afternoons, or just one or the other, if I only had one day of the weekend off. We'd drive out of the city to beautiful little country inns for long lunches, and then we'd take another long drive, listening to Johnnie Mathis and other crooners on the radio. Or we walked around the zoo, an art gallery, or went to a movie or outdoor concert somewhere in the city before going to another lovely place for dinner. His name was Ammon.

Ammon and I did develop feelings for each other, to the point we believed we were in love. One day, he told me he wanted to marry me, if I would have him. Then, he confessed he was pledged to marry a Mennonite girl his parents had chosen for him. He told me he believed, because we had so much in common and enjoyed being together so much, we could have a happy life, but he was committed to going back to northern Ohio to teach in a Mennonite college, so my life would be different from what I'd ever known.

After the freedom I had come to enjoy away from the little town I came from, with its own strict religious mores, even though a life with Ammon appealed to me, I knew a life among an even more rigid religious sect did not. Ammon had told me, months before, he was from a moderately conservative Mennonite group and both men and women dressed modestly, women in dresses with covering upon their heads, not like the bonnets the Amish wore, but small caps more on the order of a lacy piece of cloth perched atop the head. None of this appealed to me.

I really cared for Ammon, although I probably was not in love with him. I told him I would think about it. He told me not to take too long, because he would be awarded his degree within a few months and had to start teaching right after that in the Mennonite college.

He did not pressure me beyond that, so I took my time thinking about it and came to the conclusion I had to turn him down. I knew I could not be a good Mennonite, and, too, I wanted to finish nursing school and get my RN.

Clearly, he was disappointed. He confided he'd believed since I hadn't given him a definite no the night he proposed, he had a chance of winning me over to the idea.

I told him how sorry I was, but I knew I could not be a good Mennonite wife. I said if he cared for the Mennonite girl enough to go ahead with the arranged marriage, I knew she would be the better wife for him. He did not say he planned to do that, but I was certain he would, if only to please his parents. We said goodbye that night.

Then, the day before he was to leave, I had a call from him to say he was leaving Cincinnati the next morning and would like to take me to dinner that evening. Since we'd already said goodbye, I didn't understand why he wanted to see me again, but told him I would go. I'd worked that morning and had the next day, Sunday, off duty.

We drove out of town to one of the country inns we'd eaten at several times, and after dinner was finished, he drove up to Eden Park by the conservatory to a spot overlooking the river. It was a starry spring night with a silvery full moon. We were listening to WLW Radio's Moon River, one of my favorite programs that interspersed beautiful romantic love songs with romantic love poems, recited by a man with a soft but deep voice. He did no other talking, except when he was reciting the poetry.

Neither of us said a word after Ammon parked the car facing the river. Other couples were parked there, also, but not close to us. Everything was quiet, except for the sound of the soft music and radio DJ reciting the poetry, as we looked out at the glistening reflection of the lights in the river, the occasional lighted boat going by.

All of a sudden, Ammon took me into his arms and we kissed, as tears rolled down both our cheeks. He told me he couldn't bear to live the rest of his life without me and begged me to leave with him in the morning; he would explain to his parents and the Mennonite girl that he loved me, and we were going to be married.

It hurt to say it, but I told him again how sorry I was; as much as I cared about him and knew he cared about me, I also knew I could not become a Mennonite. I explained I wanted to finish school, so I would have a career of my own. He told me I still could do so if I married him. Although I never doubted his sincerity about that, I doubted it could have happened.

Our parting that night was anguish. It had been almost two years since I broke up with Buck, and my feelings, if not love, for Ammon were nonetheless genuine. It hurt to say that final goodbye to him, so much so that after he dropped me off at the dorm, I called him an hour later to say I'd changed my mind; I would marry him.

He sounded happy but understandably cautious. He asked me if I were sure and reminded me if we did marry, I would have to convert to the Mennonite faith. We talked for almost an hour. I thought I'd convinced myself I could do it, but before the hour was over, I had told him goodbye again.

I berated myself for months for doing such a hurtful thing to him and refused to go out with anyone else. Ammon was better off with the Mennonite girl than he would have been with me, with my rebellious feelings about conforming to the rules and customs of a strict religious faith. I knew myself and how outspoken I could be about things I believed strongly. Sooner or later, it would have come between us, so it was better it never had to come to that. And, I knew enough about the Mennonite religion to know only adultery was grounds for divorce, which I could never have committed against such a wonderful man as Ammon, who loved me as he had. I also knew, at the age of twenty, I was nowhere near being ready to marry anyone.

SEVEN

Misplaced Compassion

In the 1950s, a student nurse did not give medications to a few selected patients under the watchful eye of an instructor. She gave them to all the patients on the floor under the scrutiny of an instructor, until she was satisfactorily checked off. After that, she was on her own. In our hospital, each floor was a separate unit of sixty patients, except the 7th floor, which was the surgery floor, as well as EENT (eye, ear, nose and throat).

Of course, the student could call the instructor or consult the head nurse on the day shift, if she had a question about a drug order or the condition of a patient. However, if she was on the 3 –11 or 11–7 shifts, there would be no instructor or head nurse on duty and she, the student nurse, was the medicine nurse or charge nurse for all the patients with only one registered nurse, the nursing supervisor, in the house.

There was an intern or resident physician on-call to us, always, if we needed him. However, the student was expected to make the right decisions and to perform her job as if she were a graduate nurse. Yes, we were student nurses in training, but this was not a rehearsal for the real thing; it was the real thing. I realize that is an incongruous statement, but the patients, their conditions and the events surrounding them were real, even if their caregivers were students and not graduate registered nurses.

During those years of training, I remember no patients complaining because there were only students on the floor during those last two shifts of the day. I suppose most people realized this was just the way it was in hospitals in those days of three-year training hospitals and accepted it.

The decisions the student made, including calling the intern or resident, often were a matter of life or death. She did not call the supervisor on duty for urgent medical or surgical crises. This was when the intern or resident was needed, because only he could order emergency medications or treatments. If the supervisor was needed, as she was when I needed the OR oncall team to come in, we called her. After the situation was stabilized, the supervisor was made aware of it, always, and the student in charge of the floor during the shift entered the event into the shift report. At the end of the day, when she knew she'd helped to save a life by taking the right course of action when it was needed, it was a terrific confidence builder for the student involved. All the student nurses needed confidence builders in spades during those difficult three years.

In the 1950s, there was no vast selection of over the counter and non-controlled sleeping aids available as there have been in recent years, so the physicians ordered a prn sedative (barbiturate) for nearly every patient. Noncontrolled medications contain no narcotics or barbiturates. The latter were controlled substances, which were, and still are, kept under lock and key and accounted for on every shift. It always has been the responsibility of the on-coming medication nurse and the medication nurse going off duty, to count the pills together and sign that the count is accurate or discover why it is not.

Not all patients took a sleeping pill, but the order was there, if needed. And, because there were not hundreds of barbiturates to choose from in the fifties, that order was, almost always, for Nembutal or Seconal. Both were safe but strong sleeping pills, not that different from one another in their actions and effect upon the patients.

Maintaining the accuracy of the narcotic or barbiturate log was a prime responsibility of the student medication nurse. The only certain way of maintaining accuracy was to sign out a medication as soon as you removed it from the narcotic cupboard, as our instructors taught us. Or, you signed for it as soon as possible, after giving it, if you were in an emergency situation.

Without exception, as with any other medication you gave, you checked it three times before it reached the patient's bedside: when you checked the patient's order against the medication sheet, when you removed it from the cupboard and, finally, before you drew it up into a syringe or put the pill or capsule into the medication cup in front of the card bearing the name of that particular patient.

Of course, you always checked a fourth time when you were at the bedside, by looking at the patient's wrist band and calling her by name, to be certain you had the right medication for the right patient. Medication errors were taken seriously by the students, instructors, director of nurses, pharmacy and physicians, as they should have been.

One night when I was in charge of the surgical ward during my senior year, a junior year student was on medications, and we were both quite busy with our respective duties. Despite this, everything was going well until she came to me in tears in the middle of the shift. When I asked what was wrong, she said, "I signed out all my Seconals on the Nembutal sheets."

To say that was a serious dilemma was putting it mildly. One could not just tear up a log sheet and start over. Each sheet was electronically numbered, as it still is today, and the pharmacy would know right away if one had been destroyed. This mistake jeopardized her remaining in school. It also jeopardized my own future nursing career depending upon how I chose to handle it, as being the charge nurse meant the buck stopped with me, even though I was a student, also.

It was around three in the morning when she came to me, her eyes brimming with those unshed tears. The patients were asleep, and everyone who had been in pain had been properly medicated. There were no other students or hospital staff on the ward except the two of us. That was a good thing, because it gave us time to do what had to be done and a quiet atmosphere in which to concentrate upon doing it.

I sat down with her at the nurses' station. By that time, she was crying, softly. "Okay, try to stay calm. It might not be as bad as you think it is. Let's just go through the charts and see what we're up against." I knew it was about as serious a problem as a student could encounter, but I had to get her to stop crying so we could think our way through it.

She dried her tears, and we pulled and went through every chart, checking the barbiturate order, the dosage to be given and her charting of it. She had given the correct sedative in the correct dosage to each patient who needed one. We knew this because, together, we counted both the medications left in the cabinet against what she had written in the charts. The count was accurate. The charts were accurate. The logs were not, so the count still was not accurate on one paper where it mattered just as much.

I advised her to do the only thing she could legally do. "You have to go back to the Nembutal log, draw one line through each incorrect notation, write error in red above it and initial each line. Then, go to the Seconal log and sign for each one you gave."

I understand from having taken a few legal nursing continuous education courses before I retired, nurses have been advised in recent years to avoid writing the word error on any notation. Legal experts in the field of medical malpractice law tell us a jury, if the chart or log is subpoenaed to court, would misconstrue the word error to mean the nurse had given a wrong medication or had done something else harmful to the patient he or she should not have done. Now, they are to write something like "mis-entry" instead of "error," which makes more sense.

The thing I did not do that night in 1957, as I should have done, according to proper protocol, was to report this incident to the supervisor. To compound this error in judgment, I did not require the other student to write a medication incident report for each patient who received the Seconal capsule. The incident report would have specified it was an error in the log entry, not in the administration of the medication. These multiple reports would have been attached to the ward report I had to complete for the supervisor and the day charge nurse before giving my oral report to the oncoming shift prior to going off duty in the morning. Of course, copies of these reports would have been given to the nursing instructor.

I knew no patient had received the wrong medication or the wrong dose of the right medication. The phrase and motto of medical professionals, as stated in the physicians' Hippocratic oath, Do no harm, was running through my mind before I made the decision to handle it with the student medication nurse in the way I did. And, the student had done no harm to any of the patients.

Do no harm though we commonly speak of it, as I just did, in the context of the Hippocratic oath, actually came from the Hippocratic *corpus*, a large collection of medical writings of which most of the authors are not known, but it is associated with the ancient Greek physician, Hippocrates. It is not written in the Hippocratic oath. Regardless, it means the same and physicians (and nurses) try to the best of their ability, to practice their professions by it. What that section of the Hippocratic oath really translated to is this:

I will follow that system of regimen which, according to my ability and judgment, I consider for the benefit of my patients, and abstain from whatever is deleterious and mischievous. I will give no deadly medicine to any one if asked, nor suggest any such counsel; and in like manner I will not give to a woman a pessary to produce abortion. With purity and with holiness I will pass my life and practice my Art. I will not cut persons laboring under the stone, but will leave this to be done by men who are practitioners of this work. Into whatever houses I enter, I will go into them for the benefit of the sick, and will abstain from every voluntary act of mischief and corruption; and, further from the seduction of females or males, of freemen and slaves, according to :
http://ancienthistory.about.com/od/greekmedicine/f/HippocraticOath.htm

One modern Hippocratic oath translates as follows:

I will follow that method of treatment which according to my ability and judgment, I consider for the benefit of my patient and abstain from whatever is harmful or mischievous. I will neither prescribe nor administer a lethal dose of medicine to any patient even if asked, nor counsel any such thing nor perform the utmost respect for every human life from fertilization to natural death and reject abortion that deliberately takes a unique human life, according to:
 http://nktiuro.tripod.com/hippocra.htm)

I could not learn when this version, closest to the

original, came into use, but it is obvious it was translated before the passage of Roe v. Wade. Perhaps it was posted on the Internet with words missing, as, surely, the translator must have meant . . . nor fail to perform the utmost respect for every human life . . .

I should have reported what happened that night; however, because the incident could have had serious repercussions for the other student, I took a risk and did not follow protocol. I gambled, with my own future, that what she did would not be called to the attention of the instructor for that unit.

Fortunately for both of us, it was not. Neither of us ever said a word to anyone else about the incident, spoke of it again to each other, nor did we hear a word about it from anyone else. The student graduated the year after I did and I have no reason to believe she had less than a successful nursing career. I hoped that night taught her a huge lesson and she started signing for a medication as she removed it from the cabinet and charted it on the patient's chart, as she promised me she'd do if I helped her.

However, it was risky for me not to involve the supervisor, so the onus for the other student's mistake would not rest upon my shoulders. I understood that when I made the decision not to call her. Yes, the buck stopped with me, but I had a responsibility to involve my superior when the situation demanded it. And, it did demand it.

Instead, I felt compassion for the student and was so concerned for her, I took it upon myself, not to hide what happened in the log book, but to handle it with her in a discreet manner and pray it did not come back to bite either of us.

There might have been a chance she just would have received a written reprimand, a stern lecture from the director of the nursing school and been shadowed by the instructor for a period of time while giving medications, as when she was first learning to administer them. But, because of the risk she might have been expelled from school, instead, I made the conscious decision to protect her.

Even though I must have seemed calm to her, that complicity with her was nerve-wracking for me, and I never did anything like it again. Neither would I recommend any other student nurse do such a thing, if students in the few remaining three-year diploma schools today (less than 100 in the United States) are still alone without RNs on the unit at any time.

It is the responsibility of the student to relinquish responsibility to her immediate supervisor when any other student under her direct supervision makes an error of any kind, regardless of harm to the patient. That way, the supervisor can initiate the proper protocol and the onus is placed with her, not with the student in charge of the unit. To do otherwise, puts the student charge nurse, who handles a mistake by another student, in jeopardy of serious consequences against both of them.

I did not have time to dwell upon that infraction, however, because we had months on every service in the large hospital. These were called rotations. We helped the on-call obstetrics resident deliver babies and on another rotation, we cared for the preemies in the nursery for the premature babies as well as the ones who were delivered full term. Almost all of us loved the preemie nursery. To care for those tiny new beings, some smaller than our own hands, was especially rewarding. Our obstetrics instructor was the author of our OB textbook. The busy obstetrician had a hobby far removed from medicine; he crocheted beautiful lace tablecloths. All of us loved his class and did well in it. His lectures were almost verbatim from the book, even though he rarely looked at it. They were never boring.

We worked in the emergency room. We also attended a required number of autopsies (and, as in the case of my first patient death, extra ones when needed) to better learn our anatomy lessons and learn how the pathologist or medical examiner reaches the cause of death (COA), as I did after that first witnessed death.

We, for a brief time, worked on the assembly lines in the dietary department. How I disliked that service. We had to work so fast on the coffee line, I kept burning my fingers on the small metal pots I filled with coffee. I wasn't always on the coffee line, but that rotation could not end fast enough to suit me. That memory comes back to me if I'm in a restaurant that uses those small metal coffee pots for its customers. I dislike them as much today as I did then.

We also donned the smart Navy blue caps of the public health nurse, took our small black bags and went alone on a bus throughout the city, making home visits to our discharged patients to check their vital signs and carry out any treatments the physician ordered. In addition to the Navy blue cap on my head, I wore a Navy blue cape over my student uniform because I had that rotation during the bitter cold of winter. Since I was trusted to perform these duties in the patients' homes without supervision and my long woolen cape covered my student uniform, I felt more like a graduate nurse than a student on those visits away from the hospital, and I always enjoyed those bus rides through scenic Cincinnati.

I remember how excited some of my RN friends were when home health agencies sprang up all over Palm Beach County in the 1980s. One of them told me to get on board because this was going to be really big. Yes, it was a big thing since there was nothing like it in the private sector, and a nurse could make as much income as she wanted to by doing home health private or Medicare visits, if she had a dependable car and did not mind driving from one area to another to see her patients.

But, home health care did not start in the 1980s. We students were doing it routinely, just as the Visiting Nurse Association and county health departments were doing it, in the '40s and '50s, throughout the country. The big difference with what was happening in the 1980s was that the nurse was paid for each patient visit, whereas in the health department and Visiting Nurse Association, the nurse was paid her regular salary, instead of per patient. That is still the practice, although the nurse is paid mileage from the home of one patient to another. Depending upon whether she is an independent nurse contractor or an employee of a private agency, the nurse might be paid per visit for that agency, as well, and always paid mileage from one patient's home to the next.

And Then There Was One

At Bethesda, we had several months' rotation in the operating room. We could not leave the service until we had been the scrub nurse on at least one hundred cases and the circulating nurse on at least fifty others. We had to have a certain number of cases to scrub and circulate on each kind of operation, so many of us might need to work more than one hundred and fifty cases in order to fulfill our quota before we finished the rotation.

Since there were no disposable packs in those days, it was our duty to sterilize the instruments, towels, sponges, Mayo covers, etc. and to pack the exact number of each for every type of surgery before they were sterilized. We labeled in indelible ink what the pack was, for example, tonsillectomy, abdominal, amputation. This was done prior to placing it into the sterilizer, which was a large walk-in room, not a small container. The operating rooms were seldom vacant during a twenty-four hour period, so one can imagine how many packs had to be available at all times. I can remember rechecking the index cards to be certain I'd put everything on it into the corresponding packs before taping them closed.

We also had to take call for weeks during that rotation. No registered nurses were on call nor were any of our instructors. By the time you were taking call, you were ready to be trusted with that responsibility.

My maiden name, as I said earlier in the book, was Puckett and my on-call partner was a terrific student nurse by the name of Vivian Pickett. When we were called out for surgery at night, the surgeons loved it when we were in the O.R. together. They took that opportunity to tease us about our names and pretend to be confused as to who was scrubbing and who was circulating, even though we looked nothing alike. Aside from the teasing, they also respected us, because we had proven our competency, as had all our other classmates who worked the O.R. rotation without supervision. They showed their appreciation for our help by saying things like, "thank you" and "you did a good job tonight." I don't recall any of them ever complaining because they were handed the wrong instrument or for any other reason. I enjoyed those months in the operating room, except for one experience I had when I was working on the day shift.

Today, the surgeons do biopsies to see whether the patient has breast cancer and schedule the patient for surgery of the tumor and/or breast at another date, if it is positive. The surgeons in the fifties would open the patient up, send a piece of the tumor to the lab for what was called a frozen section, while everyone waited in surgery with the patient remaining under anesthesia, to see whether the tumor was cancerous. If it was, the surgeon immediately proceeded to do what was called a radical mastectomy. This involved removing all the lymph glands under the arm along with the entire breast, regardless of the extent of the cancer.

I thought it was the most horrible and gruesome surgery to witness and always wondered why they could not do a lumpectomy (as was done to me in 2006 when I was diagnosed with early breast cancer) and radiation, or maybe both chemotherapy and radiation.

Thankfully, they realized, decades later, this was the thing to do in early breast cancer not involving the complete breast and lymph nodes. Most likely, if the sentinel node is positive for cancer, it is removed with the cancerous lump, and some physicians still remove the other nodes as they always did. However, it has been discovered from a recent study of 900 breast cancer patients, this makes no difference in the five-year survival rate. (see http://abclocal.go.com/kabc/story?section=news/health/your_health&id=7947088)

One day, after the lab reported back to the surgeon that the tissue sample did contain cancer cells, he went back to work on the patient. I was the scrub nurse and had not been in the OR more than a week or two at that time. He asked for an instrument I was not yet familiar with, so I looked at the instructor and she pointed to what she thought he wanted. I handed it to him.

"What's the matter with you?" he shouted at me. "Don't you know anything at all? Someone get me what I need now!" With that, he threw the instrument across the room, barely missing another nurse. She almost slipped on a bloody towel on the floor in her effort to avoid being hit.

A resident reached over, and without touching the Mayo, pointed with his contaminated glove to the correct instrument and I handed it to the surgeon. I was never so thankful for an operation to be over as I was the day that one was. The patient came through it, as all right as one could be after such radical surgery.

The instructor, who was also the supervisor of the operating room, Ms. Dangers (pronounced like hangers), another of our favorite people with a great sense of humor, had a talk with me afterward. She told me not to let it get me down; that I did well during the surgery. She called the surgeon "a pompous ass" and said he was notorious for mumbling when he asked for something, and even she thought the clamp to which she'd pointed, was the one he wanted. Despite her trying to make me feel I had done all right during the surgery and trying to get me to laugh by calling him a derogatory name, it was the worst experience with a doctor I had as a student. There must have been others, but if so, nothing else of a negative nature stayed in my memory bank of nursing school days.

That was not to say there were not other incidents, some of them laughable. I remember one of those, when I was the scrub nurse for an emergency leg amputation one night. I was alone in the operating room after it was over, still in my bulky surgical gown and gloves, clearing things up when the OR orderly, Hans, came in and asked if he could help. He was a young German Mennonite working at the hospital in lieu of being drafted into the service. Like the Amish orderlies, he was a registered conscientious objector.

I said, "Yes, thank you, Hans. I'd like you to bag this for me." Like me, he still had on his gown and gloves, so I handed him the bloody amputated leg. The next thing I knew, he was on the floor in a dead faint, having dropped the leg on his way down with its bouncing a time or two! Straight out of a BBC sitcom, except it shocked me too much at the time to laugh.

The surgeons had already left the OR, so I called to Viv to bring an ammonia ampoule. She came into the room right away, crushed and put it under his nose, and we managed to get him to regain consciousness, gave him some juice and he was all right. Needless to say, neither of us handed him a body part of any kind, again.

The OR was the final rotation for Viv and me before we had to leave in the early fall of 1957 for Toledo State Hospital, upstate in beautiful Maumee Valley. It was at the same time, frightening and exciting, to be leaving our home hospital for our first off-campus affiliation, as they were called. They were the student nurse's equivalence of an internship, except they lasted two to three months instead of a doctor's one to two years, and we were not yet RNs. All interns are MDs.

EIGHT

Rotations to Affiliations

In these senior year affiliations at other hospitals, the purpose was to teach us their nursing specialties and to make our nursing education more well-rounded. We would become familiar with some of the options open to nurses after graduation and state boards, besides nursing in a general hospital, which was what our education and clinical training had consisted of to that point.

We spent three months at Toledo State Psychiatric Hospital. At that time, the enormous hospital was not unlike the one portrayed in One Flew Over the Cuckoo's Nest, minus the fictional Nurse Ratchet.

The hospital started out in the early 1800s as a place called the Lucas Poor Farm, to house those in society who were misfits for various reasons, not just mental illness. It evolved into the hospital complex, at which I trained, around the turn of the century. On its many acres, the facility could house nearly 2000 patients and was a huge sprawling complex of buildings. For the less extreme patients who could wander around the grounds, there were a couple dozen cottages, but there were also a couple infirm wards, two hospitals and two other large wards for the patients who were considered incurable.

Rambling throughout the property were lagoons, beautiful shade trees and groves of fruit trees and blackberry patches. There was a large library, chapel and auditorium. A greenhouse and a large open building where the less seriously ill patients made bandages with the help of assigned students, also occupied the grounds.

I remember when I was assigned to that building, I was quietly helping some of the patients make the bandages, when someone came up behind me and lightly poked me with a finger in the middle of my back. I almost stabbed myself with the scissors in my hand. Turning around, I saw one of the young female patients who worked in the building.

"Scared you, didn't I," she said with a mischievous grin.

"No, you didn't scare me, but I was startled to feel someone poking my back," I told her. It wasn't true, but we were told never to let a patient know she or he frightened us, even when we were frightened.

"Liar," she said, grinning again. "I scared the dickens out of you."

Smiling, I told her we'd better get back to work. There was no further problem with her, but when she poked me, I thought at first someone might have stabbed me. One of the instructors told of a nurse being stabbed and not feeling any pain, at first. She described it as feeling as though someone poked her in the back with something, but never suspected it was a knife, until someone else saw the blood and called for help.

One night before our affiliation was finished, all the students from the different nursing schools put on a huge production for the patients and staff. The song I sang was the popular Debbie Reynolds number, "Tammy." A cinch, right? The auditorium was huge and despite singing in public since I was ten, I had such stage fright, other students stood in the wings mouthing, "smile," and smiling to me so I'd settle down. Finally, I was able to smile and pulled it off, but not without their help. One would have thought I was auditioning in Carnegie Hall, because I wanted it to go well for the patients, in hopes many of them could somehow enjoy it, although there seemed to be no way they enjoyed much of anything about their existence in that mental hospital. I do recall some scattered laughter and applause, though, during and after the production.

Toledo State had wonderful nurses and nursing instructors, unlike some others we had encountered prior to this affiliation. They were relaxed, always smiling and related to us more like peers than instructors to students. Our Bethesda operating room instructor, Ms. Dangers, came closest to being like the Toledo State instructors.

For the first time in my life, I gained weight, until at the end of the affiliation I weighed a shocking 112 pounds, evident in my graduation portrait taken in Cincinnati not long after we returned. I would be a happy camper today if that number appeared on my bathroom scales, again, but up until then I had never weighed over 100 pounds in my life.

It was no mystery why I gained the extra weight. I ate everything the cafeteria workers handed us! We all did. Because the beautiful hospital campus was surrounded by orchards of every kind and wild blackberry patches by the thousands, when each fruit came into season, we had pies, ice cream and everything imaginable made from it. I can still taste the scrumptious warm peach cobbler today, even though peach has never been my favorite pie. The food, unlike other hospital cafeterias, was prepared and tasted like fine hotel cuisine, simply too good to pass up. It took me three to six months working back in Cincinnati to drop the extra pounds, but it had been worth every ounce.

Something unexpected happened to me in one of those wild blackberry patches one day. After we got off duty, Andy, Viv, and a few more of us went for a walk, as we did every day in Toledo. When we came to that particular patch, we stopped to pick and eat a few of the delicious berries, as always, since dinner was a few hours away.

While I was picking and nibbling on the berries, I heard a noise from the other side of the dense patch. To my horror when I looked up, there was a heavy-set man, as short as I at five feet, staring back at me with a licentious grin. I had seen him before on one of the wards and knew he was a resident physician from Turkey. Without preamble, he reached for me through the bushes.

Dropping my blackberries, I started running toward my classmates, yelling, "Help," with him in pursuit. One of them, Andy, if I'm not mistaken, grabbed my hand. Then all of us started running back toward the hospital and he could not keep up with us.

I had no idea what he intended, but my classmates teased me about it for weeks. They got a great laugh out of it and I joined in, but it might have had another outcome had I not heard him before I saw him and had I not come there with the other students.

My first assignment at the psychiatric hospital was Women's Receiving. Every Tuesday, we lined the women up for electroshock treatment. A different student was stationed at the patient's head and every extremity, to assure there would be no injury, even though the patient was strapped securely.

Tuesdays were not my favorite days. The patients who had been through EST before, were terrified of going back to be reshocked. The purpose of the procedure was to diminish or erase memories associated with causing the mental illness. They certainly did not erase the memories of the procedure! Even the ones who were heavily sedated with Thorazine, the drug of choice then, became agitated before they reached the end of the line at the door to the EST room.

One day, shortly after the Tuesday ESTs, I was assigned to sit and talk to a patient who had been catatonic for a few years.

"Talk about anything you want," the instructor told me before she walked away. The patient was unable to speak in her catatonic stupor.

The young woman was not much older than I, so I played it safe and talked about high school experiences and nurses training. During the course of the one-sided conversation, I mentioned a Bible I had won for bringing the most student nurses and Mennonite and Amish orderlies to a Youth for Christ meeting at Central Baptist church in Cincinnati, where I went on my Sundays off duty. When I mentioned that, she jumped up and started screaming, repeatedly, "Tore it up! Tore it up!"

Apparently, from what I was told later, after she was medicated with a mild tranquilizer and the psychiatrist was able to interview her, she had been under such guilt over getting angry and tearing up a Bible, it sent her into the silent world of catatonia. It was not my ability or competency which brought her back; it was hearing that single relevant word: Bible. Everyone was hopeful and optimistic about her future progress and believed she would not have to stay confined to the hospital but a few more months after that. Since each student's time was brief on that service, I never knew whether this discharge happened within the short time they'd predicted, whether it took much longer for her to get well and leave, or whether it ever happened. At least, that break-through gave her a fighting chance to begin to heal from her traumatic experience and I hoped it led to her eventual discharge back to her family and society.

We saw few patients get well enough to be discharged during our time at Toledo State. I often wondered how many more might be going home if they had not been so heavily drugged that they couldn't speak coherently or interact sensibly with others. I knew I would be unable to function at all, if I'd been drugged to the extent most of them were.

Thorazine is a neuroleptic (tranquilizer or antipsychotic) that became the "wonder drug" in the psychiatric hospitals in the mid-fifties. Doctors at Toledo

State were still in awe of its effects when we arrived late in 1957. The drug is in the class of phenothiazines that create chemical changes in the brain, equivalent to having a chemical lobotomy. I hated the thought of such a thing as robbing one of memories, for with the ones that supposedly caused the illness, the drug also seemed to erase any good memories that once added joy to the patient's life.

To my mind, it was no worse than having a surgical lobotomy, although such surgeries were stopped when the neuroleptic drugs started to be used. We heard plenty of horror stories about the lobotomies that were performed on the frontal brains of the patients. We were told there were nearly 20,000 of them performed in hospitals all over the country for eight to ten years until 1951, just seven years before we arrived. I was so thankful we did not have to witness anything like that, although we did see the effects of them, since there were still many patients there who'd had the surgery performed upon them when they were legal. When we asked why such a drastic surgery was performed in the first place, we were told it was necessary to calm out of control patients. We weren't the only country who performed these horrible surgeries, but it was Russia who banned them a year before we did.

Despite lobotomies being controversial from the time they were first used, a neurologist, Antonio Moniz, who first discovered the so-called therapeutic value of them, was awarded the Nobel Prize for Physiology and Medicine in 1949 because of it, as well as his discovery of cerebral angiography. It is still one of the most important tools in neurosurgery on the brain to this day, because the dye inserted during cerebral angiography allows the surgeon to visualize the blood vessels within the brain and how the blood is flowing, so they can tell exactly where the clot or mass is that is interrupting this flow.

The lobotomy equivalent, without cutting into the brain, Thorazine, calmed the patients, also. Young and old, they sat around like zombies. They rarely spoke to anyone, had a peculiar shuffling gait and seemed locked in a permanent fog from which we could not rescue them. Thorazine was used to treat schizophrenics. I had my doubts so many patients in the hospital were schizophrenic before they were put on them, although there were few who were not on the drug. I believed because of this, Thorazine must be responsible for their stuperous behavior and strange gait. I knew schizophrenia did not do that.

I also had my secret doubts it cured anyone. I suspected it just pushed them into a sort of prison of the mind; that if they'd been on it long enough, when they were taken off it, they might really be in trouble, psychologically and maybe, even physically. Yet, to think any of them would live forever in that druginduced prison until their deaths was heartbreaking to me.

I never saw any empirical evidence to support my gut opinion, at that time. Perhaps the ones who were on such heavy doses of Thorazine, Mellaril and other drugs did have to be on them because they were out of control or dangerous to others when they weren't medicated, as we were told in class. Still, this always bothered me and I couldn't shake the feeling some of them might be perfectly calm, and yes, perhaps even sane, if they'd never been prescribed the heavy doses of the drugs. I also wondered whether being on these drugs might cause some permanent neurological damage to these patients, since so many of them had that shuffling gait. I questioned one doctor about this but he sloughed it off as being "not even remotely possible."

Also, I couldn't stop wondering whether some of the patients had been confined in Toledo and the numerous other mental hospitals around the country for other reasons than being mentally ill, depending upon how influential and wealthy their families were. Whether, maybe their families didn't understand something about them and had them put away from society and out of their sight because of something different, though harmless, about them. I also wondered whether some of them were driven to out-of-control behavior by undesirable and unfair treatment, like constant taunting or goading, they received in their families by those who were supposed to love them, but instead, mistreated them.

These things truly bothered me about the mental hospital patients, but I had to remind myself I was a student nurse on a three-month affiliation. I was there to learn psychiatric nursing, not to save the patients from what I imagined were evil family members or doses of antipsychotic drugs I thought were way too heavy and possibly had long-term harmful effects.

On another assignment, I was put in charge of a ward of men who were considered clinically insane; their psychosis so deep, they were incurable, I was told.

Again, seeing their collective zombie-like appearance and behavior, I wondered whether they were psychotic before the drugs were put into them.

In the center of the large room, near the entrance to the ward, was a large round cage where a patient, who was criminally insane, was kept. The instructor warned me, before she left me alone in the room, "Don't go near his cage, Peggy. There's nothing you can do for him, so stay away. He grabbed one nurse, tore off some of her clothing and was choking her by the time the attendants managed to get her away from him. They can't even keep him in the state prison for the same reason."

That patient frightened me just by glaring at me. When it was time for his medication, a large male attendant would come to the ward without my calling him and with the help of the other male attendant, he'd administer it to him. The patient seemed frightened of the large attendant and reacted to his commands with meek compliance, which astounded me, considering how he was when he was not around. I wondered whether there was some kind of dark history between the two of them, but I was too busy, being the only nurse on the ward, to ask anyone. I was curious, also, about the nature of the crime the patient had committed that sent him to prison, in the first place, before they had to lock him away in Toledo, but there was not even time to peruse his thick chart. The instructor told me it was a violent crime, but offered no more because she had to leave to help another student.

I had only two attendants, a man and a woman, and the ward was at full capacity with 100 male patients. They were all in bed when I came on duty, which was just as well since, with so many of them, it took me quite a while to set up the medication trays.

While I was busy at this task, the attendants were wheeling the patients into the shower room as soon as they awakened them, where they were hosed down with comfortably hot water to make them cleaner than they were. There were too many of them for two people to give them a thorough sudsy shower every morning. I did not like this, but could understand it. I was told they were given a good shower on certain evenings after dinner, but still only a few at a time. It would not be practical or even possible to spend more than a couple minutes with each of 100 patients in the shower every morning, and then try to feed them while their food was still hot. Even that seemed an impossible task to me, but they got it done before the breakfast trays arrived.

However, I was appalled when I left the medicine room to start passing morning medications, to realize the attendants were leaving the men unclothed after their baths. They sat stark naked, restrained in their chairs, while they fed them, a bite to one and then a bite to the next one, and so forth, before starting the line all over again. Even worse, the attendants were laughing and joking about the anatomy of some of the defenseless patients.

None of this was acceptable and I was livid! It took all my patience to speak in a normal voice to them, when I asked, "Where are their clothes? You can't let them sit there naked. And, I won't allow you to ridicule them. Do you understand?" I don't know when anything had enraged me so, as seeing this.

"Yes, ma'am," they said, to me, while they probably were thinking what an upstart of a young student nurse I was, even to address this with them when they'd been doing this work for many years.

"Now, please, before you finish feeding them, put some gowns or pajamas and robes on them. They're entitled to their dignity even if they aren't well and can't tell you how what you're doing is affecting them. I'll take my medicine cart back to the station and help you dress them, before I give them their doses." Instead of getting up from their chairs and doing this, they laughed and said there was nothing to put on them and continued to feed them as they were. Searching the ward, I learned they were being truthful. There was not a gown or pajamas in sight, nothing at all to clothe these defenseless patients. I helped them to cover each of them with blankets or sheets from their beds before I resumed giving them their medications. Because they were wrapped in bath blankets to go to the shower, I never realized they were unclothed.

I wanted to call the instructor, but I'd been told to call her for an emergency situation, only. Since the attendants told me there was never any clothing on the ward, this hardly qualified as an emergency. Still, I was so sickened by this turn of events, I felt like going off the ward to talk with someone, anyone of authority, about it, immediately.

We weren't allowed to leave until the end of shift, though, so after I was relieved at that time, I locked the ward door behind me as all personnel and students had to do when leaving any patient ward, climbed the back stairs to the hospital administrator's office and placed a complaint, never thinking to go up the chain of command as I'd been taught. To my surprise, the administrator took me seriously. The next day, the patients were properly clothed in pajamas and the two attendants, subdued and respectful toward them. There even were stacks of pajamas on the shelves, so they could be changed regularly.

That evening in the dorm, I was talking about it with one of the other Bethesda students. "Oh my God, Peg, they're going to kick you out of school! Why on earth did you do such a crazy thing? Psych's come easy to you and now you've gone and spoiled everything for yourself."

"I couldn't let it go on. I had to do something, and I'm sorry you think it was a crazy thing to do, but all I could think at that moment was to go to him. As much as I admire our instructors, you'd think they wouldn't have turned a blind eye to it, wouldn't you? They take us to the ward to orient us to it, after all, and even if they don't stay there with us, they had to have known it was going on. And, God only knows how long that's been."

"I don't know. Maybe they know something we don't. After all, we have only a tiny piece of the whole picture," she told me. "You know things are run down on most of the wards here. Maybe there was no money in the budget for clothing for everyone and the powers that be figured since those patients aren't aware of anything, anyway, it might as well be they who went without, and the instructors had no authority to argue the point with them."

"Even if that were true, it's absurd," I told my classmate. "Just because those patients can't speak up for themselves and are, supposedly, out of touch with reality, doesn't mean they don't still have feelings. I refuse to believe anyone is that psychotic they no longer hurt or feel humiliated when they're well, being humiliated! God, it makes me so mad!"

"Sorry I didn't mean to upset you again, but, on the other hand, I don't understand why you feel so responsible for how they're treated and how they feel."

"Because I'm supposed to be a nurse, damn it! We're you, me, all the others we're supposed to give a damn, aren't we?"

She looked thoughtful for a moment and then said, "I never heard you cuss before, Peg. Look, let's forget about it and just go to dinner."

We went to dinner and it wasn't brought up again, but I was thankful the men wouldn't go through that teasing and be stripped again, literally, of any semblance of dignity they might have left.

I couldn't shake the feeling, though, that it was only a temporary fix and after I was on another service in the hospital, things would revert back to how they were before. I'd done something no other student had ever done, according to the administrator when we were speaking together. Something I knew I was forbidden to do, gone to the top instead of to my instructor. Maybe they were afraid I was going to go to the newspapers or something and figured they'd appease me while I was still assigned to the ward. I had to laugh to myself at one point and thought perhaps they saw me as out-of-control as some of the patients.

I realized I had no control over what happened after I left, so I tried to put it behind me and just make sure they were treated well during my brief stay on that particular ward. After all, I was only a student nurse and only at

Toledo for three months, I reminded myself, again. I'd brought about a small change and if it did turn out to be a temporary fix, at least I felt better for having stood up for the patients who couldn't defend themselves.

Although I didn't say so to my classmate, I did expect to receive a reprimand from my psych instructors, and perhaps even be expelled from training after they reported me to Bethesda. It was clearly a breach of protocol to bypass them and report it to the administrator. Instead, they commended me for the stance I'd taken on behalf of the patients and asked me, on behalf of administration, to come back to work there after graduation.

Of course, I was shocked but relieved they'd reacted that way, although I still thought it should have been one of them who had taken the problem to administration. Perhaps my classmate was right; maybe, being on the teaching staff, they didn't have the authority to advocate for the patients in that way, although that made no sense to me, either. How could they teach us to be aware of how we treated the patients, including allowing them their dignity and then turn around and ignore others who were doing the exact opposite?

I did not approach the instructor about it, though. I considered myself lucky I didn't get a reprimand, or worse, get expelled over my actions, so I thought I'd better stay quiet and not rock that boat any more than I had, already. After all, it still might happen after the nursing office at Bethesda got wind of it, if it did.

The commendation never would have happened at Bethesda. They were unwavering about chain of command. I just knew I would be expelled without hesitation, as soon as Geneva Rubins received their report. I tried to put this out of my mind and deal with it when I had to, upon my return to Cincinnati.

However, when I returned from Toledo, nothing was ever said about it except that she knew I had been asked to return to work there. If the instructors at Toledo told her why, she did not allude to it. I assumed other students were also invited to return after graduation, so thought she must have received a report of some sort with all our names on it, instead of a specific report about my actions.

I appreciated the offer of employment after I finished training and would have loved to work there as an RN, possibly even furthering my education so I could be a psych instructor. I believed it was important the mentally ill patients have advocates in the nurses; that they cared that they got well and left the place. I knew I would have been such an advocate. And, too, I hoped research might produce changes in the future that would make medications like Thorazine and treatments like ESTs obsolete one day. However, life took me in another direction from Toledo after graduation.

Even though I did not return after our affiliation, it was at Toledo State I came out of my shell, socially, in a way I never had before. I had, for the most part, always had a serious side but never seemed able to just let my hair down in a very relaxed way very often. Andy and I were roommates and became very good friends in Toledo. And, as with standing up with Mary Ann when she married Victor, I was a bridesmaid in Andy's wedding, soon after we graduated; not to Mike, whom she dated in Toledo, but to Norman Knepper, an old boyfriend who'd waited in the wings for her. They moved to Stuart, Florida, in the early sixties, with their young sons, David, the oldest, and Mike, a year or so younger. She worked in the ICU at Martin Memorial Hospital for over thirty years before they retired to Lake Wales, where they've lived for many years.

While we were at Toledo, Andy, who'd always loved to go out to play, started dragging me with her when she did. Soon, she did not have to drag me. We started going to a little rock and roll club, called The Ding Dong, which, of course, we had been warned before we left Bethesda, was off limits to us.

Rock and roll was brand new to the country, and although it bewildered many adults, all of us young people loved the happy sound. The club was near the hospital, in beautiful Maumee Valley, and the dancing never stopped.

I'd never been allowed to dance when I was growing up even the square dances at my high school on a Saturday night were considered sinful, so I sat on my front porch within a stone's throw of the school auditorium, listening to the music and others having fun dancing to it.

I discovered at 21, I loved to dance and could not have had a better dance partner to teach me than another Tom, a young man of 25, who already owned his own busy garage in Maumee Valley, near the hospital. That man could move on a dance floor faster than anyone I'd ever seen and what fun we had dancing to things like Jerry Lee Lewis' "Whole Lot of Shakin' Going On" and "Great Balls of Fire." Andy and Mike danced a lot, too, but not as much as we did. I was insatiable. I never wanted to sit down when I got on that dance floor. Tom was the same way, so we were perfect dance partners. I discovered it was fun just having fun, without thinking about where something was heading.

We also went to another smaller club, called Baldy's. Our dates had to knock on a green door, and give the right password, before we could get in. Our eyebrows lifted at that our first time there, but we found it amusing, also. "The Green Door," made popular around that time, by another singer, Jim Lowe, was one of our favorites. I smiled many years later in the early 1970s, when I heard Tony Orlando and Dawn singing, "Knock Three Times," remembering that little club and the fun I had with my friends there.

The owner, Baldy, a genial bald-headed man in his fifties, liked to promote local amateurs, so I was encouraged by my friends to play the piano a few times. The first time he heard me, I played Chattanooga Shoe Shine Boy in the style I'd grown up playing, like Jerry Lee Lewis. After it was over, while everyone was cheering and applauding, as friends are prone to do, he told me out of earshot of them, by holding his white apron over our faces and making them think he was stealing a kiss, I should give up nursing school and perform professionally. Of course, that had always been my dream, but I loved nursing by then, knew I was a good nurse and would never have given it up. He was a former Vaudeville performer, so coming from someone like him, it was nice to have my ability validated, despite not wanting to leave school to use it.

I never drank anything stronger than 7-Up all through training or did anything else a proper young lady should not do, except go into the clubs we were warned were off limits. When Baldy came to our table one night, where there was always a lot of laughter, he said that was the first time in his history of owning night clubs he ever saw anyone get drunk on 7-Up, because I never stopped laughing. And, I never stopped laughing, because I was having so much fun. None of us did.

I was more content during that affiliation than at any other time during my three years of training. Yes, I loved psychiatric nursing and felt I brought something positive to it for the sake of the patients, despite the feelings I had about the heavy drugs and other treatments, but it was more than that. It was also the relaxed atmosphere of the classroom, the treatment by, and the camaraderie with, our instructors and never feeling intimidated as at Bethesda, depending upon which instructor we had at any given time.

Certainly, the dancing with Tom, Andy and Mike every weekend added to the relaxing experience I had while in Toledo. They were such nice men and really treated us with respect. Sometimes, we had another student or two with us. We had a large group at Mike's house to watch football a Sunday or two, also. Andy and I kept the popcorn coming and the guys paid for the pizza. Before then, I'd never paid attention to football on TV, but grew to love the game. Actually, that's not a true statement. I grew to tolerate it and didn't become a real fan until I moved to Florida and started watching the Miami Dolphins, even attending a home game now and then.

The buildings of Toledo State Hospital were demolished in the early 1970s and today, a state of the art hospital stands in its place. Our class was one of the last to have a lengthy in-residence affiliation at Toledo State. After that, student nurses observed patients on a psych unit in a local Cincinnati hospital for a few days. That was the extent of their psychiatric nurses training.

Toledo State, after the new hospital was built, was called the Northwest Ohio Psychiatric Hospital, serving 120 patients. "The field of psychiatric care has made great strides over the past 50 years," it says on its website, " and we are proud of both our facility and the state of the art treatment we provide, which encourages patient-led recovery and family and community involvement."

I was happy to read that. It was what I'd hoped for the patients. Maybe things are looking up for those with emotional/mental illness since I was a student there fifty-three years ago.

Another positive thing that has happened in that field of medicine is that the use of Thorazine is not widespread as it was in the fifties, although I understand it is still used in small doses, and rarely, to treat intractable vomiting.

In preparing to write this book, I found some interesting and fascinating quotes on the use of Thorazine and the other neuroleptics, which at first, I was hesitant to include, but because they do concern the long-term effects of the drugs, I've decided to add them to the book; well, all except those claiming the CIA initiated the Jonestown, Guyana "study," that the controlling Jim Jones was a CIA operative and the FBI found over 11,000 Thorazine capsules in one footlocker after the poisoned Kool-Aid deaths of all those people in Jones' cult. If anyone cares to delve into that, it can be Googled on the Internet.

Here are a few of the quotes I found relevant to my thoughts on the drugs in the late '50s:

"Since 1954 in the United States, the administration of one class of twenty psychiatric drugs called neuroleptics — Thorazine, Haldol, Mellaril, Stelazine, Prolixin, and others— has caused between 300,000 and one million cases of motor brain damage." Rappoport, Jon , American journalist and author.

"The miracle drugs (neuroleptics) caused the worst plague of brain damage in medical history." Peter Breggin, M.D.

"I believe more than 1 million Americans suffer from TD. It seems conservative to say that in 1991, tens of millions of TD victims are alive around the world...Psychiatry has unleashed an epidemic of neurological disease on the world. Even if TD were the only permanent disability produced by these drugs, by itself, this would be among the worst medically-induced disasters in history." Peter Breggin, M.D.

"The risk of developing severe TD from antipsychotic drugs probably lies between 20% and 40%, but mild symptoms appear in up to 70% of patients." Jack Gorman, "Essential Guide to Psychiatric Drugs," 1990.

The "TD" these physicians are referring to is Tardive Dyskinesia, which is an involuntary neurological movement disorder. It seems I had reason in 1958 to be concerned about the heavy doses of neuroleptics being prescribed for the patients. I do not, for one moment, believe the physicians who prescribed them meant to do the patients harm. I believe, from hearing them talk about them, they truly did think they were miracle drugs. Unfortunately, as in so many other things in the inexact and unpredictable science called medicine, the patients suffer because the full permanent effects of the drugs or treatments do not become known for decades after they're used in abundance, because they're believed to be such great healing agents.

Another three-month affiliation where a few other students and I were invited to join the staff after graduation was Children's Hospital in Cincinnati. As much as I loved working there, I did not accept that invitation, either. Contrary to how I loved working at Children's, after I became a mother in the sixties, I could no longer bear to work in pediatrics in any hospital. After my children were born, it was impossible for me to take care of sick little children with the same kind of objectivity I possessed in 1958.

Today, nurses learn pharmacological formulas, but today's IVs and meds are already mixed by the pharmacy, except for those that just need liquid added to the small five or ten cc bottle of powdered med to add to IV fluid or give as injections. Not so with the IVs we had to administer to the children while we were on pediatric affiliation in 1958.

One night I had a ward filled to capacity with babies, nearly all with intractable diarrhea. The resident or private pediatricians ordered IV fluids for all 100 babies. When the pharmacy sent the completed order to the unit, the other student and I had to do the formula according to what we learned in pharmacology class, and figure how much medication to mix (by sterile procedure) with the fluid in the bottle actually, an IV flask, not a standard IV bottle and put a piece of wide adhesive down the length of the bottle, upside down, since it would hang upside down when connected to the tubing. Then, we marked off the amount the IV fluid was supposed to be down to each hour; again, according to the proper formula. This was time-consuming, but had to be exact for each baby, according to what the physician ordered.

What a headache, but I had no problem doing it then since we'd spent so much time in pharmacology class, just as we had in every other class. If we didn't know how to figure each formula, we didn't pass the class, so we all knew how. We still could call the pharmacy at any time, if we wanted to confirm the amount, so it wasn't as though we were out on a limb, alone, if we questioned our figures.

After all the IV flasks were hung, we had to go to each bedside every hour to check that it was running on time. Many of the babies also had Coca Cola hanging, along with the antibiotic or whatever med the doctor ordered. He ordered the Coke to counter-act the severe dehydration the babies were experiencing from the intractable diarrhea that had gone unabated before the babies were admitted to the hospital, and the cola also helped to control the diarrhea.

The student I was working with that night, Jane (not her real name, because she might not want anyone to know about this), set out to prove to me it didn't matter what you called babies; they'd respond to the way you said it and the smile upon your face. She said you could stand there and swear at them, but if you said it softly and with a smile, they'd respond as though you called them honey, precious or sweetheart. I said, no way can that be true.

After we got all the IVs hung and meds given, she told me to walk along with her and watch what happened. So, I played along since we had a few spare minutes. She walked up to a little baby girl who was crying. After assuring she was dry, she said, "Watch, Peggy." Then, she leaned down toward the little girl, smiled broadly and said, "You're such a nice little —, aren't you."

"Jane! That's awful. The poor little baby," I protested.

"Just watch her face," she said, as she repeated what she'd said. I couldn't believe my eyes. The baby, who'd just been wailing with all her might, smiled at her and stopped crying! "See, I told you, didn't I. They're not responding to all your sweet little words, Peggy. It's the soft tone of your voice and your smile."

"Okay, you've made your point, but I still think it's awful to call a baby such a name."

She laughed and said, "I don't do that. I just wanted to prove to you they'd respond the same if I did."

She certainly had proven it, but all the same, I was glad she didn't make a practice of doing it. I never could bear for anyone to hurt a baby or child of any age, even if that baby or child did not realize she was being hurt, as Jane had proven with that baby girl.

That affiliation was an exciting and often heart-wrenching experience for me. Children's was and still is a leader in research. Dr. Albert Sabin developed the oral polio vaccine at Children's Hospital in Cincinnati. (Although we never saw him during our affiliation, it was said Bethesda's former resident pathologist, Dr. Hans

Gerth, whom I'd had the little secret crush on at the age of nineteen, went to Children's as one of the physicians who assisted Dr. Sabin with his research on the vaccine.)

I saw diseases and syndromes in that hospital I have never seen since, and the surgical results, especially the reconstructive surgery, were nothing short of amazing to all of us.

I was particularly interested in the delicate heart surgeries and was privileged to observe the Blalok operation of a fouryear-old patient with Tetralogy of Fallot. Student nurses were not permitted to work in the operating rooms at Children's Hospital or even to observe the surgeries, because of the large numbers of doctors and nurses required in the OR during the lengthy operations. But, when I went out on a limb (which I was known to do a time or two throughout my career after the Toledo incident) and asked my instructor if I could observe my patient's surgery, she spoke with the surgeon.

To her surprise as well as mine, he consented to my observing the surgery. I was given a stool to stand on, away from the sterile field, of course, and out of the way of the nurses and physicians, where I could see everything that was happening to the patient. The surgeon even gave me a running dialogue of everything they were doing during the very interesting operation, from the moment they began to lower her body temperature until the heart was successfully repaired and they raised the temperature back to normal. The surgery was one hundred percent successful for the little girl.

Hopefully, this began a precedent because these are fascinating operations, which, unless she works in pediatric surgery after she gets her RN, no nurse has a chance to witness in her career.

The child who tore my own heart out was a three-year-old boy with platinum ringlets covering his head. His name was Ricky and he was dying of leukemia. It was the dead of winter, in early March. The winds were fierce, snow was piled deep everywhere and the temperature was bitter cold.

One night, when the little boy's fevers became so uncontrolled nothing would touch them, the pediatric resident, Dr. Holland, instructed me to move the other children out of that end of the ward, and he opened all the windows wide to let the cold air in to bring Ricky's temperature down faster.

Neither his opening the windows to the frigid March temperatures, our giving him aspirin suppositories nor his instructing me to place the freezing and screaming little patient into a tub of iced water, not once but several times, decreased the fevers for long. Little Ricky died, mercifully, the next morning.

His memory haunted me for a long time after that. In the quiet of the night, I could see him and hear his, "Please, please, don't do it," as I lowered him to the icy water. His screams would become louder and through my own tears, I kept telling him how sorry I was, but we were trying to help him. He didn't care about that. He just did not want to hurt anymore, and God

knows I did not want him to, either. Despite the fifty-three years that have passed since that night, I still remember what that precious little boy looked like. I've rarely seen such a beautiful child.

Peggy Butler

Thankfully, we've come a long way since 1958. The medical profession accepts death and dying today, and children are permitted to die, peacefully, when it is time to let them go.

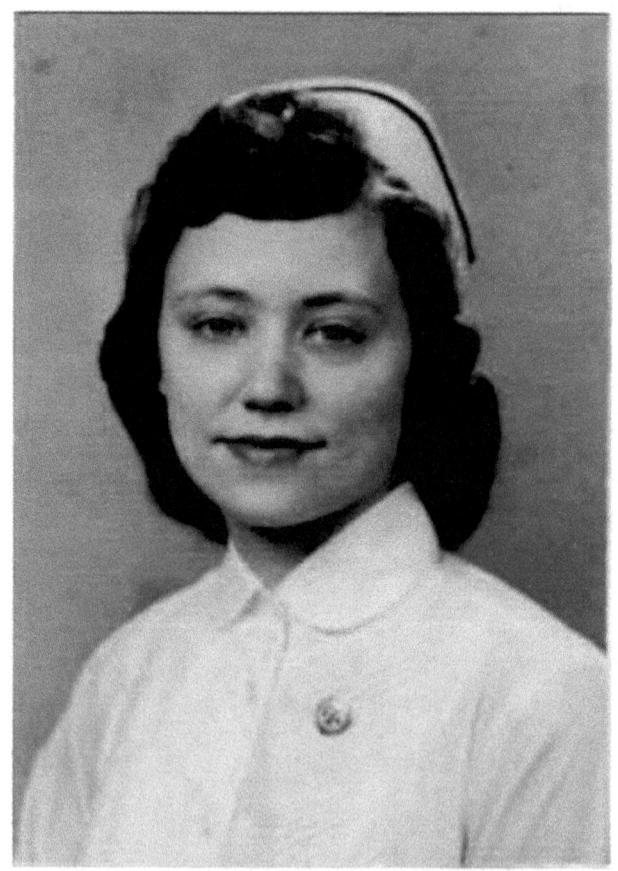

Peg, in uniform with cap and pin.

NINE

Final Affiliation and Graduation

My final affiliation, in 1958, was at a private hospital for tuberculosis patients. This affiliation, unlike the two three-month ones, was for two months. I did not know it then, but I would soon be grateful for that.

As I said in the beginning of this book, had anyone told me, then, it was the beginning of a love affair with TB nursing, I would have rejected that notion in a heartbeat. Dunham Tuberculosis Hospital in Cincinnati was a nightmare for me.

Dunham was the first city-owned tuberculosis sanatorium in the United States and was named for Dr. Henry Kennon Dunham, who served without pay from 1909-1940. It was situated on 150 acres above Lick Run Valley on Guerley Road in Cincinnati. It is now the Dunham Recreational Center, part of the Cincinnati Recreation Commission. The hospital closed in 1973.

Knowing Dr. Dunham dedicated his life and service to that hospital for 31 years and never took a penny for it, did not leave me with a good feeling about myself for finding little redeeming value in my TB nursing affiliation at his hospital.

Conversely, Andy loved her TB experience there. When I asked why, she said, "Lots of reasons, not the least of them being the ice cream they gave us students every night, the wonderful nutritious meals they served us and having the woods to hike in when we were off duty." She also recalled the patients' beds were out on the porch, and the students could put their beds out on the dormitory porch at night.

The biggest difference between her experience and mine was that I had mine in winter and hers was in the summer. During the winter, none of the patients could go outside. It was too cold for us to sleep out on our porches or do much hiking in the woods. We were, of course, served the nutritious meals and delicious ice cream at night, which I agree with Andy, made it nice for us students when we were away from the patient wards.

In the late 1950s, hope had arisen for a cure with the new medications, INH, PAS and PZA. Before then, with just Streptomycin, there was no cure for the disease, tuberculosis. And, still, in the '50s, the early medications barely arrested it unless it had been caught early.

That was the greatest problem. Most patients were in denial, so did not want to learn they had TB. A most vivid example of this is in Verdi's opera, La Traviata, written in the mid-1800s. As early as the first act, Paris courtesan Violetta Valery, who fears she has consumption, faints in her salon as she's greeting arriving guests to her party. While she is alone, resting, Alfredo Germont comes into the room and declares his love for her. Because of her fear of the illness, she sends him away by pretending to love another man. When Alfredo learns the truth, both about the other man and her serious illness, he rushes to her side, only to have her die in his arms. That last scene before the final curtain never fails to elicit tears from my eyes, knowing how often it must have played out in the lives of real people during those times when TB was feared by so many, and with good reason.

Even into the early 1900s, TB still was the plague of the century, a stigma upon anyone who had it. The fear of being shunned and sent away to the TB sanatorium for many years, being isolated from others and possibly dying without ever seeing your family again, was a valid one. Your family also might be shunned, even if they did not contract the disease from you. Because there was no cure and so little still was known about TB, people feared they might get it if they associated with family members of the patient with TB.

Because of this, it was easier, most often, to stay in denial for as long as possible. As a result, too often, the illness was life-threatening by the time the patients received medical attention, so drastic measures had to be taken in order to try to save lives.

The most drastic of those were the extensive surgical procedures: removing a lung or large segments of the lungs and ribs and placing ping-pong balls into the chest cavity to expand it. The premise behind this plumbage surgery was to allow the lung to rest, but it was next to useless effort and some patients got worse instead of improving because of it. Many of these operations caused permanent disfiguring, especially the removal of a lung, or large portions of a lung, and ribs. The patients were left severely depressed for some time over the drastic changes in their appearance.

If you see someone in her late eighties, nineties, or older, with one shoulder several inches lower than the other and who leans to one side when she walks, more than likely she might have had far-advanced TB in the '40s or early '50s, requiring drastic surgery.

At the time I was at Dunham, everyone received Streptomycin injections with their other antituberculosis drugs and almost everyone was on Codeine injections for the intractable cough. There were no disposable syringes and needles, as there are today. In order to draw up the Codeine into the glass syringe, we had to first dilute it in a spoon over a hot Bunsen burner, a time-consuming procedure.

Andy recalls, with a laugh, on the days she was on Streptomycin assignment, she would load up her table, go out to the porch where her patients were and say, "Bottoms up!" All the patients, she said, would turn over in unison like the Radio City Rockettes, and wait their turn to be injected.

Until 1958, my senior year in training, it was not known INH could provide chemoprophylaxis in tuberculosis-infected persons who did not have tuberculosis disease.

That left no way of preventing family members from contracting TB, if their diseased relative was coughing and living among them for a long period of time before his disease was diagnosed. Consequently, we saw whole families coming into the hospital. Patients were not treated at home, either, after it was diagnosed, as most of them are now because of the multiple drug therapy.

Most of the medical community was as fearful of contracting the disease, as was the general public, so treating it in the sanatoriums was the only option for many years.

We wore cotton masks, surgical gowns and surgical gloves always when on duty. We only removed them before going to lunch or dinner and before walking back through a very long tunnel to get to the nurses' dormitory at the end of our shift.

One of the patients, a man in his fifties named Ted, had surgery, was no longer infectious, and was well enough to have the run of the hospital. It was his favorite pastime to hide behind a stairwell out of sight of the guard's flashlight to try to steal kisses from us, as we walked through the dark tunnel. He never forced himself on us, but consistently tried. I understand, on occasion, he was even successful. Most of us were wary of that tunnel walk because of him, even though he seemed harmless, and because it was just plain spooky. But it was the only way for us to get back to the dormitory adjoining the hospital.

The area, as many in the sprawling city, was not the safest for a young woman walking alone. Although it was more country than metropolis, students' walking at night was discouraged. We did enjoy walking during the daytime because it covered such a vast area, but, even then, we did not walk alone or often, because it was so cold outside.

Conditions in the 1950s in the TB hospitals were

horrendous. Very few patients were as well as the stairwell Romeo. There were many deaths from complications such as gross hemoptysis (as opposed to spitting up a little blood). Not every patient was a candidate for pneumonectomy, pneumothoracotomy or plumbage the operations described earlier, which, taken as a whole, saved many lives.

I remember always being very hot under my mask and gown. There was no such thing in the fifties as air-conditioning. There was not an abundance of windows, either, and the entire hospital seemed dark and dreary that winter, as compared to every other one we'd worked in throughout our training.

As much as we tried, we rarely could get these seriously ill patients to use cough precautions to protect us from their sputum. I was glad to know, from talking with Andy, they were moved to the porch in the summer weather. That would have made the experience much nicer for me, I know. Their coughing into the air wouldn't have had such serious consequences, when they were outside, since the droplet nuclei containing the TB bacilli (Mycobacterium TB or MTB) would dissipate quickly, as compared to coughing in an enclosed room.

By the way, prior to starting my Dunham affiliation, I had been taking care of a patient at Bethesda for three weeks, with diagnosed miliary tuberculosis, a form of extrapulmonary tuberculosis.

The patient was in strict isolation, but was not coughing, since he did not have pulmonary tuberculosis nor did he have abnormal chest x-rays. I was always gowned, masked and gloved, which one had to be when the patient was in strict isolation. And, even had I not followed strict isolation technique, it would have been next to impossible to contract tuberculosis or TB infection from a patient who was not coughing from pulmonary tuberculosis.

Yet, I was sitting in class at Dunham, the day after my first PPD test was administered, listening to the physician instructor talking about the induration of a positive PPD, "like that one," he said, pointing to me. Talk about embarrassment!

He walked back to me and measured the induration. "This PPD measures 20 millimeters, class, and that is substantial. One might expect this kind of reading in someone with active tuberculosis." Oh joy, I thought. They'll find I have TB and I will have to stay here for years.

It was never the staff or instructors who made it a less than stellar experience for me. As Andy said, they were all good to us, including the instructor who noticed my positive PPD. He was kind to me, reassured me I probably had nothing to fear and made certain I had the best work-up for TB, which he didn't have to do, since it was my responsibility to report it to Health Services.

I did not have TB nor could my positive reaction (infection) be traced to a known case of pulmonary tuberculosis. I never had symptoms of TB. However, it was not a false positive. It reacted the same when repeated a month later, and six months later. Of course, in order to have such a positive Mantoux (PPD) test, I must have had close contact with someone with the disease, at some time in my recent past. However, it could not be traced to any patients I had taken care of prior to that time.

It could have been from contact with someone with undiagnosed pulmonary TB, before I entered training. If so, despite my being vulnerable to illness, it did nothing to me. I knew of no one with TB from my family or school. Since I did not have it, there was no contact investigation, as there has been the past four decades. My grandfather coughed, ferociously, from the time I was a toddler and became aware of him, but whether the cough was productive of sputum, I have no way of knowing. I don't recall seeing him spit anything from his mouth, except tobacco juice. He also had a cigarette dangling, constantly, all those years. No one became ill from being around him, so I suspect his cough was lung cancer and/or emphysema-related. He never went to a doctor as long as he lived, and, at 59, he died in his sleep, from a major heart attack.

Still, a 20 mm PPD certainly was indicative of active TB or close contact with someone with active TB, but the source in my case remained a mystery. I was thankful not to have the disease, because I could think of nothing worse than having to live at Dunham TB Hospital for years until I got well enough to be among people again.

Because of the possibility of necrosis of the tissue on my arm from repeated administrations of the PPD and based upon the fact the positive status had been confirmed three times, I was never tested again but had a screening chest x-ray, always negative, every year thereafter while I was still working in the health care field.

This was standard practice with an individual with a positive PPD reading, unless the person was rendered positive from a tuberculosis vaccination. This vaccine was given in most under-developed countries without adequate medical personnel, supplies or drugs to treat tuberculosis. Annual screening chest x-rays are no longer performed on individuals like me with the positive PPD readings, unless at some point, they begin to show symptoms of TB, which I never did.

If the vaccination, BCG, was administered ten years or more prior to the patient's presenting for examination, and the PPD is positive at the time of the examination, it is now believed to be an infection from exposure to the TB bacillus, not from the vaccination. Then, the physician proceeds with the work-up to rule out active tuberculosis. Having been born and raised in America, I never had the vaccine.

Because of my history of hepatitis, even after the advent of INH chemoprophylaxis later in 1958, physicians and later, CDC consultants, with whom I worked, believed the risk would have been greater for me to get another severe case of hepatitis from taking the INH than not to take it and get TB. I am in my early seventies now and have never contracted tuberculosis.

TB interested me in training and the surgeries were fascinating, if not gruesome, but, oh, how glad I was to finish that affiliation and see the last of TB patients.

Mike and Tom came to Cincinnati for our senior prom a few weeks before we graduated, after all the affiliations were over for each student in our class and before we started our two weeks of comp exams. They brought another friend, Herb, whom we'd gotten to know when we were in Toledo. He was the date for one of the shyest students in our class. After I saw the first episode of Seinfeld years later and saw the character of Kramer, I thought, ah, Herb. Herb was quiet and not a silly guy like Kramer, but there was something similar about his appearance.

Janet Miller was a natural blonde and wore glasses. Like I had in Toledo, she came out of her shell that night. Off came the glasses when Herb got her out on that dance floor and the transformation was startling. She could really dance, something none of us realized until that moment, and her shyness melted away. In place of that reticent student with glasses, stood an exceptionally pretty young woman, with beautiful eyes, who couldn't stop smiling. She outshone the rest of us and we were happy we'd included her in our party.

We never had a high school prom at Rarden, so that was another first for me. The prom was held at a large beautiful hotel in downtown Cincinnati with one of the big bands that played wonderful standards like "Sentimental Journey," "September Song," "Blue Moon," "That Old Feeling" and "At Last," in addition to faster rock and roll numbers, of course, and we rarely left the dance floor.

Needless to say, I was in the proverbial seventh heaven. We had a wonderful time that night and every night we were all together, but because of the distance between Toledo and Cincinnati, Tom and I kept things light. We never made any commitments to each other, though we enjoyed our time together very much and saw each other for awhile after I graduated. I'll always remember him as a very nice young man.

Once, not long after Toledo, I went out with another embalming college student, Adam (not his real name because I can't recall it). I'd met him when I was seeing the other Tom. A few months later, he called to ask me to his senior prom held the week after ours. Totally hooked on dancing now, I said I'd love to go and did. What a good time we had. I came back to the dorm that night with large holes in the feet of my nylons, because except for the beginning of the prom when we had a bite to eat, we never sat down the entire night except when the band took a break. I had to carry my shoes into the dorm, hoping all the while Suzy wouldn't see me. Lucky for me, no one was at the desk when I signed in. I'm sure if she had been there, I'd have heard, "No lady walks in from a date without shoes on her feet."

Adam was a wild one not wild as in drugs and crime, just wild in a sort of embalming student way. After dinner on our first date, he showed me around the funeral home, walking from coffin to coffin to explain why some were more expensive than others. I could not believe my eyes when he took off his shoes and got into one of the satin-lined coffins, with his arms crossed over his chest, imitating Dracula.

Those students learned to be embalmers by working at the mortuary, as well as in the classroom, just as we worked in the hospital and classroom. And, as we student nurses learned, more than one of them took his date to the mortuary after dinner or the movie. Tom (from Warren) had never done anything outlandish on our dates, which I'd always appreciated since I'd heard rumors about the others who did before I learned it firsthand on that first date with Adam.

I almost didn't go to the prom with Adam, because it had felt beyond creepy being in a funeral home late at night. He even took me into the embalming room and gave me a ghoulish description of the procedure. That, I definitely could have done without. Attending autopsies to learn cause of death was one thing; being told how the deceased is embalmed was quite another. As I said, he was a wild one.

Even though our class work was finished and affiliations behind us, there were the comps to study for and they were similar to college SATs. They were called comprehensive exams because that is exactly what they were exams to test us on everything we learned in every class and on every service of our rotations, long after we took the final exams for those classes.

It was also rotation time again. All of our rotations from that time onward were to give us extra time in charge of the wards, which had been considerable before this. It was an enjoyable and relaxing time for us senior students, knowing we were on the last leg of our three-year journey toward realizing our goal as registered nurses.

To say comps were not easy is an understatement. I had to study very hard to maintain a C or above C average throughout the three years of training, as Geneva Rubins predicted in 1955.

However, that was nothing to how hard I had to study to pass all the comps. And, if I didn't pass each one of them, I failed nursing school, with no second chance.

I did pass all my comps, as did all 46 of my classmates who had successfully made it to the end. We were about as relieved as any group had ever been to know it was finally over. The pressure was off and nothing was going to stop us from becoming graduate nurses. We still had State Boards to face, but that wouldn't be for several months. There was much celebrating to do because we passed comps, and we did it all night long, even those who had to be on duty at a quarter till seven in the morning. They could have cared less about the lack of sleep. It was almost like a dream, but it really was over.

May of 1958 came too quickly. Nearly all of us had mixed emotions on Graduation Day. Yes, we were excited and eager to leave training; after all, school had occupied the past fifteen years of our lives. We could not wait to go to Columbus, take our boards, receive our licenses and be able to write RN after our names. But, we had gone through a lot together as a class, and nostalgia draped us like a San Francisco fog.

A time or two some of us had considered giving up, because training was so difficult. Mother pushed me, and my suitcase, up the Greyhound bus steps once, because I started to cry and told her I could not go back. She knew how hard I'd worked to get into school, and how hard I'd worked to stay there. She didn't care that I was twenty years old; I was not quitting. This was before affiliations started, and I had almost a whole year stretching before me. It was impossible to picture its being over.

And Then There Was One

    The bus driver, Joe, knew me, since I'd taken that same bus so many times over the three years. He did not say a word as I sat in the first seat to his right and sobbed quietly. There was no one else on the bus at the time. Afterward, we talked about training and how difficult it was. Like my mother, he told me I had only a short time to go, even though it didn't seem like it then, and I would be glad I completed it when it was over. He told me, no matter what happened in my life after I got that RN, I would always have a job to support myself and wouldn't have to be dependent upon anyone else, unless I wanted to be. I appreciated his being so kind to me that night.

    Of course, I was glad Mother was adamant I stay the course, because she was right; I did want to graduate, despite, at times, feeling so stressed I thought I could not do it one more day. How I would have regretted it, had I not listened to her and not gone back to Cincinnati that night.

That day in May, 1958, Mother, Dad, Bebe, and Kathi, my youngest sisters, and my maternal grandmother, Lottie Gardner, were seated in the audience of the large church in Cincinnati when I walked down the aisle in my new white uniform and white cap with the narrow black velvet stripe across the top of it, signifying I was now a graduate nurse. I could never forget that uniform, even if I had no photographs of myself in it. It draped beautifully, had a hint of a shimmer, a Peter Pan collar, long sleeves with wide pearl-buttoned cuffs and small pearl buttons down the front. It was the most beautiful dress I had ever seen, after having to wear those heavy blue dresses with white pinafores over them for three years. And, instead of being almost to my ankles, it was hemmed to right below my knees.

When we new graduates walked into the sanctuary and down the aisle of the church to take our places to receive our diplomas, we were singing, "You'll Never Walk Alone," while carrying lighted candles; not an easy thing to do. As soon as we started singing it, my emotions kicked in and the tears started to fall. I had to hold my candle out further than we were supposed to in order not to put it out with my falling tears. To this day, I don't remember whether it stayed lit or my tears extinguished it. I was ecstatic to be graduating but sad to be leaving my friends, my sisters from Bethesda.

To this day, the tears start falling whenever I hear "You'll Never Walk Alone." Even though it was only on a music box, when I bought one with the song on it as a going-away gift for my youngest granddaughter, Emily, before she went away to the university in 2010, I sobbed as I wrote a special verse to go with it, knowing I'd miss her and remembering my own graduation.

Our Bethesda Hospital School of Nursing Pin was another source of joy for me. The pin was made entirely of 10 Karat gold and in its center was the Maltese Cross, a symbol of hope and safety, which dates back to the early Christian era and was adopted by the Knights Hospitalliers. Surrounding the cross was a round band with the words Bethesda Hospital School of Nursing, Cincinnati, Ohio, and surrounding the pin was a circle of olive branch. It also has biblical significance and symbolizes peace, good will and healing.

I loved that pin, the size of a nickel, and before I sold one of my cars many years ago, for some reason, my pin had been taken off and put up on the dashboard. A friend was helping me clean the inside of the car and accidentally flipped the pin into the vent system, when he tried to pick it up to hand it to me. Try as we might, we could never reach it to recover it and, to my dismay, it went with the car when it was sold.

After the commencement ceremony and all the diplomas had been handed out, we attended a graduation tea, together for the last time. Students were introducing the instructors to their families and I was no exception. Ms. Drysdale, the medical instructor the upperclassmen had called The Great White Lady, told my mother when I introduced them, "I was very hard on Peggy when she was on my service and I know she didn't appreciate it." She smiled and rationalized this with knowing I had "the potential to be a really good nurse if I continued to push her." I could have used a little less of a shove, but I smiled and said nothing to that. I was just thankful it was all over and I had nothing else to prove.

What naïve thinking that was! In the real world, away from the classes and instructors, nurses constantly have to prove to their supervisors, their peers, physicians, patients and patients' family members that they know what they're doing. They must exude confidence, despite not feeling confident in every situation that presents itself.

There is a new challenge every day for the registered nurse, even when the day seems routine as it begins. A life or death emergency can be right around the corner, and with it comes something that might cause the registered nurse to question herself. This is something she cannot allow herself to dwell on in an emergency situation. She must always act with decisiveness from her strong base of knowledge and within the bounds of her license. There will be plenty of time, after it is over, to play Monday morning quarterback with herself. The RN will discover, in most instances and the longer she is a nurse, she expects more of herself and is harder on herself than anyone else ever could be; there will be times, throughout her career, she is her own worst enemy.

Our graduation day was a happy but sad one; a proud but overwhelming day and way too soon, it was over. All of us who shared our lives, hopes, dreams, heartaches, pain and joy with each other for three long years, went our separate ways, never to be all together again for the rest of our lives.

Andy and I had thought we'd go to our 40th reunion, but circumstances got in the way. It's been 53 years since that day and we've never made it yet. Serious illness and death have already claimed several of our classmates. We can only hope those of us remaining will see each other again one day.

PART TWO: A. G. HOLLEY STATE TB HOSPITAL

And Then There Was One

With youngest sister, Kathi, age 6, in 1960, after moving to Florida

TEN

Move from Ohio to Florida Leads to TB Hospital

After passing my boards and becoming licensed, I worked in Ohio in a small hospital and then as a nurse in a doctor's office. My parents and siblings had moved to Florida in 1959. In 1960, I followed, because my mother had a positive pap smear and her gynecologist was not doing any follow-up to rule out cervical cancer.

After I moved to West Palm Beach and started working at Good Samaritan Hospital, I became friends with a young gynecologist, Curtis Cannon, MD, who'd just finished his residency and moved from Jacksonville to practice in West Palm. Curt agreed to see Mother. He did not criticize her gynecologist but, conversely, he scheduled a D & C right away on her. He told her if it looked like cancer, he would do a hysterectomy.

Mother was relieved, as were we, after the surgery, to

know, even though the lab confirmed cancerous cells, it was in the early stages, and the surgeon got all the cancer when he did the hysterectomy. She remained cancer-free for the next three decades, until breast cancer laid its claim on her. With the rest of my immediate family in Florida, I did not return to live in Ohio.

A year later, I contracted infectious mononucleosis, a disease mostly found in young adults. The Epstein-Barr virus causes the illness. Because one of the ways it can be spread is through saliva, it has the colloquial name, the kissing disease. In addition to the mono, I developed secondary hepatitis, my spleen was quite enlarged and I was ill for several weeks.

When my physician discharged me from Good Samaritan, it was with the provision I go to live with my family in Lantana and do nothing more strenuous for six months than take slow walks to the beach every day when my energy level allowed. Lantana was a few miles south of West Palm Beach and my parents lived a block from the Intracoastal Waterway, so I took his advice.

Since the physician specifically told me not to return to work for six months but said I could return to the lab class I had been taking at Palm Beach Jr. College, a few miles west of Lake Worth, between West Palm and Lantana, I continued the class. It was during our break from class when I collapsed with mono. I was glad to get back to class, which met twice a week at night.

A lab classmate, Opal Ford, a nursing supervisor at Southeast Florida State Tuberculosis Hospital in Lantana, kindly gave me transportation to and from class. One night on the way home, I was lamenting being tired of the idleness and despite what the doctor told me, I wanted to get back to work.

All I had been doing for the past three months was walking to the beach every day, swimming a little, lying in the sun reading paperbacks and going to the lab class two evenings a week. I laugh as I write this, because many who read it will think I've lost my marbles, especially if they do not have access to a beach or that much down time, since it seems the ideal way to spend one's time. And, it was for a while. Florida was still new to me and I loved the ocean, but I was a twenty-four year old nurse, also, and in love with nursing. I'd worked just three years since passing my boards and truly missed taking care of patients.

Opal said to me, "Why don't you come to the TB hospital and apply for a position? I have an opening on one of my wards and since it's on days, you could still finish the medical technology course with me." She told me, compared to working in a general hospital, working at "Lantana," as she called it, was comparable to being on perpetual vacation.

I applied the next day, was hired on the spot and went to work the following morning on 2B, a women's ward. I had a sweet and knowledgeable head nurse, Eleanor Briggs. All I did was pass meds twice a day, do a few minor treatments and visit with her, the doctor, the patients and other staff after my charting was finished. Opal was right; compared to what I'd been used to in the general hospital, it was a vacation; a wonderful one, at that.

I could not believe my luck in getting the job. It was the best of all possible worlds. I was able to get back to nursing without jeopardizing my complete recovery from the illness and the atmosphere of the workplace could not have been better.

Unlike Dunham, Lantana was a bright cheery five-story hospital, including the basement offices and lab, with wall-to-wall awning windows on both sides and solariums with the same windows on three sides, on both ends of the building and in the center on each patient floor. There, the patients relaxed, conversed, read, and played pool and board games.

Because of the climate, the windows throughout the hospital were always opened to the sub-tropical breezy air. This kept any droplets of tuberculosis bacilli, coughed by the patients, circulating to the outside air instead of lingering inside the building. There were acres of beautiful trees and tropical foliage on the hospital grounds.

One of the nicest surprises for me was that staff members did not wear masks as we did at Dunham, unless we were taking care of fresh post-op patients in order to protect them. And, we wore cool scrub dresses or regular uniforms, whichever we preferred, and of course, we nurses wore our nursing caps.

The 2B patients were classified as convalescent and a step from discharge. They had not been infectious to others for a considerable length of time. They wore their own street clothes and had the freedom to leave the ward to go outside whenever they desired. They could go to occupational therapy to work on crafts and anywhere else in the hospital they desired to go, except 3A and 3B.

On 3A, the patients were sicker than on the other

wards, usually with far advanced tuberculosis, which responded slower to the medications because it involved more of the lung tissue.

3B was the surgical ward, so those patients had to stay away from the others to avoid infection after surgery.

Unless they were not feeling well, the 2B patients went down to the patient dining room for meals. They received shopping passes twice a week to walk to the small shopping center a half block from the hospital.

These little shopping excursions were healthy for them and their self-esteem, because they felt as normal as everyone else. They did not look like they had TB, so there was no way the other shoppers could tell they were hospital patients.

TB still carried a stigma in many circles and for this reason, the patients needed to understand they were normal people who were temporarily sidelined by an illness, not people who should feel ashamed and hide from the public eye.

The patients received dinner passes when their families came to visit. There were no restrictions from visiting, except no visitors could be in the hospital after visiting hours were called at 8:30 every night.

In addition to all that, most of them got weekend and holiday passes to go home, so the workload on weekends and holidays was even lighter. In fact, so much so that half the staff got to take holiday leaves during Thanksgiving week and the other half, during Christmas week, because there were hardly any patients left in the hospital.

I discovered I loved everything about working in TB. Amazing to me after the experience at Dunham three years prior to coming to work at Lantana. I learned most of the staff had worked there for over a decade since the hospital opened its doors in 1950. Furthermore, because of the good teaching each of them reinforced upon the patients on a daily basis and their own sensible precautions, none of them ever contracted tuberculosis, despite the close daily contact with patients even before their sputum converted to negative status.

Each patient had to submit three bottles with sputum samples for laboratory examination every week. Patients produced sputum by coughing deeply from the lungs. They could not just spit saliva into the bottles. Those unable to cough up the sputum had to be assisted with producing induced sputum. This was obtained by inhaling a misty solution of saline (salt water) to stimulate coughing. Another method of obtaining sputum was gastric washing. That was particularly useful when the patient was a child and could not understand how to cough up a specimen.

My patients on 2B no longer needed to have Strept injections, and Eleanor instructed me to leave their oral medications at the bedside, unlike in the general hospital where the nurse always had to observe the patient taking the pills. No stress for them, and since I was not delayed by trying to chase them down to take their meds right then, no stress for me, either.

We never had to worry about non-compliance on the convalescent wards. Those patients were too close to being discharged after confinement in the hospital for one to two years, to take such a risk. They'd been told consistently there was no guaranteed cure for TB yet, because the newer drugs had not been used long enough to be certain of it. Also, the chance of relapse was great if they didn't take the medication on a regular basis, as it was ordered. The alternative was crystal clear, so they gladly took their medication before they went off the ward or as soon as they returned if they were gone just a short time.

Every week, Dr. Adil, our ward physician, would meet with the patients and staff out in the big sunny solarium. These informal porch meetings were great morale builders and gave the patients the chance to vent to the staff as a whole, so problems never became serious before they were resolved. The meetings gave the patients the feeling they were part of the team in charge of their health, not just people observing what others were doing to get them well. This was true, as in no other hospital.

I sometimes got to float to other wards at Lantana, something I'd hated to do in general hospitals. I loved to do it at the TB hospital because it was always a pleasant experience and I was eager to learn all phases of the patients' care. Even on the wards with the sicker patients, it was nothing like it had been in 1957 in Ohio when so little could be done for the patients.

That's amazing when I consider the implications of it. I had been out of nursing school just three years at that time, and yet, there had been that much progress made in the treatment and care of patients with tuberculosis. When I was a young nurse, I had no idea I was living such important history.

The staff at Lantana was different from anywhere else I'd ever worked. They were relaxed and friendly and they genuinely cared about the patients with TB. They even came to 2B on their breaks for no other reason than to meet me, the new nurse. That was saying something about the calibre of personnel who worked there; they would go out of their way to make a new nurse feel welcomed. And, to be fair to nurses in general hospitals, these nurses had the time to do this. In general hospitals, there is rarely time to sit around and do nothing but visit with each other, or to leave the unit to go to another one to meet someone new. Too often, it is the rule, not the exception, that the general hospital nurse does not get to leave the floor, even for a meal. The work simply is too constant and demanding of her time.

Having a new employee in the house was a novelty at Lantana, because most of the staff had been employed there since the hospital opened its doors in 1950, eleven years before I stepped a foot inside it. It was like being queen for a day, but that day turned into months. Everyone wanted to know what the new nurse was like, and most of all, if she enjoyed working at this place they held dear.

One of those who introduced herself to me was a young RN from Tampa named Maurine Butler, who like me, was not long out of nursing school. She worked in the operating room with her RN supervisor, Betty Wright. Maurine's husband, Bob, worked in the State Lab located in the hospital basement in the '60s instead of the separate accommodations it has now, still on the A. G. Holley grounds south of the hospital.

She was eager to get to know me, not only because I was new and she was as curious as the next person who'd worked there for years, but also because her brother-in-law, Ron, who worked in the serology section of the lab, processing VDRLs during his summer vacations from Florida State University, told Bob and her during lunch the first time I walked into the cafeteria, he was "going to marry that nurse."

Maurine, who married Bob a few months before and believed everyone else should be married, too, wanted me to go on a beach picnic with the three of them on the 4th of July. As much as I liked her when I met her and still do, the thought of going on a double date with a man who, without even speaking to me, had decided at first glance he was going to marry me, was pretty scary. But, I told her I would go, just to be sociable.

As the July 4th weekend approached, I suffered a severe case of cold feet and tried to persuade Eleanor to let me work the weekend, so she could be with her family. She saw through the ruse and said, "Nothing doing. You're going to go out with that nice Ronnie Butler and have a good time."

She even recruited Dr. Adil to help her persuade me. I relented, in the end, and went on the picnic with the Butlers. I did have a good time with the couple and the slender, smiling young man with dark brown hair and great sense of humor, who'd decided at first glance he was going to marry me for whatever his reason. Of course, he'd dared not mention that on that first date.

During my time on duty, I continued to absorb all I could about the hospital, tuberculosis treatment and medications.

It still astonished me how much I loved working at that

hospital on those beautiful grounds, after having had such an unpleasant experience in nursing school.

To be honest here, it wasn't the hospital in Cincinnati, as much as the futility I felt in trying to teach those patients to take care of themselves and protect us, their caregivers.

Sputum care was such a simple thing for them to do; it was also one of the most important. I found the majority of them too downtrodden and depressed about having the disease, to make the effort. What I was teaching them was low on their priority list. I could almost hear the unspoken mantra: *What's the use of trying when I'm going to die, anyway?* Although more were getting well, I think few believed they were going to get well enough to go home.

Part of that might have been the season, for when one goes through a long and dreary winter, there is that natural physiological tendency to get the blues. In my own case, I looked forward to and loved that first snow and it seemed to begin every Thanksgiving in southern Ohio. There was nothing more beautiful to watch than large snowflakes covering the space between the ground and as high as one could see. It was magical and made the air I breathed crisp and clean.

I didn't mind when it continued to snow until Christmas, or when I had to walk gingerly to avoid slipping when the snow mixed with ice. I wore boots or shoes with the kind of soles that gripped rather than slid on the ice. With all that white snow covering the ground, it was difficult to tell when there was going to be a patch of ice mixed with it, right below the surface, so one had to be prepared for it.

However, as December turned into January, and then, March into April or later, with the sky still a dreary gray and the ground still covered with snow and dirty slush, it was not unusual for me to experience those winter blues, as well, and long for green grass, blossoms on the trees and flowers springing up everywhere to signal an end to my dreary-looking world. When this spring phenomenon happened, my world became beautiful once again and my somber mood gone.

I wasn't alone. Even now, there are millions who are affected by this. There's even a medical term for it: *Seasonal Affective Disorder* (appropriately known as SAD). It is caused by a genuine chemical imbalance of the hypothalamus gland from the lack of sunlight and shorter hours of daylight.

As much as I did not like to be inside Dunham TB Hospital with that gray world surrounding it, I could not begin to imagine how it felt for the patients to have to lie there and see it day after day, without end in sight. It must have quadrupled their depressed, often hopeless, spirits. As much as I didn't want to be there, I tried to understand this and them, so it would not color the way I cared for them. I believe I was able to accomplish that attitude within myself.

I continued to use gentle repetition to teach them the proper way to care for themselves, and in the process, protect those of us around them. I tried to understand why this was such a difficult thing for them to do, and I felt in jeopardy from them when they ignored the sputum precautions to protect us from exposure to their disease. It was a constant struggle for me to truly emphasize with them.

It was as different as night and day to come to work every day and see that Lantana blue sky outside those windowed walls, the swaying palm trees and thick bushy ficus trees, the hibiscus and lush bougainvillea that beautiful green and multi-colored world that kept us all in good spirits when we glanced out the windows throughout our day and felt the silky warm breezes caress our faces, ever so softly.

Of course, the patients at Lantana were not without their problems. I don't mean to paint a picture of a perfect rosy hospitalization for them. It wasn't. They were still away from home, if they had homes, and their families, if they had families. There were better places to be than in the hospital, unless one was homeless, despite how nice it was there.

But, not having their illness coupled with dreary winters seemed to make it easier for them to bear than for my original group of tuberculosis patients in Cincinnati. I cannot say how many times I made rounds in the afternoon, at Lantana, when most of them were resting in bed after having their afternoon meds and eating a good lunch, and saw so many of them lying there awake, some with books and glasses nearby, just looking out the windows with what seemed a peaceful meditative spirit. We never disturbed their afternoon tranquility.

I'll always believe it was that beautiful place with its subtropical weather, coupled with the caring staff, rest and medications, that healed them. A dreary winter season was one less thing they had to be concerned about, and I loved it, too, coming from a place where winter could last from November to the end of May, as it had the last day of my residence in Ohio.

ELEVEN

Improvement in Medications and Patient Prognosis

A patient's dying from tuberculosis was becoming less common in the sixties. That was because the multiple drug TB chemotherapy, now primarily INH, PAS, PZA, Ethambutol and Streptomycin, was working better than in the fifties.

Instead of the injectable Codeine, most of the patients who coughed were given oral pills called Tessalon pearles, a noncontrolled medication. A few were given Codeine pills, but because of the addictive nature of the narcotic, that was not encouraged unless Tessalon could not control the cough.

The TB hospital was becoming a place to get well instead of a sanatorium to come to be isolated from loved ones, until death took you. And, at Lantana, it was a bright, cheerful atmosphere where patients and staff were like family, and where the patients' families were always welcome, if only to visit with them outside under the vast canopy of trees on the beautiful hospital grounds, if their sputum status was still positive.

It was also a place where the patients could enjoy themselves, thanks to the efforts of the Special Services Department under the direction of a caring gentleman by the name of Dick Conlin, who always had a smile on his face. They played pool or other games in the end and middle solariums, watched movies in the auditorium and us, the staff, as we performed for them on stage at special staff programs.

Over the years of my involvement with the Lantana TB hospital, I was privileged to dress in a pretty gown and lose my nurse persona for a while more than once. I loved singing the blues and country for them at a couple of those shows.

Once when I deviated from accompanying myself at the piano and sang to a Tammy Wynette record, it was especially fun for them and the other staff. I wasn't sure why they were clapping and laughing at the same time at one point, but I soon learned it was because it was difficult for me to hear the record and I was ahead of the music. That would have been embarrassing to me any other time, but everyone who was there, including me when I realized what was happening, had a good laugh because of it.

It was a pleasant break for all the staff members who were able to go to the auditorium to watch and partake in the show, if they so chose. We had some talented musicians among the staff who enjoyed wearing that other hat, and playing their instruments for an afternoon's entertainment. It gave the patients the opportunity to see a different side to their nurses, x-ray technicians and other members of the hospital staff.

The medical ward, 3A, and the surgical ward, 3B, were the busiest wards in the house. The senior resident physician and surgeon, Dr. T. S. Feng, a mountain of a man and an excellent surgeon, was performing patients' bronchoscopies and chest surgery, mostly lobectemies (partial lung removals by that time), almost every day.

Of course, being confined for such a long time, the patients developed other (non-TB) problems and some required general surgery. The resident surgeons performed cholecystectomies, appendectomies and herniorraphies more often than any other general surgery, so the O.R. workday wasn't confined to chest surgery. The operating room nurses also scheduled routine and emergency gynecological surgeries, if the patients could not be temporarily transferred to a general hospital because of their positive sputum status. Dr. Curtis Cannon was the gynecologist consultant for the hospital, and his scheduled days were filled with back-to-back surgeries.

Chest surgery patients always came back to the post-op rooms on 3B with chest tubes for re-expansion and drainage into chest bottles and spent at least a week being specialed. This meant one nurse and specially trained nurses aide would have the responsibility for his or her care on each shift. Better private duty care could not be had anywhere else.

The patients stayed in that room, in strict isolation for their own protection, being cared for by the nurses and those specially trained surgical aides for at least a week and sometimes for two or more weeks, depending upon the progress of their recovery.

One of those surgical aides was a young woman by the name of Margie Knowles. Had I ever needed chest surgery, it would have been her big, bright, confident brown eyes I would have wanted to see above that surgical mask when I awakened, knowing she would do everything in her power to get me through it. She was more than capable of doing just that. I'll have more to say about Margie, later.

Our social services department, under the capable direction of social worker Shirley Bennett, was busy assisting patients with matters no one else could, such as signing up for their social security and other benefits, being the liaison between their families and the hospital and helping with any problems the families encountered, while they were on their own, by collaborating with their county social services agencies. This was a great relief to the patients.

Once a week, each patient was seen on rounds. Dr. Adil and Eleanor or I placed all the patient charts onto a treatment table and went to each patient's bedside. Dr. Adil reviewed their cases with them and decided whether a change in medication orders or activities was needed.

Patients were involved in their own care, knew what medications they were on and what was expected of them. They took rounds seriously, were in their rooms without our having to look for them and had their questions ready for Dr. Adil.

Every Tuesday, Conference was held in the first floor

conference room, a practice continued to this day, except the conference room is on another floor now. The ward secretaries, without whom no ward could function, kept track of when each patient's monthly chest x-ray was due, sent the patient to x-ray for this and scheduled him or her for conference that week.

The fresh x-ray was compared with the one from the previous month while the ward physician presented the case to the other physicians and staff who were present. Together, they made a decision for continued hospitalization with or without a change in treatment regime.

Or they would rule in favor of discharge from the hospital to the county health department for outpatient care, depending upon whether there was improvement in the patient's general condition, his chest x-ray and sputum status.

Working in partnership with our ward physicians made all the nurses, aides and orderlies into tuberculosis experts. I was no different and my mind absorbed everything like a sponge.

When the word came back to the patients who had been discharged in Conference, there was a great deal of celebrating on that particular ward, and with good cause, since, as was pointed out earlier, in those days each patient was confined to the hospital for a year or two. Some were there much longer because their sputum status remained positive despite the medications.

Before he could be discharged, a patient had to have three consecutive TB negative sputum cultures, improved chest x-rays and have a place to live in the county that had admitted him to the hospital.

That is true today, as well, if the patient is in the hospital, although I understand if it is determined he has a bona fide place to live elsewhere, now, he may be discharged to that locale and followed by its county health unit.

The patient was discharged to the care of TB Control at the county health unit. This meant being seen in Chest Clinic on a regular basis to have chest x-rays and weight monitored, submit sputum samples, have blood drawn to check his liver function and be examined by the TB Control physician who would re-evaluate his medications and change or continue him on the same regime, as indicated, just as did his hospital physician.

Most of the TB Control physicians were young men and women assigned to the county by the United States Public Health Service. They were intelligent and knowledgeable. TB Control staff learned much from them and vice-versa, since this was, more often than not, their first experience in TB Control.

The TB Control nurse would then speak with the patient and give him the prescriptions he would take to the health department pharmacy to be filled at no cost to him. At each visit, before he left the clinic, she reviewed the side effects of each of the medications he was taking. These included nausea, vomiting, rash, itching, jaundice, blurred vision and numbness or tingling of the extremities. It was rare to experience any of them, and most did not. She would caution him to take the pyridoxine (vitamin B6) daily, while he was on the tuberculosis medication, because it would help to prevent the peripheral neuritis he might experience, otherwise.

Though repetitious, this review of side effects at each visit was of the utmost importance because, unlike when he was in the hospital where he was observed by nurses and physicians on a daily basis, he was on his own at home and needed to know to call TB Control for an appointment right away if anything was amiss. If he called with a side effect, he would be advised to hold (not take) the medications at that time.

The nurse spoke with the physician as soon as the patient reported side effects. He, in turn, made a decision to change the medication regime at that time or wait for the results of the lab work. Regardless, the patient was advised to come into the clinic right away to see the nurse so she could draw a blood sample for a liver function test (SGOT) to determine whether his liver was being adversely affected by the medications. Unlike in the disease hepatitis, the liver affected by a TB drug usually recovered at a rapid pace when the offending medication was discontinued.

So, the patient knew, before his discharge, what was in store for him on the outside because TB Control referred him to the hospital; rarely was a patient sent to the hospital without first being seen in Chest Clinic. For the most part, the patients were compliant with this routine.

However, when they failed to keep their clinic appointments and take their medications, the TB Control nurse sent the field representative in search of them. If they continued to be recalcitrant with coming to Chest Clinic and taking their medications, proceedings would get under way to get them back into the hospital. Sometimes this would require court-ordered commitment to a locked ward in the hospital. Since the patients knew about this, most of them went willingly.

For the hospitalized patients who were taken to Conference month after month without the good news they were discharged, they were disappointed, of course. Most of the time they knew from what the ward physician told them during rounds, even before Conference, whether they might go home or not. Despite his not encouraging them to believe they were ready, they still hoped the other doctors in conference might disagree with his assessment and rule for discharge. This rarely, if ever, happened, but who could blame them for having a desire to go home to be with loved ones when they had been away from them for so long?

And Then There Was One

Peg's Wedding, 1961

TWELVE

Relationship of Patients to Nurses

Patients in the TB hospital got to know the nurses, aides and orderlies on their floors because of the quality time they spent with them. Most of them felt comfortable venting to the staff about their hopes and disappointments. Staff was never too busy to stop and listen to them. And, because of the nature of the work, they had the time to do this more so than those who worked in other kinds of hospitals.

Lantana staff did a lot of sitting around talking with one another, reading or relaxing with a cup of tea or coffee, also, especially in the afternoon when the patients were lying in their rooms, sleeping or reading. The nurses spent afternoons finishing their charting and the charge nurse wrote her report for the supervisor, but after this was finished, their work was through for the day, unless a patient needed them, until they gave the oncoming charge nurse the ward report.

No one reprimanded them, the aides or orderlies for

not being busy during these down times. If they'd finished their routine duties, their care plans updated, the ward was clean and orderly, and the patients did not need them for anything, what would there be to reprimand them about? Nothing.

The TB hospital was so different from any other hospital I'd ever worked in, and there was a lot of down time after the work of the morning and early afternoon was completed.

If a patient needed someone to talk with or explain something to him, of course, he was not ignored. The aide or nurse would spend as much time as the patient needed, until his problem or concern was addressed.

That was the first thing that hooked me on TB nursing in Lantana. It had been a frustration to me in the general hospital setting to hurry from one patient to another, when it would have helped some of the patients had I simply had time to sit and listen to them for as long as they needed me.

When I was one of two, or sometimes the only nurse on the unit in the general hospital, I had too much responsibility, of an urgent nature, to do this for the patients. I often felt I was cheating them of good care because of it, despite doing everything the physicians ordered for them.

Being one of two, or the only nurse on a TB ward, more often than not, I could take all the time I wanted to sit down and listen to the patient. This was so much more gratifying to me than working amid all the chaos of the general hospital setting, as exciting and challenging as that could become at times. I remained alert to anything of emergency nature, but emergencies were much fewer in the TB hospital than in a general hospital.

Most hospital workers had no desire to work in a sanatorium treating TB patients, out of fear of contracting the disease. And, for the most part, it lacked the excitement general hospital staffs can count on almost every day.

Those who did take care of the TB patients were not afraid of catching the disease from them and cared about them. The patients seemed to sense that. This was one of the factors that contributed to making their hospitalization tolerable and, often, even pleasant.

The patients, in turn, learned to care about the staff as well. I learned this in a dramatic way a few months after I started to work at the hospital. I continued to date Ron Butler and he persuaded me to marry him. September 2, 1961, was the planned date for our wedding, to take place in a small Lantana church. The entire hospital got into the act, including the patients.

One day I had just finished my late lunch when the operator paged me. "Peggy, there's an emergency in 2A solarium," she told me, when I picked up the phone.

"That's odd," I said, since Eleanor was on the ward and the supervisor was in the house, but had not been paged. Perhaps she had been on the ward when whatever happened, happened.

Why would they also call me? But, "I'm on my way," I told her. Of course, I took the stairs to the second floor and hurried to the east solarium, quite a long walk from the stairs or elevators.

The emergency was a surprise bridal shower Dr. Adil,

Eleanor, the other nurses on second floor, the aides, secretaries and all of the 2A and B patients had thrown for me. I don't know who was more excited the patients or me!

Another surprise shower, given to me by the entire female hospital staff, followed this, in the lobby of the nurses' residence, where I lived on the northeast side of the hospital grounds next to the parking lot.

In addition to this, the staff bought the flowers for our wedding, and one of our nurses aides made the bridal veil to go with the dress my younger sister, Bebe, made for me. Dr. Feng took wedding pictures to add to those of the professional photographer, and Opal and Maurine organized the reception. Most of the off-duty staff attended the ceremony.

I had found a second family at Southeast Florida State TB Hospital and was sad to leave it for Tallahassee when school restarted for my husband at FSU a few days after our wedding.

I transferred to W.T. Edwards State TB Hospital in Tallahassee and was 3-11 charge nurse on the surgical floor and assistant 3-11 supervisor of the hospital, meaning I relieved the supervisor on her days off. I enjoyed working there, but even though it was smaller than the 500-bed Lantana hospital, it was nowhere near the same.

My mother, Norma Gardner Puckett, a dedicated nurse's aide, joined the staff while I was in Tallahassee. I was kept apprised of the Lantana hospital happenings through her and my new in-laws, Maurine and Bob Butler.

At W. T. Edwards, some of the patients were prone to violence, which was rare at Lantana. They did not have the recreational facilities and activities the Lantana hospital had, and I believed this contributed to their restlessness.

One night when I was covering the house, the operator paged me. "Peggy, there's a fight on 4."

"I'm on my way," I told her.

"Bosey has a knife and threatened that kid again."

"Okay, we'll take care of it. Thanks for warning me."

The young patient in question was frightened, as would be expected. The offender, Bosey, had ripped every button from his shirt with the knife. He was not injured, not even a scratch, but was traumatized from believing he was going to have the knife thrust into his chest. It took skill to rip those buttons off his shirt without hurting him. For that reason, I thought the other patient intended only to scare him.

I instructed him to go to the surgical ward and tell the nurse in charge to hide him in the bathroom. I told him to lock the door, until he was told it was safe to go back to his ward.

I took the orderly on duty, a handsome, older gentleman with shiny grey hair, to Bosey's ward on the fourth floor, and we walked up to him in the wide hallway.

"Don' come any closer, Miss Butler. I don' wanna have ta hurt ya, ma'am," he warned me. Jesse, the orderly, hovered behind me.

I told the patient, "Bosey, please give me the knife and go back to your room."

He was a pleasant looking man with a ruddy complexion, in his late forties. Six feet tall, he had a medium build and looked as though he'd been working out since he began to heal from his TB. I could smell alcohol on his breath, but he was not unsteady and his speech was not slurred.

As they had at Lantana, the Tallahassee alcoholic TB patients managed to find a way to get the booze, shoe polish or cough syrup whatever was handy that might contain an iota of alcohol to substitute for beer or liquor, when there was no one to make the run to the liquor store.

"I'll have ta give it to ya in the belly, ma'am, if you come any closer. Ya know I don' wanna do that, Miss Butler."

"Well then, you know what I have to do," I told him, as I stopped within a couple feet of him, to give him the space he'd requested.

"Yes, ma'am, I know. Ya have ta git the sheriff."

"That's right, Bosey. Is that the only choice you're giving me?"

"I s'pose so, ma'am. I'll wait right chere."

Bosey was what is known as a Florida cracker. He was born in the panhandle region of Florida along the Gulf coast. Not all, but many Crackers have thick southern accents, unlike Floridians who were not born or did not live most of their lives in northcentral Florida or the panhandle of Florida, near Alabama and Louisiana. They, like southerners from other states, are polite and courteous in their manner and speech, especially to women, just as this patient was toward me, despite threatening to plunge the knife into my belly if I tried to disarm him. I knew he would have done it had I given him reason.

"Thank you, Bosey." I turned to walk to the elevator with the orderly, who was walking backwards and begging me not to turn my back on the patient with the knife.

"Jesse, just walk with me and don't look back at Bosey."

"But, Peggy, he said he'd stab you."

"Only if I tried to get the knife from him. And, I certainly was not going to attempt that. That's for the deputy to do or for Bosey to relinquish voluntarily. Now, please, let's walk to the elevator and don't look back at him. I promise it will be okay, Jesse," I told him with a smile. Finally he was convinced and turned his back on the patient before we reached the elevator.

Despite his being intoxicated and armed, because I had a reputation for being fair toward the patients, I knew Bosey trusted me to treat him fairly, even if that meant calling for law enforcement to handle the situation. I was confident he would hurt no one if we did not look back and antagonize him.

Having those three months at Toledo State taught me to handle agitated patients like Bosey and gave me the confidence to do the right thing, like walking with my back to him after we'd reached the agreement to involve the sheriff's office. It taught me to assess every situation, before taking action. It was imperative to do this on a case-by-case basis, since doing one thing in the presence of one disturbed patient might not work in the presence of another. Another patient might have knifed me in the belly without warning me or in the back when I started to walk away. I knew Bosey would do neither.

When we returned ten minutes later with the armed

Leon County Sheriff's deputy, Bosey was standing with the knife still in his hand, in the same place in the hallway where Jesse and I left him. I had not been concerned he'd hurt anyone else. His argument was with the young man who had taunted him one time too many. There was not a sound from him or any of the other male patients who stood in their doorways, watching this tableau unfold. He dropped the knife and held out his arms so the deputy could cuff him as we approached.

"Thank you, Miss Butler," he said, as the deputy led him to the elevator, after picking up the knife and bagging it for evidence.

"You're welcome, Bosey. Take care of yourself in there." He knew he was out of control. He did not want the situation to escalate any more than we did. When he was released from the county jail, he might have been transferred to the committed ward at Southeast Florida TB Hospital in Lantana to complete his tuberculosis treatment. He most likely pled out on his assault charge after he was well, but we heard nothing further about him in Tallahassee.

When I got back to the surgical ward after the patient left with the deputy, the young man who'd been the object of his *knifing*, was still locked in the bathroom. The charge nurse saw the deputy and Bosey walk out, but hadn't told him the coast was clear. She grinned at me when she nodded her head toward the door.

"You can come out now. He's been taken to jail," I told him after knocking on the bathroom door.

"Are you sure?"

"Yes, I'm sure. I stood on the steps until they drove off

with him."

"Okay, then." The boy unlocked the door and sheepishly walked out of the bathroom. "Thanks, Miss Butler."

"Hey, don't thank me. You should be thanking Bosey for cutting your buttons off instead of cutting you. You were taunting him again, weren't you."

"No I I . . ."

"Look, Billy, you were lucky tonight. That man has told you many times to leave him alone, but you just kept coming back at him. You're the youngest patient we have right now and Bosey was well liked by the other men. I think it would serve you well to toe the line on that ward from now on."

"I don't understand what you want me to do." He was just seventeen and had a cocky attitude.

"Billy, what I want you to do is stay in your room, read, watch TV or just be quiet, for a change. You can't continue to tease these men who are older than you. They don't like it and if you keep it up like you did with Bosey tonight, you really are going to be hurt by one of them. They don't like being here any more than you do, so don't do anything to get them stirred up."

"I didn't mean anything by it," he said with a grin.

"Yes, you did and you know it. But, that's beside the point." The smile left his face. "The point is it's going to get you hurt before you have a chance to get well and get out of here, so starting tonight, I don't want to hear you've gotten yourself into trouble with another patient. Do you understand?"

He looked down at the floor. "Yes, Miss Butler. I'll stay

out of their way."

"I hope you mean that. Now, it's past nine, so you'd better go up and get ready for bed. If anyone says anything to you about Bosey, I want you to ignore him and walk away. If he tries to hurt you because of what happened, get away from him, take the stairs and come down here. Penny will call me right away and we'll figure out where to put you. All right?"

"Yes, I'll do that. Goodnight, Miss Butler. Goodnight, Penny."

"Peggy, he needed to hear that, but you know as well as I, he's going to start needling one of the other men, now that Bosey's no longer around."

I sighed and said, "You're probably right, but I had to try, Pen. I really am afraid for him. He's so close to going home and I'd hate to see something happen to him before then."

"Well, don't worry too much about it. Maybe you did get through to him. Anyway, the night's almost over so finish rounds and try to relax before you go home."

"Thanks for hiding him, Penny. Is your report ready?" She handed it to me and we said goodnight.

Billy never got into trouble again after that night. His sputum converted to negative and he was discharged from the hospital the following month.

And Then There Was One

Oldest daughter, Karen: left, age 6 months; below, age 2 on Easter Sunday; bottom, age 2½ learning to read.

THIRTEEN

Happiness is Having a Baby

When we returned to south Florida in 1963 after Ron got his degree, we had with us our beautiful five-month old daughter, Karen. We found a duplex apartment in Boynton Beach, south of Lantana. Ron took a position in Environmental Health at Palm Beach County Health Department and I tried to get back on at Southeast Florida State TB Hospital.

My meeting with Maggie Smith, the Director of Nurses, was not as productive as I'd hoped. Dr. Adil was still there, also, but was not in the interview with us.

"Peggy, you were assistant supervisor at W. T. Edwards and we don't have a supervisory position open right now."

"Maggie, I never asked to be supervisor up there and I'm not asking for it here. I just want to come back here to work."

"And, Dr. Adil and I would love to have you on

staff again, but I won't allow you to do that to yourself. It isn't a wise career move for a young nurse to go down the ladder."

Again I told her I was willing to take any position she had open in order to work there again.

"I promise to let you know if an opening for supervisor comes up, but I'm sorry, I just can't let you come back as less than that. It wouldn't be fair to you. Will evenings be all right, if nothing comes up for day shift?"

"I'd prefer to be home at night with the baby, but yes, I'll take anything that comes available."

"Don't be down about it now," she told me, with a smile. "You'll thank me for it if and when I can bring you on as supervisor."

"Thank you, Maggie," I said, we shook hands and I went home, about as down as I could be, because it hadn't gone as in 1961 when I was hired on the spot and started to work the following morning. I knew how draining general hospital work was for me. I wanted to give more than what energy was left over from that, to Karen. She was everything in the world to me.

Becoming a mother made such a difference in my life. For a while during my labor, it looked as though one or the other of us might not make it; in fact, at one point the obstetrician told my husband he had to think about which of us should live. I couldn't believe the doctor had asked him to make that choice, after it was all over and he shared this with me.

Also, unknown to me until Curt told me years later, he'd called my obstetrician after a call from Mother to let him know what Ron told her was happening. He told the other obstetrician he could not lose either the baby or me; that I meant a great deal to him. After his call and at his urging, when I was on the delivery table for the third time, the doctor internally and manually turned Karen so her face was in the birth canal.

I was in agony from a day and a half of painful, constant (popcorn) back labor, lying on my left side and not being allowed to turn over, in an attempt to get the baby to turn. This did not happen; she stayed firmly wedged in the same position. I'd made clear to the obstetrician I wanted natural childbirth, with no anesthetic, although I screamed for him to give me some right before he pulled her out, with the help of the forceps. Of course, he had to refuse; the time for anesthetic was long over.

After she was safely out, and he put her into my arms, the long hours of labor pain and the pain of delivery were all but forgotten. I had never seen such a beautiful creature and marveled that I'd had anything to do with her creation.

The doctor apologized to me the next morning; he told me his measurements of my pelvis must have been in error; that as large as she was and as small as I was, I should have been scheduled for a Caesarean section.

I enjoyed being home with Karen so much and would be sad to go back to work, anywhere, because it would mean leaving her. I saw small changes in her personality, almost daily, as the months went by.

However, we needed another income, so I went to work at Bethesda Memorial Hospital, south of where we lived in Boynton Beach, on the 11-7 shift, which I'd always had problems with because I couldn't sleep in the daytime. I had no choice but to take this shift; we had only one car and no extra money to buy another until I'd worked a while.

Karen was not a day sleeper, and some nights I went to work after only twenty or thirty minutes of sleep for the entire day. This continued until a few nights after President John F. Kennedy was assassinated on November 22, when she was six months old.

That was such a sad and unbelievable time for the country and it affected all of us. Americans over the age of 62 (with President William McKinley's assassination in 1901), age 82 (with President James Garfield's assassination in 1881), age 98 (with President Abraham Lincoln's assassination in 1865) were the only ones to have lived through such horror before that bleak day in November, 1963.

That particular night, around three in the morning, not long after I'd had my cold sandwich and my third or fourth cup of black coffee to keep me awake and alert, I was sitting at the desk going over doctors' orders from the last 24 hours, as the night shift routinely did in every patient's chart, to be certain nothing had been missed.

All of a sudden, I had a severe pain in my upper abdomen and had to run to the bathroom to vomit. When I vomited, it was projectile (with great force) and dark coffee ground material. I knew it wasn't the coffee; it was from bleeding.

Of course, the supervisor sent me home, and as soon as the doctor across the street came into his office a few hours later, I went over. I was so weak I could barely walk, but I asked Ron to stay home with Karen until I got back. The doctor told me what I'd feared. I probably had a bleeding stomach or duodenal ulcer.

"I'm ordering a GI series for tomorrow morning and I want you to start taking an antacid right away as soon as it's over. You have to go off the coffee and cigarettes right now." I never smoked except at night while I was at work. He stopped writing and looked up at me and said, "And, you have to stop working. Working at night, especially, is not good for you right now."

"But, I have to . . ."

"Peggy, I'm not giving you a choice. You're to call the nursing office today and tell them I ordered you to quit your job, or I'll call for you—your choice. I know you nurses smoke, eat cold sandwiches and drink black coffee all night long to stay awake. You can't do that and get this ulcer to stop bleeding. You need lots of rest and a bland diet."

"Okay, I'll resign today," I said, my feelings ambivalent. On the one hand, we needed the money I was making, but conversely, I missed being able to be with Karen all day, without trying to sleep in order to be alert for work that night.

My GI series confirmed the presence of a bleeding duodenal ulcer. After a few months of being home, eating a bland diet and taking the meds, the ulcer healed, but I was in no hurry to go back to work right away, nor did Dr. Forlaw want me to, at least not for a few more months.

I felt like a new woman, being able to be with my little girl all the time and visiting with the family and our friends when I wished. At nine months, Karen was taking her first steps and saying many new words every day.

I'd never enjoyed cooking, but during that time, I tried all sorts of exotic recipes and made a different kind of bread from a different country every two to three days. I learned if I had plenty of time and was not pressured to hurry so I'd get to work on time, I could cook almost as well as the next woman.

Before I knew it, Karen had her first birthday party, with all the cousins playing with her in the back yard. Her first year had been uneventful except for repeated ear and throat infections, which robbed her of 20% of her hearing. Before she was two, though, something quite frightening happened. She was in her playpen in the backyard and I was sitting in a lawn chair, reading. When I noticed she was rubbing her eyes and looking sleepy, I picked her up and carried her into the house to her crib.

When I put her down, she let out a single cry, turned dusky and then almost black within a matter of seconds. She was in full respiratory arrest, but did have a thready pulse. I was stunned at what I was seeing but picked her up right away, totally forgetting about the doctor across the street, and was doing everything possible to get her breathing. I was crying and begging her not to leave me. Bertha, next door, heard me but thought I was laughing and playing with her. Finally, I held her upside down, gently poking on her back and after I stuck my finger into her mouth, she took a deep breath and started to cry. It was then I realized, with a shock, I'd forgotten about Dr. Forlaw across the street! I ran with her as fast as I could and his receptionist took me back right away.

The doctor started her on oxygen without delay and

said he could tell she'd had a serious episode. He asked me what she'd been doing before I put her down in the crib. When I told him she was playing in her playpen outside, he said she'd probably picked up a little blade of grass and put it into her mouth. Then, when I lay her down on her back, the grass probably went into her throat, got stuck in the trachea and shut off her breathing. He said it no doubt had cleared when I held her upside down and cleared her throat with my finger, even though I saw no blade of grass.

She was fine after he gave her the oxygen, though she was a bit listless for a few hours after that. Thankfully, there were no further episodes of respiratory arrest, so I'm sure the doctor's diagnosis was correct. I watched her like a mother hawk, though, for months after that, worried history would repeat itself.

Even though I was a nurse, and CPR had been demonstrated as a life-saving measure in the mid-50s, it was not accepted and taught as a standard resuscitation procedure until 1970, so I had to rely upon all the other methods I'd learned. I was in a panic and near hysteria when none of them seemed to be working. Yes, I was a nurse and had saved other people's lives, but I'd never felt so helpless and frantic as I did during those few moments I was trying to save the life of my own little girl.

When I went to work as college nurse at Palm Beach Jr. College, in 1971, I took a CPR course from Davy Crockett (yes, that was his real name), then Town of Palm Beach Fire Chief. A month later, Davy certified me as an American Heart Association CPR instructor, and I taught the course to faculty and staff in every department in the college and to all the dental hygiene students enrolled at the college. Also, as AHA volunteer, I taught the lifesaving procedure to church groups, physicians' and dentists' staffs and others throughout the county for the next ten years. It was my mission to make certain as many people as I could reach learned this simple life-saving technique. I taught both adult and small child CPR. I wish I'd had that knowledge to help my own little baby in 1964. Perhaps I wouldn't have been so frantic had I known that uncomplicated technique, instead of trying hit or miss techniques on her.

When Karen was two, we moved to West Palm Beach into a nicer rented house in a quiet neighborhood of other young families. They were going to start building interstate I-95 in 1968, from Miami north to Ft. Pierce and it was to run close to our street, which ran east/west almost to the FEC railroad to the west. Our house was in the center of the street, not at the cul-de-sac. A high school was on Forest Hill Boulevard and our street, Forest Court, was across from it.

    There were several other young mothers like me on the street and we enjoyed a quiet camaraderie. Sometimes we'd get together at one house or another during our mornings, so our children could play together. Karen enjoyed these play times with the other children, especially with Barbara Ann, the little girl next door.

    One day while I had her in the backyard with me as I hung the laundry at the end of the big yard, I left her for a moment while I carried in a laundry basket of dried items. When I started back out the door to see to her, she stood in front of me with a huge smile on her face and tried to hand me a gift a little snake or maybe it was a glass snake, which I didn't know at the time was a lizard with a long tail. "Look Mommy, it's for you. Isn't it pretty," she told me with that big smile intact.

"Karen, put it down! Put it down, honey!" I screamed to her. She dropped it and it scurried off. Her smiling little lips puckered and she started to cry. I picked her up and said, "I'm sorry, honey, but that was a snake and it could have bitten you." Nothing I could say helped. Here my little girl thought she'd found a colorful wiggly gift to give her mommy and I dismissed it with my ridiculous screaming. I felt like a bad mother at that moment; surely I could have handled it better. "Sweetheart, thank you for wanting to give me that pretty gift, but some snakes can hurt little girls. Others are okay, but until you're a little older and know which ones won't hurt you, it'll be better not to pick any of them up. Okay?"

"Okay, Mommy," she said, her lips still trembling with her sobs. I held her tighter, and then took her inside for a dish of ice cream. Soon she was laughing again and playing with her dolls.

I swore after that, no matter what happened, I would speak to her in a calmer manner. Sometimes it worked; other times, it didn't, but I continued to try. This being a good mother was not as easy as I thought it would be!

Karen was a bright little girl and paid particular attention to the words the children were taught on Sesame Street. She'd sit in front of the TV and mouth them until she could pronounce them correctly.

One day she asked if she could learn to read the books we bought her. I told her I'd see if I could teach her and she was happy about that. I found a book in the bookstore called, "How to Teach Your Baby To Read," by Glenn Doman, a physical therapist who worked with brain-injured children. He used the concept of large flash cards with whole words on them, rather than just phonetics. I can do that, I thought, so I took Karen to the store and we got poster paper and colored markers. She was excited because she knew it was for her classroom in the corner of her small bedroom.

I printed the words, starting with parts of the body and then generic names for family members, like mommy and daddy, on the poster paper. When I pointed to the word, shoulder, and at the same time touched my shoulder as the book suggested, she said, "Shoulder." Even when I mixed the words up and did not point to anything, it wasn't long before she could read them.

Every day, whether I had to work or not, we had a lesson.

I was careful not to tire her, so I limited them to half hour sessions. She never wanted class to end. We progressed from parts of the body and names for family members to all the words contained in the first book she chose to read, "The Cat in the Hat," by Theodor Seuss Geisel, known as Dr. Seuss.

By the time she was three, Karen could read "The Cat in the Hat" with no problem at all. From there, she read one book after another. Her favorite, also a Dr. Seuss book, "Green Eggs and Ham" with the character, Sam, I am, was worn out from reading it over and over again.

Some suggested she would never learn her phonics if I taught her to read by recognizing whole words, but we'd always sound the word out, also, especially if she had difficulty with it. She excelled in reading when she got into Montessori School a year later. And since she is literate and teaches in a college today, I don't believe learning to read at two, by the Doman method instead of by phonics, was a hindrance for Karen.

The landlord tried to get us to buy the house on that little street, but Ron didn't want to stay there if that major highway was going to be so close. I didn't understand that, since we could barely hear the trains that ran along the track next to where the interstate was going to be built. I doubted the cars on the highway would be any louder, if we heard them at all. The landlord told us we could get a good price from the house if we wanted to sell it before the highway was built. He would have let our previous four years of rent go as the down payment and I thought it was a great deal.

I loved the house, the friendly neighborhood, what could be Karen's future high school across Forest Hill Boulevard at the end of our street, and would have liked to buy it. I lost that argument. His mind was made up, and since I was not working at the time, I believed I had no right to insist upon it. I'd forgotten about the millions of wives who never worked away from home but had equal say in decisions affecting the family. I'd also forgotten about the two years I'd worked to support us, while he was finishing his education in Tallahassee until my seventh month of pregnancy.

Sometimes, being a working partner in a marriage made me feel guilty during the infrequent times I was not working outside the home. It should not have, since staying home, making certain things ran smoothly and caring for one's children was no easier than working outside the home. Of course, when a mother works outside the home, but still has most of the work to do to run the household, that is never easy, either. When I had to work in the evenings, Ron took care of Karen, cooked dinner, and put her to bed, but I had the laundry, ironing, and cleaning to do before I went to work or on my days off in addition to caring for her.

I'm glad today's parents are more inclined to be equal partners in most everything about the marriage, especially if both are also working outside the home, but it was not always that way a few decades ago.

In the meanwhile, a new hospital, JFK Memorial, was opening west of Lake Worth, just a few miles south of us. The innovative director of nursing, Mary Ellen Hazzard, RN, was offering flex days and flex hours to nurses who could not work full-time. The nurses were free to choose their own days as well as the hours they wished to work. No one had ever tried such a concept before, to my knowledge.

My friend from Good Sam, Jo Hogan, and I decided it might suit us, so we both applied to the hospital and interviewed with Ms. Hazzard. Jo and her husband, Tom, had two little girls, Carol and Annie, near Karen's age, and we socialized often. She was Aunt Jo to my girls and I was Aunt Peggy to hers.

We went to work, on different floors and units, two to

three nights a week from 6-11. It was a beautiful hospital and everyone was friendly. Coming on at 6, I was able to get dinner over with and Karen ready for bed before I left. Ron got home a little after 5 so it worked out well for us.

Since I could start a good IV, Helen Bonner, the head nurse on 3rd north where I worked, would save most of the IVs for me to start after 6. This was before they invented intracatheters. The needle we stuck into the patient's vein stayed in it to funnel the fluid through it instead of coming out and leaving a plastic tube in its place, as when the intracatheter is used. Laura Frost was her medication nurse when she was on duty and Laura and I also became life-long good friends.

Word caught on that I was getting all the IVs done after I came on duty, so the supervisor started giving Helen a list of them on other floors for me to do, also, so I spent the better part of my short shift starting IVs throughout the hospital. This was before they formed the IV team who took over that duty, if they were needed. I didn't mind that and working only five hours a night and no two nights in a row, I had plenty of energy left over for Karen.

Ron was hinting I might start thinking of going back to work full-time, but I wanted to continue the flex days and hours for as long as possible. Karen was so happy when I was home, and since I didn't go to work until almost her bedtime and not very often, she didn't seem to notice my absence so much.

FOURTEEN
Back to Lantana and More Medication Regime Advances

When the State TB Board approved another 3-11 slot in 1967, when Karen was four years old, Maggie Smith offered it to me. Rather Dr. Adil, who was now Medical Director, offered it for her by appearing at my gynecologist's office the day I had my routine check-up.

In the most casual manner he could muster, but with a sly grin, he said, "It's a surprise to see you, Peggy. You know, Maggie has just gotten a third supervisor position approved for 3-11. Maybe you should go to the hospital to apply for it."

I looked at Curt. He was grinning, also, but I didn't think anything about the way the two of them were looking at me. I just said, "That's great, Dr. Adil. I'll head down there right now." More and more we needed another full-time salary, but I'd been resistant to working full-time at the general hospital when Karen was so young.

"Good, I'm sure Maggie will be pleased you still want the job."

"Of course, I want the job," I told him. I said goodbye to both of them, still standing there smiling in that peculiar way at me, and left the office.

Curtis Cannon had been the GYN Consultant for Lantana since 1961, the year I started working there, so Dr. Adil's visit to his office the same day I had my appointment was no coincidence, he told me later. I'm not sure how it came about they'd discussed me, but there Dr. Adil stood in the outer office when we came out of Curt's office.

I was so happy to learn of the State's decision to allow Maggie to hire another nursing supervisor that I drove straight to Lantana and completed the process to accept the position.

Maggie told me the job was mine when I reached the hospital. I just had to go through that formality. There were two other supervisors on the shift but she said, "I've divided the responsibilities by sections of the hospital so most of the time, there will be two supervisors on each night."

"Great, I'd like that," I told her.

I started that week and it worked out well for the three of us. The other two supervisors were Emily Komperda, RN and Candy Radcliff, RN, capable and nice nurses with whom to work. When there were two of us on duty, I usually covered the first and second floors and the other supervisor, third and fourth.

Sadly, Emily had a massive coronary on duty one night a few years later and died at JFK Memorial Hospital. She was only in her mid-60s. I was on duty that night during a hurricane. I was told, "Komperda had a heart attack. They're stabilizing her over on 3A if you want to see her before you start working."

I was stunned. Even though she was not in the best of health, she had been there for so long; to see her get knocked down like that with something so serious was a shock to everyone. I felt like someone had kicked me in the stomach from hearing about Komperda. No one called her Emily. It had always been just Komperda. When we met, she asked me to address her as Komperda, so I always did.

It was all I could do not to cry when I saw her. "Hi, they told me I'd find you over here. How do you feel?"

She wiggled her hand to say so-so and said, "A little weak but most of the pain's gone for now."

"I'm not going to stay long, because I know they want you to rest before they transfer you to JFK, but is there anything I can get you before I leave?"

"No," she said, in a weak voice I could barely recognize as hers. "I'm just going to try to sleep for awhile. Thanks for stopping to check on me, Peggy."

"I'm glad I got to see you," I told her, feeling myself on the verge of tears, because I didn't believe I'd see her again. "Maybe I'll catch you later. Have a nice sleep." I squeezed her hand and tears came to her eyes, as she nodded her head. I'm sure she knew she wouldn't make it. That was my un-doing, but I got away from her bedside before my tears fell.

And Then There Was One

That was the last time I saw Emily Komperda. She died the next day at JFK. It was a sad time for the staff, as everyone at Lantana knew each other so well. Most of them had worked together since the hospital opened and it was like losing a family member.

Komperda was a no-nonsense woman with a laid-back manner. Some nurses called her a warhorse because she'd been around for so long and survived the trenches. I loved to talk with her and listen to her stories of how things were when she was a young nurse. She could also make me feel intimidated at times when she insisted her way was the best way. Since she'd been the 3-11 supervisor for a long time, I deferred to her, even when I thought things might have been better done another way.

Candy was also laid-back. She had a little more nervous energy than slow-moving Komperda, but I liked her, also. Her sense of humor was quirky and it was enjoyable to be on duty when she was, even though we covered different floors and sometimes saw each other only during report and on breaks.

Although I was happy to get back to the best place I ever worked, Karen was unhappy I was away from home so much. She was upset I wasn't there to tuck her in at night and she let me know it. Because the staff did not have their unit assignments, until after the supervisor got there and looked at the schedule and needs of the night, it meant I had to leave no later than 2:15 to 2:20 in order to make it by a quarter till three. This was especially important when I covered the house alone.

Some days, she clung to my legs tightly, screaming,

"Please, Mommy, don't go. Don't leave me. Please, Mommy."

"I'm sorry, honey, but I have to go now. I'll be home as soon as I can tonight and come to see you before I go to sleep." I'd tell her I loved her and wished I could stay home with her, but it did no good. All she cared about was that her mommy stayed with her. Nearly every day, I'd end up having to forcefully pry her fingers off me and hand her to my next-door neighbor, Bobbi, the mother of Barbara Ann. Karen stayed at Bobbi's until Ron got home from work.

When I'd have to leave her like that, I'd end up crying, too, almost all the way to work. How I hated leaving her, even to go back to Lantana where the work was easier on me and didn't take so much of the energy I needed for her. But, my full-time salary was necessary, so I had no choice.

Despite this ambivalence, I was glad to be in tuberculosis nursing, again, and saw even more changes in the field. More drugs had been added to the treatment regime. PAS was still used in combination with INH, PZA and Ethambutol and now another new drug, Rifampin, was added to the multiple drug therapy regime. Streptomycin was still given to the sicker patients.

Instead of a year or two, most patients were being discharged within months of having been admitted, because their sputum cultures were converting to negative for mycobacterium tuberculosis within months. However, their treatment continued for another year or two through TB Control at the public health department in their counties, as before. Today, I'm told, that time frame is even shorter.

I usually had a staff of eleven or twelve when I covered the house alone on the 3-11 p.m. shift, with one to two other registered nurses, two to three LPNs, medicine aides and other aides.

The specially trained medicine aides were in charge of the wards like 1A, 2A, 1B and 2B where the patients were ambulatory and convalescent. They knew their limitations and TB medications. I would get the sedatives out of the narcotic cabinet and sign for them to give them to the patients. I would sign for and give all narcotics, as the patients needed them for pain relief. The medicine aides did the rest of the work and knew when they needed to call me.

Medicine aides are no longer used because of the Nurse Practice Act, but they were a necessity during those years when so few nurses wanted to work in the field of tuberculosis and we had 4-500 patients nearly all the time.

Margie Knowles, the surgical aide spoken of in an earlier chapter, was still on 3B, but she was now an LPN and assistant charge nurse on the surgical unit. I was glad to see she was moving up in nursing and still on the surgical unit. It had been obvious to me when I met her that someone with her intelligence, ability and knowledge of tuberculosis treatment would be an asset to the professional nursing staff.

One day I was half-joking with her when I said, "Margie, you keep this up and before you know it, you'll have become an RN and then, by golly, you can just take over this place."

"Yeah, right, Peg. First, I'd have to go back to school

and I think I've seen enough of school for a long time," she said, with a hearty laugh.

"Well, don't rule it out. They could certainly do worse than having you as director of nurses."

She laughed again and said, "Weren't you making rounds or something?"

I laughed, also, as I waved at her while walking toward the next ward, 3A, but I was thinking to myself, wouldn't it be great if she would move on up the ladder like that. It was rare I was taken by any other nurse's ability as I was by that of Margie Knowles, and I did hope she wouldn't stop with the LPN.

Shortly after I came back on board, two nurses unknown to me were transferred to 3-11 for a short while from their permanent positions on the day shift. They had been hired at different times but were transferred at the same time. They were Liz Phillips, RN and Carol Norris, LPN (not their real names).

They were excellent nurses and I thought they were a perfect fit for the Lantana TB family. Liz was an attractive shorthaired brunette with an amazing sense of humor. She could tell the funniest stories of any woman I ever knew. Like me, she had two children, but they were close to their teens. Carol, shy and glamorous, had short blonde hair and bangs. Her make-up always was impeccable.

We fell in love with both of them and they, with us. They became loyal and generous friends, dropping whatever they were doing to help another member of the Lantana family.

I was the recipient of their generosity on more than one

occasion throughout the coming years. Jumping ahead to 1980, to one day when I called in sick, because I'd been up most of the night with abdominal pain: Maggie was no longer there and I'd asked to come off night duty supervision to the day shift because by then, I was a divorced single mom. Our roles were reversed and Liz was the supervisor, not I. I was head nurse on 4A.

From the way I described my pain, Liz suspected appendicitis but, in my vehement state of denial, I said it was just an upset stomach or perhaps a virus. I loved taking care of patients but hated being one, especially in the hospital, so was always quick to deny anything was serious enough to warrant going to one.

She or Carol called me often throughout the day and each time, my pain was worse instead of better, making talking difficult. When they got off duty at 3:30, they drove straight to my apartment, where they found me crawling across the floor from the bathroom, in agonizing pain.

"How long have you been like this, Peg?" Liz asked me.

"You mean unable to stand?" I tried to laugh, but couldn't because of the pain.

"Yes, how long has the pain been this bad?"

With difficulty, I answered, "Pretty much the whole day."

"Damn it, Peggy Butler, you know better. Come on, you're going to the hospital." My daughters were on vacation at their dad's at that time, so I didn't have that concern if the doctor admitted me, though I still didn't like the idea of going.

To this day, I have no idea how I got there; whether they called 911 or carried me to the car, but I was rushed to the hospital emergency room, probably protesting all the way it was nothing serious, even though by then I was almost delirious from the severity of the pain.

When the surgeon came into the cubicle to examine me after my blood was drawn and I was found to have an elevated white blood count, he touched my rigid abdomen with the tip of one finger. I screamed from the pain. Of course, that cinched the deal, and I was rushed into surgery for an emergency appendectomy.

Liz and Carol came to my rescue, again, a year later. My car had broken down and could not be repaired for under a thousand dollars. I was told it was too old to bother with such an expensive repair job so was saving for a better car. As I said, I was a single mom and money was scarce, so I could not afford to buy another one right away.

I started riding my bicycle ten miles each way to work every day. I felt so healthy doing that and was in no hurry to get another car. It was refreshing to start out an hour early and ride through the park around beautiful Lake Osborne in Lake Worth and Lantana, avoiding the fumes and noise from motor vehicles in the process.

At that time, I still worked on 4A. After parking and locking my bike, I climbed the back four flights of stairs, because I was wearing shorts instead of my uniform, and changed into the uniform in the nurses' station restroom. I was in such great shape from the bike riding I never got short of breath walking the four flights of stairs. In those days I never weighed more than one hundred pounds, so everything was easier even before the bike riding became necessary.

One afternoon I left work and took my usual route around the lake. After I left the park and approached Lake Worth Road, I just had a couple more miles to go. When I crossed Lake Worth Road, going between twenty and thirty miles an hour on my ten-speed, I tried to make a left turn onto the sidewalk. I was only a few feet from the intersection to my road.

Unfortunately, I forgot one has to slow down to make such a turn. The bike went out from under me and I landed on the ground beside the sidewalk, missing a thick steel light pole by inches. One of my arms was pinned under me and I couldn't move it. Otherwise, I was not in too much pain.

I still had my white nylon hose on under my black shorts. I was afraid of getting my uniform pants caught in the bike chain, so always changed back into the shorts before heading home. As it turned out, it didn't matter what I wore since I crashed anyway. The ground upon which I landed was loaded with sand spurs, most of which were stuck to my legs. Anyone not familiar with Florida's sand spurs has no idea how much they can hurt, especially if they are twisted as they come out of you. They are shaped similar to miniature arrows on the end but are not perfectly smooth spears, making it a precarious situation when one is removing them from one's body.

A young teenager on his way home from school stopped to ask whether he could assist me. Having no other friends or family who would not be at work at that hour, I gave him Liz's number and asked whether he would go into the office building next door to call her. He did as I asked.

It was not long before Liz and Carol drove up and found me, still on the ground, trying to pretend I was just resting with my head against the light pole. "Resting are you, Peg?" Liz asked, innocence dripping from her lips. They tried very hard not to laugh, because they could see I was in pain.

"Yeah, can't you tell," I said, wincing as I pulled out another sand spur. I was trying to get as many of them out of my legs through the white nylon hose as possible and the young boy, who would not leave my side until they arrived to help me, was also removing them despite my embarrassment and protestations. I thanked him for calling for help and he left soon after they arrived.

Then, they did laugh. "Oh be quiet," I said, unable to keep from laughing, myself, between moans. After they helped me up from the ground, they drove me to the emergency room, once again, where the physician saw me, ordered my arm x-rayed and to my relief, I had a bad sprain, but no fracture. They stayed at the hospital with me until I was discharged a couple hours later.

They drove me home, all the while teasing me about the boy's picking off the sand spurs from my legs as I sat there in excruciating pain, pretending to rest from my bike ride. Of course, it was another amusing story for Liz to tell to our coworkers the next day. It was even more comical when she told it than it was at the time, and I laughed with the rest of the staff, despite the pain from my arm in the sling.

FIFTEEN

Celebrity in the House

In 1967, when I came back to work at Lantana the second time, we still had the entire hospital complex for TB and seldom had a census below 500 patients, did minor and major emergency surgery on 3-11, including tracheotomies on the ward with less than adequate lighting, when it was imperative it be done stat, or immediately. Despite this drawback, it always went well because we had excellent surgical residents and competent staff nurses and nursing assistants, as the aides were called by then.

Dr. Feng, still a superb thoracic surgeon, was now in private practice in West Palm Beach. Dr. Abe Vargas later became a successful thoracic/cardiovascular surgeon in Miami, performing some innovative surgical procedures rarely, or never, performed in this part of the country, and Dr. Rudy Sheerer became a prominent thoracic surgeon and internist in West Palm Beach. They were among our better residents. I had the privilege of working closely with both of the latter physicians when I was 3-11 supervisor.

I was covering the house alone the night Louie, an oriental patient who could not understand or speak a word of English, was diagnosed with tetanus. I had barely given out the ward assignments to the staff when Dr. Akin, the 3A (medical) ward physician, had me paged to come to the patient's room across from the nurses' station, stat.

"This man has tetanus," Dr. Akin told me. "It's gone to his chest muscles, so we have to put him on the Morshmuller immediately."

"I'll get it brought over here right away," I told him. I'd never seen the Morshmuller Respirator, much less had cause to use it, but with the help of the day supervisor, it was located and we had it brought to the floor.

After Dr. Akin got the patient's breathing stabilized, despite the respirator, he kept going into respiratory distress and we worked on him all night.

"It's too light in here, Peggy. We need these windows boarded up. He has to have absolute quiet and darkness to keep down his agitation. Any unnecessary stimulation is going to make him worse."

I called Maintenance personnel to come in to board up the windows with plywood to keep the room dark. They came right away to attend to this. Within twenty minutes, they'd measured and had the boards installed.

None of us had ever seen tetanus before, so it was an educational experience for the whole staff. Sometimes the first symptoms of the disease can be a severe headache, restlessness and irritability. Louie seemed to be exhibiting all of these symptoms in the beginning, from what we could see, although he couldn't tell us this.

We never believed the patient would pull though that critical state, despite all the staff working so diligently to save him. His tetani progressed so rapidly throughout his body, it was frightening to witness. I don't remember how many times we lost him that night, but resuscitation efforts were always successful.

Louie's tuberculosis was far advanced, so he could not be transferred to a general hospital population. This was a blessing in disguise, Dr. Akin told us, because he could not have survived all the noise and bright lights in the general hospital setting.

We had no idea how the patient contracted the illness. We knew only that he must have stepped on a nail or had another deep dirty injury. Or, it might have been from a deep insect bite; anything that would have enabled the tetanus organism (clostridium tetani bacteria) to bore into the contaminated wound.

The danger from tetanus comes from the nerve toxins produced by the bacteria multiplying. The toxin gets between the nerve and the muscle it stimulates and causes the muscle to tighten in continuous spasm.

People most often believe only the jaw becomes locked in spasm since tetanus is known as lockjaw, but it can affect any neuromuscular juncture in the body, or the entire body, including the intercostal muscles that help the patient breathe; the reason for Dr. Akin to rush us into getting Louie on the respirator. He would have died without that immediate life support ordered by this astute physician who recognized the symptoms of tetanus so quickly, in spite of the language barrier.

Despite the seriousness of Louie's condition for so many months, he did improve and we were thrilled to watch him go out the door to return to his home several months later. He was feeling well and had a huge smile on his face and a tear or two on his cheeks to match those of some of the staff members who had seen him through this ordeal. He was truly one of the greatest miracles we'd ever witnessed at the Lantana hospital.

A few years later, a young woman came close to mirroring Louie's miraculous recovery after serious complications. Her name was Ruby and over a long period of time, she had several lung operations. She always seemed to have a difficult time, but nothing like what occurred after the last surgery.

She hemorrhaged profusely from the suture line at the back of her left chest and it looked as if that might be the end of the road for Ruby. Liz, the supervisor coming on duty, and Dr. Paul Winokur, our surgical resident at the time, had other ideas about that.

She called him at six in the morning, after she assessed Ruby's dire situation. At first, he told her he'd be over in an hour, but Liz insisted. "No, you have to come right now, Dr. Winokur. Ruby might not be here in an hour."

With such urgency in her voice, the resident told her he'd be right there. When he arrived, without hesitation and to the shock of the nurses at his side, he removed all her wire sutures and packed her with gel foam. That was taking quite a risk that with nothing to hold her suture line together, she would bleed out right away, but as quickly as he removed them, he'd packed her with the gel and the bleeding stopped.

Thanks to Liz's quick thinking and the physician's unorthodox procedure, the bleeding never resumed. Ruby recovered with no further major problems during that hospital stay. She finally got well, returned to her home and lived a healthy life for many years.

Some hospitalized patients still died from TB, despite miraculous recoveries like those of Louie and Ruby. It was the same old story as that of the TB patients at the turn of the century by the time some of them sought treatment and were diagnosed, the disease was too far advanced, or they suffered complications from other diseases as well as TB. Their battle was already lost.

However, most of the patients were getting well and leaving the hospital. Then as now, we had our revolving door cases because of substance abuse, overcrowded homes or homelessness. This in itself was not good, but what made it such a negative factor in a patient with tuberculosis was this: it contributed to non-compliance. Non-compliance led to drug resistance from taking the medications so irregularly, reactivation or new TB disease. This was the most difficult problem caregivers working with tuberculosis patients encountered. It was almost always a win-lose situation. We'd work so hard to help them get well, but then, when they got away from the hospital, the battle they'd fought so hard to win would begin to go downhill.

Despite this, we never gave up on them and neither did our counterparts in TB Control at the health departments throughout the state. They'd search until they found them. If they continued to be too ill or too non-compliant to treat on an outpatient basis, the TB Control physician would order them back to the hospital for treatment.

Not all of our patients were hospitalized because of

substance abuse, being homeless or living under less than optimal conditions. Many were upper and middle class with good living conditions, positive family lives and no substance abuse.

These patients had procrastinated about seeing a physician until their disease was so far advanced they were too debilitated to take care of themselves or their families. Or, because they smoked, they ignored the cough, thinking it was just irritation from smoking. They rarely thought it might be lung cancer, either, in those days, because the full extent of the connection between smoking and lung cancer was not yet known. However, it wasn't lung cancer; it was tuberculosis, a disease much easier to cure.

These patients were among the most successful in recovering after their diagnosis if treatment was not started too late. They took their disease and its treatment seriously and rarely were recalcitrant. They had a life and a job to get back to, as compared to many of our non-compliant patients. Incentive was the best medicine for TB patients.

It amazed us how quickly the very young children with tuberculosis healed. We seldom had them in the house but when they were admitted, their recovery course was rapid. Of course, many of them came into the hospital in a mal-nourished state from their illness, so, as with the adult patients, in addition to the tuberculosis medications, they were given vitamins to built up their strength. Their energy level became so high we had to stay on our toes to keep up with them.

The exception to this quick recovery were the infants, but, by the late '60s, health officials had the parents of the young removed from the home as soon as their TB was discovered, so babies did not get the disease very often.

Five months before I left to have my second child in 1968, a celebrity was admitted on my shift, the first one in several years. He caused quite a stir among the baseball fans in the house, both patients and staff.

Rico Carty was the left fielder for the Atlanta Braves, a strong and healthy looking twenty-five year old batting champion from the Dominican Republic, who had no tuberculosis symptomatology.

During his spring training physical exam, a routine chest x-ray showed a cavity in one of the upper lobes of his lungs. Tuberculosis was suspected and, regardless of his situation, the doctors could not ignore this discovery. He was rushed to the Southeast Florida State Tuberculosis Hospital in Lantana.

Due to his being on a major league baseball team, with its spring training headquarters in West Palm Beach, this discovery made the local television and radio news broadcasts and newspapers right away. By the next day, the national media and press had picked up the story.

Understandably, Rico was devastated by this interruption of his career. He realized if he had to be in the hospital for months, he'd miss spring training and without spring training, even if he happened to get out of the hospital within a short period of time, he would not be permitted to play during the regular season.

He was placed on ward, 3C, nearest the supervisor's

office. At first, he was sullen about being in the hospital, but soon adjusted to the routine of his ward. Like many other Caribbean islanders, he was, by nature, a happy individual and was often heard singing in the hallways.

One rule Rico resisted was wearing a mask in the elevators and lobby while his sputum smears were still positive for acidfast bacilli. Positive AFB almost always cultures out as mycobacterium tuberculosis, but can be non-contagious mycobacterium, as well. The mask was essential, until we were certain which it was.

Although he needed this constant reminder to wear the mask when needed, he complied with his medical treatment, and his sputum smears soon converted to negative. This rendered him non-infectious to others. He was happy when he was told he could dispense with the mask after that. It took several more months for his sputum cultures, which were mycobacterium tuberculosis, to convert to negative and he could be discharged to outpatient treatment.

The first baseball season after his discharge was Rico's best ever. He, along with the great home run king, Hank Aaron, Felipe Alou, Felix Milan, Phil Neikro, Clete Boyer, Orlando Cepeda, Pat Jarvis, Sonny Jackson, Bob Tillman and the rest of the Atlanta Braves team took the National League pennant which entitled them to play in the '69 World Series.

The Braves lost the Series, but it was a terrific comeback for that slugger from the Dominican

Republic who wasn't going to let TB stop him. He was living proof to the world that anyone from any walk of life, even if they were as healthy as a major league athlete, could get TB and recover from it if they complied with treatment.

And Then There Was One

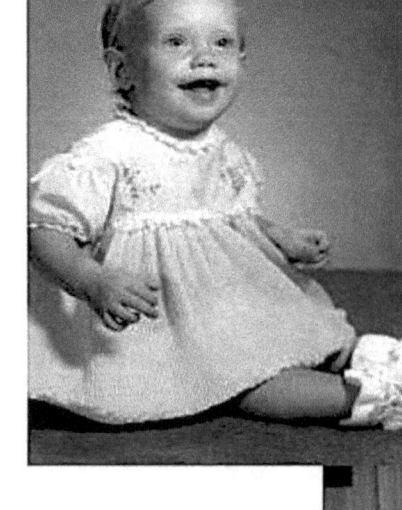

Suzy: center, age 6 months in 1969; top left, age 5 after first train ride in Miami; top right, 1973 with Karen and cousin Mike, during Karen's fundraiser for muscular dystrophy kids; bottom left, 1970, learning baton-twirling from big sister Karen, holding her trophy; bottom right, with Karen at Aunt Kathi's wedding.

SIXTEEN
Joy of Another Baby

I had become sterile, both from advanced endometriosis and using the birth control pill for a year or two after Karen's birth. I was distressed over being unable to have more children. I wanted another baby so badly and she wanted a baby brother. Curt, who had diagnosed the endometriosis before I got married, promised me if I were unable to conceive, he would try to help me with a tubal insufflation. We were both surprised I was able to get pregnant with Karen, although it was believed passing three kidney stones prior to conceiving had something to do with the Fallopian tubes also being patent.

Good to his word, he performed the procedure, and to the delight of Ron and me, I became pregnant right away. Karen, who was five, was over the moon about the pregnancy, despite our cautioning her the baby could be a girl instead of the baby brother she wanted.

While my beautiful Suzy was being born at St Mary's Hospital on Veteran's Day that November of 1968, Karen was having her tonsils out at Good Samaritan, a few miles southeast of St. Mary's in West Palm Beach. I felt so guilty because I could not be with her. She was so frightened of needles, and I knew she must have been scared when they put the IV into her before surgery. My guilt was compounded when Ron told me he arrived at the hospital after leaving Suzy and me, to find Karen's little hospital gown covered with blood after she'd hemorrhaged. I'm sure she could not understand why her mommy who'd been there for her since she was born, was not there to help her at the time she needed me the most.

To make matters worse, Karen got chicken pox a few days after I got home and Suzy, only five days old, got them immediately afterward. I was fortunate to be able to be home to take care of both of them. Suzy's case was not as bad as Karen's, but soon they both were rid of the itchy blisters and life settled down for a while.

At first, my oldest daughter resented the baby because she wanted me to bring home Greg instead of Susan, but soon she got used to her being a girl and was won over by her winning personality. Suzy's face seemed to light up every time she saw her. Karen still is her rock, to this day.

Like her big sister, Suzy had a sweet disposition from the beginning and was always smiling. This, despite the fact she never got to walk until she was nearly four, because she had a cast on one foot after being born with it rotated outward instead of straight. Dr. Brandon, her orthopedist, told us it was caused by a too shallow hip socket. At different times, she had the cast alone, the cast with a hip splint, and then after the cast came off, corrective shoes fastened to a horizontal bar that kept her hips rotated in such a way, she sat Indian fashion when we'd put her on the floor.

Although she'd seemed to take all of this in stride, the one thing she hated was wearing the corrective shoes, even after she was finished with the splint and bar, and walking. One day when she was around four and a half, she ran out and gave them to the garbage man before he pulled away from the curb, saying we'd forgotten to put them in the trash. They were destroyed with the rest of the trash before we realized what she'd done.

Another time, we had to get a plumber because we could not get the commode in the hall bathroom unstopped. He found her latest pair of corrective shoes stuffed down the toilet.

I never punished her for those antics. It was punishment enough for her to go back to the shoe store with me to buy yet another pair of corrective shoes. She'd cry and tell me, "But, Mommy, they're so ugly." Eventually, she resigned herself to wearing them and never threw them away again, thank goodness, since they cost almost $20 a pair, a high price for a little girl's shoes in the early seventies.

When the time came to wear normal shoes, besides the school shoes and sneakers I bought her, she told me she wanted a pair of black, patent leather Mary Janes for church and Sunday school. After she'd been denied regular little girls' shoes for all those years, of course, I bought them for her. She loved those shoes and wanted to wear them everywhere.

Unlike Karen, Suzy did not talk until she was nearly two and had no interest in learning to read early when I offered to teach her from Karen's lessons we'd saved for her. I didn't push her, because she had enough to contend with by having that physical disability. I knew she was a bright little girl and starting late in her developmental skills was not going to hinder her later in life. Since she is a registered nurse supervisor on a busy hospice team today, it proves that a late start didn't render her incapable of becoming a successful adult.

After she lost the cast, the splint and the metal rod and started walking, we discovered what a tomboy we had on our hands. It was not at all unusual for us to find our good sterling silver pieces out in the backyard, where Suzy had been digging to find her latest catch a wiggly worm or lizard. She was enraptured with lizards and like Karen had with the little snake all those years before, she took pride in carrying them into the house to present to us. She enjoyed playing with Togo, our little black poodle, as did Karen, but was fascinated with the wiggly kind of pets, unwilling as they were to be her pets.

Although Suzy was almost always smiling and possessed a pleasant disposition, she could become angry just as any other little child who could not have her own way all the time. She demonstrated this, dramatically, one day when we were alone in the house. She was not quite five, yet.

I had arranged the living room furniture, with the sofa facing into the room, its back to the front foyer. Unlike the living room, the foyer was uncarpeted. Suzy had asked to go somewhere I did not want her to go, so she was unhappy with me. She went out the front door to sulk on the porch swing, and I heard her say, "Bitch," as she walked by the sofa. She had never said a derogatory word in her life, but she was going to pre-school, so I assumed that's where she'd heard the word. Of course, I was taken aback, but I did not act as though I heard her.

All of a sudden, as I continued to sit on the sofa mending something, I heard the front door open again and the sound of rocks and gravel hitting the tiled floor of the foyer. I still said nothing; nor did I turn around to see what was going on. I wanted to see how this little tableau played out if I left everything up to her.

When they built the house a few months before we bought it, we loved everything about it but wished they'd have extended the roof over the front door, as we were constantly sweeping the gravel and tiny rocks from in front of the door.

This continued for awhile and then, suddenly, I heard the door close. I waited to see what else was on her agenda. I still had not said a word, nor had I turned to look into the foyer. Soon after this, the vacuum cleaner was turned on, and I heard her dragging it down the hallway and into the foyer. I was a bit horrified at the prospect of all that gravel and rock going into it, but then reasoned they surely were small pieces and I could change the bag before I went to bed that night.

The noise of the vacuum cleaner droned on for several minutes and then it stopped, and I heard her drag it back down the hallway and into the hall closet where it belonged. I still said nothing. Soon, I heard her footsteps coming into the foyer again and before I realized what was happening, she came into the living room and threw herself into my arms, sobbing loudly. I put my sewing onto the end table so she wouldn't get jabbed with the needle, and held her to me.

"Mommy why am I so bad?" she sobbed.

I held her tighter. "Sweetheart, you aren't bad. Sometimes, like many other little girls, you do things that aren't good."

I never wanted either of my daughters to grow up with a low self-esteem as I had, so I always was careful to assign their behavior as not good, but never them, when they misbehaved, which wasn't often.

She continued to cry and whimpered, "I'm sorry I called you a bitch, Mommy. I shouldn't have throwed those rocks on the floor."

I smiled but didn't correct her grammar. The lesson she was learning was more important than the words she used to tell me she was sorry she'd done something wrong. I held her out where she could see my face. "Suzy, I accept your apology. Thank you for cleaning up the floor, honey. But let me ask you something. That word you called me; do you know what it means?"

"No, Mommy."

"Did you hear it at pre-school?"

"Yes, another little girl said it the other day. And, you know what the teacher spanked her." She almost whispered this last part of the sentence, as though it were a secret. I couldn't resist smiling at her again.

"Honey, besides not being a nice word, that's why I don't want you to say it anymore. You might forget and say it at school. I signed the paper that says the teacher can't spank you, but she might forget and do it instead of calling me. I wouldn't want that for you. Do you understand?"

"Yes, I won't say it again. It's a silly old word, anyway."

Then, a little bit of a Suzy smile came on her face, and I smiled and pulled her to me.

"Yes, it is a silly old word," I agreed. She never did say it again, to my knowledge, and until her hormones started raging at fourteen, she rarely became upset after that, except for the occasional sibling argument with Karen, which never lasted too long.

That was the day I learned that it paid not to hook into the challenges our children threw at us. If we did nothing, they would soon enough realize they were wrong, just as Suzy did when I remained silent. Their guilt over it would teach them not to do it again; much better than if we yelled at them, or hit them for it.

I'm not saying I never yelled, as too many times I did, but I never believed hitting your children taught them anything except how much it hurt to have violence used against them. That could cause them to do one of two things: either resent the parent, turn it inward and feel unworthy, or grow up to emulate the parent by doing it to their own children. That does nothing but keep the cycle of violence going and I wasn't going to do it. This was something Ron and I agreed on before we married and had children.

During Suzy's first year and a half I stayed home, but as with Karen, she didn't have a full-time mom very long before I had to go back to work. Since there were no positions at Lantana, I went back to work part-time at JFK, although unlike when Karen was younger and it first opened its doors, I didn't have the shorter flex hours and usually, didn't get to pick the evenings I worked.

Jumping way into the future for a moment, when Suzy received her RN at the age of thirty-six after graduating with honors from Palm Beach Community College and taking her boards, she worked on a med-surg unit at JFK, before she switched to outpatient hospice nursing for Hospice of Palm Beach County from which I retired from nursing in 2002.

When I left JFK in 1971, I spent four years as the college nurse at then Palm Beach Jr. College, where I, too, earned my A.S. in Nursing when I was thirty-eight. Karen also became a student at Palm Beach Community College when she was thirty-six, like Suzy and me, teaching math after graduation. She graduated with honors from FAU with a BA in Mathematics and after a brief respite, earned her Master's. She still teaches math there, but PBCC is now Palm Beach State College, a four-year degree school. I graduated from FAU with a BSW (Bachelor of Social Work) at the age of 50.

Karen, as I write this, is working on her PhD in administration leadership from FAU. She has accepted a new position in management at Palm Beach State, although she'll continue to teach math, as her time allows. Suzy, still a nursing supervisor at Hospice of Palm Beach County, is working on her bachelor's in nursing from Palm Beach State College. Her interests lie in nursing research and, in particular, genetics.

So, both my daughters and I were late bloomers in earning our degrees and seemed to follow each other around to the same schools of higher learning and the same places of employment over the years.

When Suzy was five, the college opened its Early Learning Center. I was fortunate enough to get her enrolled in its first class. That was great for us both since she could ride to school with me, I'd park the car and walk her to school down the sidewalk north of my office before I opened Health Services at 8. Then, when school was over for her at 3, I'd walk over to get her, bring her to the clinic and she'd stay there until I closed at 4:30.

My boss at the college, Director of Health Services Helen Diedrich, R.N., loved to see Suzy come into the clinic. She particularly loved to hear her giggle. One day when she had the giggles about something, Helen smiled and said, "She's just like you, Peggy; your little heartbeat." I accepted the compliment and thanked her.

As I knew she would, Suzy loved going to 'real' school and since the ELC was based on Montessori principles, I knew she'd get a good start before elementary school the following year, just as Karen had five years before. She did well at the school and not having to take her to another school for that year took a great deal of pressure off me, as well.

Karen, in the meanwhile, had developed a love and natural ability for theater, and before she reached high school, she played the little girl, Melinda, in Inherit the Wind. This was the play based upon the real life drama between Clarence Darrow and William Jennings Bryan, the lawyers who argued for and against John Scopes, the science teacher accused of teaching evolution in 1925. It was dubbed the Monkey Trial.

This play was presented at Palm Beach Atlantic

College, now Palm Beach Atlantic University. In the mid-90s, I was also college nurse for that institution.

When she was a senior in high school, she turned in a phenomenal performance as Annie Sullivan, Helen Keller's teacher, in The Miracle Worker. We were so proud of Karen. We could not believe our eyes when we saw how calm she was the night of the play, even though we were emotional wrecks inside. She played Ms. Sullivan with poise and grace. Her ability to sign to Helen was nothing short of amazing, for having just learned it after she started rehearsing for the play. It was beautiful to watch her hands as she spoke to the little hearing-impaired girl. She could have been a great actress, had she followed her dream, but as with my career choice, life took her in an entirely different direction, academically, after she became a mother, and she is a wonderful teacher.

Because of my task force work to get a rape crisis center in Palm Beach County, I was recruited to serve as acting coordinator and paralegal counselor after it became a reality in 1976, as the Sexual Assault Assistance Project (SAAP), working under State Attorney David Bludworth's office in West Palm Beach. This was a departure from nursing but fulfilling work for me.

Two weeks after I went to the sexual assault program, something I knew was going to happen soon, did. Curtis Cannon, who always said he wanted to retire from medicine at 50 and travel the world, died of cancer two months after he turned 50. I met Curt three weeks after I moved to Florida in 1960, the day he started his practice and appeared on the women's unit at Good Sam where I was working. His death was a tremendous loss.

I didn't have time to dwell on it, however; being acting coordinator and counselor kept me busier than I'd ever been in my life. I had very little time at home because I was called from one crime scene, hospital or law enforcement agency to the next all night long, seven nights a week.

In the daytime, I was in court with survivors or called elsewhere throughout the eight hours. Intermingled with that were speaking engagements to promote the program. As a result of this effort between another counselor, dedicated Jennifer Elliott, and me, we were able to bring the reporting statistics up to 110% within the first six months, as more women learned of the program and support they'd have throughout the criminal justice process. Our office secretary, Lavonne, was invaluable in keeping these stats for us.

I loved working with law enforcement, Jenny and the survivors of the rapes and molestations. I'd thought it would be difficult to learn the language of law enforcement and the criminal justice system, but it came easy to me and within weeks, I was very much at ease with all of it. It bothered me that 95% of my cases were children, mostly molested by their own fathers or a father figure, but I had to put my personal feelings aside as did everyone else, including the cops and deputies to whom the crimes were reported, in order to do what had to be done for the victims and their families.

I was a single mom by then, and I could see my doing that kind of work was taking its toll on Karen, 13 now, and Suzy, 8. They began to bicker back and forth more than they'd ever argued in their lives. It seemed to happen more and more, when they were with me, especially right before I had to go out on another case. It was difficult, but how could I blame them? There was no way those two precious girls could count on me even to sit down to dinner with them every night. To say I was on a guilt trip because of it was putting it mildly. As much as I loved the work, I could see I had a tough decision to make in the near future.

SEVENTEEN

Unexpected Final Week

Because my time away from home was taking such a toll on my daughters, with reluctance, while they were at their dad's until school started the next month, I resigned my position from the sexual assault program, effective, July 11, 1977. I thought my last week would be uneventful. I could not have been more wrong.

On July 4, 1977, seven days before my final day to work in the program, I was called to Delray Beach early in the morning because a young woman had been brutally raped. I drove straight to the hospital to be with her during the rape kit and then, after the exam was finished and evidence collected, the two of us got into the back seat of the detective's car. A crime scene detective sat with him in the front seat.

While we were driving around, searching for the small apartment that was the scene of the crime, she was telling me how the rape happened. Since, as a paralegal counselor for the victims, I had immunity against having to testify when the cases went to court, nothing she told me was official, unless she were also giving a statement to a police officer or detective at the time. I was there to support her through the process and if that meant allowing her to vent to me, that was part of my role as her counselor and advocate.

As this young woman was speaking, I felt tiny hairs on the back of my neck raise. I never really believed it when people said this happened, but it was true. A month before she was raped, a nineteen-year-old college student working alone in a convenience store in Delray was robbed, kidnapped, raped and stabbed to death. Her father had been on the way to pick her up after work, but arrived minutes after they took her from the store. It was believed the perpetrators had stalked her and knew the exact time her father picked her up each night. Her body was found among the garbage in the Lantana landfill, but there had been no arrest at the time I was called to support the other Delray Beach victim.

Although I worked closely with the Palm Beach County Sheriff's Office detectives who worked all major crimes, not just sex crimes, and would hear them discussing cases, I could not officially get involved with them. Sometimes, because they said they trusted my instincts, they'd run something by me, but I never advised them in an official way or did anything involving cases other than my own.

From their discussions, as well as reports on the local news of the kidnapping and murder, I knew the perpetrators drove an old white car, stole a brand of beer that came in gold cans, and one of them stabbed the young woman in the neck before he disposed of her body.

Witnesses coming upon the scene at the store, described the perpetrators' clothing as like that of mechanics, with a logo ending with oco on their shirts, so it was assumed they were mechanics who possibly worked at a local gas station.

What got my own antenna up was that the rape victim, riding in the back seat with me, described an old white car, with gold beer cans strewn over the floor. She told me the man driving it, who picked her up as she was walking on the street outside her motel (she admitted she was a street prostitute), was dressed in "mechanic's clothes that had Amoco on them."

Then, she said, after they had sex for which he paid her $50, he started to get rough so she said no, that was enough. She got up, went into the bathroom after telling him she wanted to leave, and started dressing. He threw open the bathroom door, put a knife to her throat and said he'd kill her if she fought him; that he'd decide when enough was enough. This time, he tied her to the bedposts with sheets, forced himself upon her, and then said he was leaving but would be back with his cousin. She tried to get loose but before she could, he came back with a younger man in his mid to late twenties, while the other man looked to be around thirty years old, she told me. The younger man, whom he said was his cousin and was dressed the same as he, also raped her. They left again and warned her not to try anything, because they were coming right back.

As soon as they left, she continued to try to free herself and was successful in freeing her legs from the sheets. She tugged the sheets that bound her hands from the bedpost and then, without bothering to dress, with her hands still bound, she fell backwards out an open window, knocking the screen out as she fell. She threw the money on the ground as she ran to the nearest lighted house. The $50 was found on the ground under the window, along with her bare footprints. When the people, to whose house she ran in the darkness of that early morning, called the police, they took her directly to the hospital for the rape kit to be performed and called my service so I could be with her throughout the exam.

After a short time, she was able to identify the small apartment where she was raped, as well as another one where the man said he was living, so we drove to the police station, and the detective was going to drive her back to the Lake Worth motel where she was living and from where the rapist picked her up. I left her for a moment in the interview room and talked with the detective. I told him everything she told me, enumerating the old white car filled with the gold beer cans, the knife to her throat and the Amoco uniforms of both perpetrators.

I asked whether he agreed it sounded like the murderers of the young college student. He said, no, because the younger man's father, who owned the Amoco station where they both worked, had just called the police station. He told them the two cousins, one his nephew who'd been placed, recently, into his guardianship after paroled from prison, came to him and were afraid they were going to get charged with raping the prostitute. The detective told me there was no way they could be the murderers because they were so fearful of getting into trouble over what happened that night and, "besides, she's a prostitute, so it wasn't rape."

Instead of arguing with him on that point, even

though I was livid about the ignorance of the remark, I asked him to, at least, take the victim to a women's shelter rather than back to the place where the older perpetrator knew she lived. He refused to listen to that, also.

Driving me back to the hospital to get my car after he dropped her off, he told me he was going to un-found the case since she was a "hooker and solicited the man for money." He wouldn't consider it was forcible sexual assault after he put the knife to her throat.

Again, I didn't argue the matter. My heart was beating so rapidly in my ear, it was distracting, because I knew what I was going to do about it, since he intended to do nothing. I told him if he un-founded his case, I needed to have their names and addresses so I could un-found mine, also. This was true since, if I had been called to a case, I was required to keep a record of the crime scene, alleged perpetrator and victim, plus their addresses. He told me their names and addresses plus the name of the Amoco station (across the street from the convenience store where the college student worked when she was kidnapped) owned by the younger cousin's father. I wrote the information down on my worksheet under the victim's name.

We said goodnight, I got into my car and drove straight to the central sub-station of the sheriff's office, off Belvedere Road in West Palm, hoping some of the detectives were still there. It was 6:30 a.m. by then and I'd been working all night, but that didn't matter to me. I knew I was right, and I was not going to let the possible perpetrators of this horrendous murder get away, just because a police detective did not take me seriously enough to run with the information and bring them in that night for questioning. I felt the victim of the rape had handed us the truth on a silver platter and couldn't believe he wouldn't have taken it seriously.

To my relief, as soon as I climbed the steps to the side door I knew would be open at that hour and went into the station, I saw Crime Scene Detective Bill Brown. I asked him if he'd been working the murder case and his eyes widened. He said it was the Delray sub-station's case, but they were all on the alert for the perpetrators. I asked whether he'd like a couple names and addresses. Bill smiled and told me to come with him.

We sat at his desk while he took all the information I had on the case. Then, he called the detective who was in charge of the case, Delray Sub-station's Sgt. Emilio Diamantes. The sergeant told him the two men were suspects from the beginning of the case, but they had no real probable cause to arrest them until I brought the information to the sub-station. They handled it from there and I drove forty miles to Belle Glade. I couldn't go to bed yet. I'd been paged to go to another crime scene. Fortunately, Karen and Suzy were still with their dad for summer vacation, so I didn't have to worry about their being alone in the house.

When I returned home in the afternoon, still July 4, 1977, I just started to go to bed to catch some much needed sleep, when I had a call from Jenny Elliott who had worked, until recently, with me in the program. She told me to get down to the Delray Sub-station; Sheriff Richard Wille was holding a press conference (her husband, John Peterson, was a Palm Beach Post reporter) about the arrest of the murderers. He was giving me credit for having put it together and giving them the information that provided them with probable cause to make the arrests. John wrote the front-page story of the arrests.

When I arrived at the station (to hugs and cheers from everyone), the younger cousin was in the interrogation room giving his confession to Chief Assistant State Attorney Jack Scarola. He implicated his cousin as the one who told him to wait at the car while he took a walk up the hill with the rape victim. He told Jack he begged him not to do it, because he knew he had a knife and knew if they walked up that landfill, the young woman was not coming back, but his cousin led him to believe he was taking her up there to release her.

I was at the arraignment of the one who stabbed the student. My name and picture had been in all the newspapers, and at one point, he looked back from the defense table and stared straight at me. The look he gave me was so piercing, I knew the meaning of "if looks could kill." At that moment, I felt like sobbing for both his victims, especially that poor innocent student he murdered, and thought how terrified she must have been of him during the time they had her in the apartment and especially as he was forcing her up the landfill hill.

Months later, when the judge sentenced them for the kidnapping, rape and murder of the student, there were no surprises. The younger cousin, Gary Forbes, 19, even though he'd cooperated with the sheriff's office, was given a life sentence and his cousin, Nollie Lee Martin, 36, was sentenced to death by electric chair. He lived on Death

Row for fourteen years, until 1991, when he was one of the last to die in what is known as "Old Sparky" at Florida's Raiford Prison.

Right after the arrest, I was in the central sub-station on another case and Lt. Richard Sheets walked up to me with an application in his hand. They wanted to put me through the police academy at Palm Beach Jr. College; I'd be put on road patrol for a year or so to get some experience and then brought on as a detective in the major crimes squad, they told me.

There was nothing I would have wanted more than to work with the detectives on major crimes, especially with Detective Jo Ann Potter, whom I'd worked with the most as a counselor. I respected her so much and loved to work with her. The beginning salary of a sheriff's deputy was only half of what I would get by going back to nursing, and the hours would be just as long as what I'd been working as a paralegal counselor, if not longer. I had to think of my daughters, again, and declined the offer, so he wrote me a wonderful letter of reference, with the help of Jo Ann, to take with me when I left since I did not have a full-time job lined up, yet.

Assistant State Attorney Jack Scarola and I received written commendations from State Attorney David Bloodworth with a personal note from him for a job well done. That was unexpected, but it was nice of him to take the time to do it and it meant a lot to me, since even though he was not my direct supervisor, we worked under his department with the assistant state attorneys. He'd always been kind to Jenny and me.

That night after work, with my daughters still at their

dad's, to get away from my ringing phone (not for calls to crime scenes, but family, friends and neighbors calling to congratulate me for helping the S.O. with the case), I went to a little piano bar where my friends, Laura and her husband Ed, were playing. I'd already told her I was coming to escape from my "fifteen minutes of fame," but Ed did not know this.

When I walked in to a packed piano bar with one spare seat in front of his piano, Ed told the crowd, "Hey everyone, Peggy Butler just walked in."

Laura rolled her eyes at him, saying under her breath that I'd wanted to get away from all that for a little while. Before I realized what was going to happen, everyone applauded and middle aged and elderly men and women left their seats to crowd around me. They hugged me and shook my hand. They all thanked me for, as one of them put it, "helping to rid the county of those evil murderers."

The next day I was driving to meet a sheriff's office detective at another crime scene. I had my radio on and one of the DJs, who'd made a reference to the arrest of the two men, earlier, dedicated the song, "Undercover Angel to the boys in Delray." That was all I needed, since when interviewed, the Delray Police Department had accused me of "interfering with their investigation by taking the information to the PBSO." They forgot to say the lieutenant I had worked with on the rape case of July 4th, had discounted the information as invalid. When Sgt. Diamantis called to speak with him, he was in bed asleep, not working the case I'd supposedly interfered with, and his captain knew nothing about it.

I had worked with several others in the Delray Police Department prior to July 4, 1977, and their work was top-notch, despite the song dedication's inference that the entire department was inept. The other road patrol officers and detectives were good police officers, and I never had a reason to fault any of them. They were hard-working and dedicated and I was always impressed with their professionalism.

Sheriff Wille reported at the news conference, after the perpetrators were arrested, that Delray was charging them with false imprisonment and sexual battery in the case of my brave survivor.

There was one thing for certain; everyone, including the radio D. J., was getting into the act because they were so glad it was over and the perpetrators of the heinous crime, that had upset the whole community, were behind bars where they belonged.

Lt. Richard Sheets, when asked by a reporter whether he was relieved the pair had been caught, said, "Oh, that's not the word for it. That's not the word for it." He said Martin had implicated himself in the crime, but didn't call it a confession at the time.

A secretary from the PBSO told reporter John Peterson, they'd cancelled their weekend, "but at least they got 'em. It was worth it."

The murder victim's parents were benevolent in their attitude toward the two men. They were a religious family and she had been attending a Christian college. When the reporters asked for their reaction to the murderers being caught, they said they held no malice in their hearts for them and were praying for them. I don't think I could have been that generous had it been one of my daughters they'd destroyed like that.

I felt sorry for the father of young Forbes, the one who'd confessed to the crime and told the detectives Martin had stabbed the young woman. Mr. Forbes had been so generous toward Martin, who'd been paroled from North Carolina where he'd been convicted of second-degree murder in an arson case. The fire had killed his girlfriend and her two young daughters. The elder Forbes had vouched for him with the court and Martin told him the night of July 4th he hadn't done anything to get into trouble since he was paroled. He'd taken him in, given him a job at the Amoco station he owned and said he seemed to be working out. He said he couldn't believe either of them had anything to do with the kidnap, rape and murder, despite their telling him they raped the prostitute. Forbes sold his home and the station before moving from the area to an undisclosed location. His son is still in prison.

EIGHTEEN
Hospital Name Change

During this time, many changes had been taking place at the TB hospital in Lantana. The name, A.G. Holley State Tuberculosis Hospital, was one of the changes during the late 1960s. A. G. Holley owned a hardware store in the Florida Panhandle and was a longtime member of the State TB Board. Against the objections of the Palm Beach County delegation, then Rep. Wayne Mixson pushed through the name change of the Southeast Florida State TB Hospital in 1965, but it was not effective until the end of the decade. Mixson later became Lt. Governor.

I returned to A. G. Holley in November 1977, as night (11-7) supervisor and one weekend a month for almost a year, I also worked as relief ship's nurse on the S.S. Emerald Seas cruiseship out of Miami while my daughters were with their father (we shared joint custody). This was a nice, but busy diversion from the hospital work. While still in the sexual assault program, having accumulated so much overtime in my first month of employment, I had to take the comp time off, so I relieved a nurse on his ten-day vacation from the M.S. Fairwind cruiseship, out of Ft. Lauderdale. This cruise took us to the tip of South America and since I'd enjoyed that time as ship's nurse, I welcomed the opportunity to relieve the other nurse in Miami once a month.

In 1977, A.G. Holley State Hospital was just the eastern half of the large building in which I had made rounds, night after night, just nine years before. The hospital had just 150 beds now instead of 500. Some portions of it were utilized by other state entities not affiliated with the tuberculosis hospital.

In the photograph in this book, the hospital in 1977 ended where the cafeteria was to the far right, beyond the palm tree nearest the flagpole at the entrance to the hospital. The western end of the building, which was the Lantana Correctional Institution for male inmates with drug dependencies, on the other side of the cafeteria, is a duplicate of everything seen in the photograph.

The men's residence opposite the west end of the hospital, where Ron lived when we met in 1961, now housed the Work Release Program for prisoners working within the community near the end of their incarceration. It had no connection to the correctional institution.

A sad word here about Ron: He left Palm Beach County Health Department in the 1970s and retired after 30 years with the State, as Director, Hernando County Health Department in Brooksville, in central Florida, forty miles east of Tampa.

After retirement, he lived in Ridge Manor for a few years and then came back to West Palm Beach, where he shared a home with Suzy and her husband, Brian. He'd been divorced from his second wife for a while at that time.

Ron's health deteriorated during those years after retirement and after a fall in 2004, in which he suffered a fractured hip, he went into heart failure and died at Hospice of Palm Beach County shortly afterward. Prior to that, he seemed to be improving, but then, his heart failure came on so rapidly our daughters had no time to process what was going to happen. Of course, it devastated both of them. It has been a long road back and I sometimes recognize a haunted look in their eyes, even now, seven years later, especially during the holidays, and I know that hole in their hearts never will heal completely.

Right before this past Thanksgiving, Karen and her husband, Stephen, become grandparents for the first time. This precious baby girl is bringing so much happiness into all our lives. I know Karen and Suzy will have a bit of that empty hole in their hearts filled by her, just as the emptiness left by our divorce was erased a little at a time with their marriages and the addition of each of our grandchildren into their lives.

Tuberculosis medication changes were evident, also, when I returned in 1977. PAS, for the most part, was now passé. PZA, used in tuberculosis for two decades now, was being hailed by many in the TB field and literature as the drug that affected a cure, when used in combination with the others. No one had ever used the word cure with such assurance before this. So, it was exciting to know what was suspected and hoped for in the early '50s was now true.

INH (Isoniazid) was another change. We seasoned TB Control staff members still called it INAH, as in Dinah. Now, it was being called I-N-H by the new generation of TB workers. We were happy to see young new professionals coming to work in TB Control, not just because they needed jobs, but from a true desire to work in TB; what they called the medication was of little consequence.

Unit Dose became the big thing soon after I returned. The pharmacy now sent up cards of sealed unit doses of medications for each individual patient, so the nurses simply punched out the dose as they reached the patients' rooms with the medication cart.

That was an improvement over counting and pouring meds from bottles into the tiny soufflé cups before placing them all on large trays. We still put the meds from the unit doses into the cups but no longer had to pre-pour them and put them onto the trays. Since most of the patients came out into the hallway to get them, we seldom went into the rooms to leave the meds, anymore, either.

The carts had compartments for supplies such as syringes and alcohol prep pads plus a locked compartment for controlled drugs. The carts, themselves, also locked.

All things considered, it was a secure way to administer medications. Unit dose became a universal method for administering medications in all the hospitals around the country, not just in A.G. Holley State Tuberculosis Hospital, and the locked medication carts became the standard in all hospitals. Medications no longer were stored in cabinets in the nurses stations, a great improvement over the past.

The MAR (medication administration record) became universal, as well, replacing pages of hand-written medication records in the patient's charts. All we had to do was write our initials beside the correct date and time under the correct medication on the MAR of each patient.

Alcohol addiction was, and always has been, one of the greatest obstacles to keeping hospitalized and outpatient TB patients compliant with their medication regime. It was a constant struggle for the nurses and physicians to try to keep the patients from drinking. If they drank, they did not take their medications regularly, and that was the only way they could avoid drug resistance and get well from tuberculosis.

Despite all our efforts, many of them continued to slip out to the nearest liquor store, The Duke, on Dixie Highway (U. S. 1). They would hide their purchases among the trees in the woods on the hospital grounds before they returned to the wards. Of course, they were fooling nobody. It had been known for almost three decades it was going on, just as it went on in the other two tuberculosis hospitals before they closed. Finding their stashes was another matter, since staff members did not have any occasion to rummage through the acres of woods searching for whisky bottles. Every now and then, one of the hospital security guards would find a bottle when they were out on patrol at night, driving around the grounds in their golf cart.

The State developed a special program for the alcoholic patients, similar to Alcoholics' Anonymous. It was called AGHAP (A. G. Holley Alcohol Program) and the counselors were a constant presence on the wards. Their success was marginal at best, because as soon as most of their clients were discharged from the hospital, former influences came back into their lives and they resumed the drinking. AGHAP was terminated after a brief number of years, but not because its staff did not give it their best effort.

When I returned this time, Marge Thompson (nee Knowles) was a registered nurse, supervisor and acting DON. My prediction and hope for her had all but come to fruition. She was seldom called Margie, anymore. Just as with my former classmate, Barbara Lumpkin and her nickname, it was no longer fitting. Marge had grown so in stature and had become a confident administrative nurse, as I knew, a decade before, she would. The nurse who replaced Maggie Smith, Agnes Naughton, RN, left as I was returning. She interviewed me for the returning position, but left so soon after that, I never got to know her.

The same nursing assistants who were there in 1961 and 1967 still worked at the hospital in 1977. Most of them went to work when it opened its doors in 1950 and had no desire to work anywhere else. There were a few new ones, also.

Without complaint, they were still reinforcing to the patients the need to cough into their tissues and fold the tissues into clean ones before throwing them into the paper bags taped to the side of their beds every shift, and then disposing of the bags properly when they became full.

This repetitive teaching by all the staff, but mostly by the nursing assistants, as much as anything else, accounted for the staff remaining free from tuberculosis. The patients knew, by not coughing into the air, they were protecting us. Although they had to be reminded from time to time, to my knowledge, no patient ever blatantly ignored this important part of living with TB among other people.

The nursing assistants became mother, sister and confidant to those patients who lived at A. G. Holley for months at a time. When they were recalcitrant and had to return to the hospital, it was the nursing assistants, as much as the nurses and physicians, to whom they had to listen because they'd ruined their chance, once again, to remain healthy and free of TB. They were not surprised they didn't get off easy with those knowledgeable staff members. On the other hand, they knew A. G. Holley was one place they would be welcomed back like family, no matter why they'd had to return. And they always were.

Unlike at most general hospitals, where the patients only see the nursing assistants when they need them, at Lantana, the nursing assistants were visible components of the nursing team and were there for the patients the entire time they were on duty.

They performed the repetitious duties such as passing fresh drinking water, changing bed linens and other things their peers in the general hospitals performed, but they did, and still do, so much more than routine duties. They listened to the patients and talked straight to them, so the patients soon learned to trust them and learn from them. They always have been vital members of the nursing team at A. G. Holley Hospital.

The hospital was no longer under the small State TB

Board in 1977. It was now under the gigantic bureaucratic umbrella of HRS (Department of Health and Rehabilitative Services).

Had this drastic reorganization not occurred, we all believed the 500-bed hospital would still exist, exclusively, for tuberculosis treatment, instead of being relegated to 150 beds in one section of the hospital.

As the incidence of TB declined, so did the bed capacity. Currently, although the hospital is licensed for 100 beds, it only is funded for 50 and the medical director, Dr. David Ashkin, has had to fight for its existence on a continuous basis.

In 1977, Liz was supervisor on the 7-3 shift and Carol, also, was still on 7-3. Maurine and Opal were no longer working at Lantana. Opal moved away from Florida and Maurine was working for the Visiting Nurses Association in West Palm.

Sadly, Maurine's husband, and my brother-in-law, Bob, died of cancer at the age of thirty-nine in 1969, a few months after Suzy was born, leaving Maurine with two young sons, Mike and Sean. Ron was never the same after Bob's death, and Maurine never remarried. She has been in hospice nursing in Tampa, her hometown, for the past several years since her sons grew up. During tax season, she also works for H & R Block and helped me with my own taxes many times.

The State chose an unknown nurse, Charlotte Fitzsimmons (not her real name), from another state to be Director of Nurses shortly after I returned. Charlotte had no working knowledge of TB nursing prior to her appointment, which puzzled all of us who knew how important this was.

Cecil Teague, the Personnel Director since the hospital first opened its doors, was still in that position. He confided one morning that he was no happier than any of the rest of us that the state wanted someone who knew nothing about the hospital, its staff or tuberculosis, to be the director instead of Marge.

Some things were just out of the hands of local control, he told us. That darned bureaucratic umbrella again.

Marge had grown up at the hospital and risen, through hard work and study, from an aide to RN supervisor; an amazing nurse who knew more about that hospital than any other nurse and doctor there because she never, decisively, had worked anywhere else. She'd made the hospital her life's work. Marge could see the broad picture about A. G. Holley TB Hospital and its needs, as few others, including this writer, ever could.

Charlotte stayed for ten years but, in reality, Marge Thompson always was the true director of nursing and Liz Phillips, the assistant director, although Marge had the title of assistant director and Liz was still, on paper, the 7-3 shift nursing supervisor.

That director of nursing never seemed to learn or understand much about TB disease, despite all those years of working in the hospital. She never seemed to understand what the patients were up against or understand the treatment of TB, so she relied upon Marge and Liz to make patient decisions with the other staff.

One never had the impression Charlotte was

interested in tuberculosis, and we wondered why she had come to work at a TB hospital. She already had a pension, a lovely home and did not seem to need the additional income. On rare occasions, she was present during physician rounds. If no one was speaking to her, she had the annoying habit of rocking back and forth from heel to toe, whistling through her teeth. The whistling was not loud, but she still could be heard. This was especially embarrassing if a visiting physician was with us during rounds.

If there was a saving grace in having Charlotte Fitzsimmons as the director, it was her military background. She had risen through the ranks in the military to a high command and that was the source of her pension. Thankfully, with this background, her strength was in her ability to delegate. This benefited the hospital and the patients, despite this seeming lack of knowledge and interest.

Most important, and the one truly positive thing about Charlotte, because she made the effort to round on every ward every day and talked with the patients, she knew most of them by sight and many by name. And, to her credit, even though she sometimes seemed not to have a clue about how to resolve anything for them, she brought their problems and needs to the attention of her nursing staff so they could be resolved. And, to be fair to her, since she was retired military, she probably believed that was the way things should work in the civilian world, as well as it did the military.

NINETEEN

Physician Turnover

Because Karen, now 15, and Suzy, now 10, needed me home at night and I wanted more quality time with them, I requested a transfer to the day shift in 1978. I knew there was no supervisory position available, nor was it likely there would be in the near future. HRS, in addition to taking more than half the hospital from TB, cut back on staff as well, so I requested the next day position of any kind. As night supervisor, I never got to know the newer physicians; now that I was back on days, I enjoyed getting to know all of them.

Dr. Adil had left State employment and had a large private practice, with many patients in Palm Beach, as well as West Palm and other areas of the county. He was no longer known as Dr. Adil but by his full name Dr. Adil Sokmensuer. To this day, however, he is still Dr. Adil to those of us who knew and loved him as our TB ward physician and medical director. If he ever had occasion to call us for anything after he left, he would say, "This is Dr. Adil," never Dr. Sokmensuer.

Dr. Osvaldo Espino, who worked with us in the '60s as a ward physician, also was gone, but still worked full-time in TB Control, at the county health department in West Palm Beach, and as the physician for Belle Glade and Martin County Chest Clinics, as well as some other counties further north in the state.

In addition to his chest clinic duties, as CDC Consultant for most of the state, including Palm Beach County, Dr. Espino had the awesome responsibility for reading, interpreting and dictating his findings on every chest x-ray taken on every outpatient in all those counties, after he left the Lantana hospital.

A handsome Cuban in his late fifties, he had a smile for everyone. It was amazing how he and his secretary, Grace Floyd, took care of this monumental task with no other assistance. Yet, one never saw them harried or behaving as though they had such an enormous amount of work to carry out every day, even though we knew they had. Grace, a tall, attractive and gracious lady, wore her black hair sleeked back in a chignon most of the time. She, like her boss, was well liked and respected by everyone at the health department.

Dr. Jorge` Manas, also at the hospital from my early days, was still working at Lantana in the late '70s after having worked in the ER at JFK Memorial Hospital in Lake Worth for awhile. He was a tall, somewhat heavy man, who, from the time we were all much younger and I first met him, always walked with his head down and never hurried, reminding one of a slow-moving, friendly relaxed bear. Everyone liked Dr. Manas and he related well to the rest of the staff.

Dr. Herman Cutler, who was a Harvard graduate and proud of his alma mater, was new to me this time around.

Herman was a lecturer. The most trivial thing, elementary to those of us who had worked in TB for a long time, could produce a lengthy lecture from him, if he believed it was something we nurses might not understand. He would have been a great professor because he was a natural orator. I often wondered why he was at the hospital rather than teaching at a college or university. He had a medium build, thinning hair, wore glasses and always appeared harried. Even when he laughed, one had the feeling it was forced, as he always seemed to take himself and life seriously, even when the occasion did not call for it. He never relaxed, it seemed, even at informal staff gatherings.

Also new since my last tour of duty at the hospital, was Dr. Bruce Cominole, a former Navy physician and one of the most gifted diagnosticians I've ever had the privilege of knowing. All who knew him, including his fellow physicians, conceded this about him. Privately, he scoffed at such a thought. He never believed he was the physician everyone else knew him to be. Bruce, handsome, slender and not much taller than I, had perfect posture, giving him the appearance of someone who was taller. He had thick white hair and wore horn-rimmed glasses. He also looked enough like Senator Barry Goldwater they could have been brothers.

One of my favorite stories about Bruce was this: One day he was having dinner in a restaurant when another patron he had never seen before, walked up and shook hands with him. Just as the man started to tell him how much he'd admired his work in the Senate, Bruce stood and shock registered on the man's face as he realized he was not the tall senator, after all. Bruce had a gift for putting people at ease, so he dismissed the man's apology with the wave of a hand and said, "Nonsense, you paid me a compliment."

Dr. Jake White was another new physician I'd not met before. He transferred from Southwest Florida State Tuberculosis Hospital in Tampa when it was closing, about the same time W.T. Edwards State Tuberculosis Hospital in Tallahassee became Sunland for the profoundly retarded. Jake was a handsome physician of medium height and a bit on the heavy side, but like Dr. Manas, he was not obese. Jake reminded me of the singer, Lou Rawls; both in looks and the way he spoke. If he also sang like Mr. Rawls, I never had the privilege of hearing him.

There is an amusing story involving Jake, as well, which happened a few years later. Liz and I were having a late lunch in the hospital cafeteria. Jake and Bruce were there, also. It happened to be a holiday weekend and Jake had brought in some eggnog in a gallon container. All of us had some and my, but it tasted good.

Bringing alcohol onto State grounds was forbidden and carried a large fine, so knowing this, I thought nothing of drinking the eggnog. And, of course, Liz and I were still on duty, as was the assistant superintendent of the correctional facility, Don Findley, who came in and sat with the four of us.

When I got back to the ward, all of a sudden I looked at Carol, who was setting up the afternoon meds, and told her, "I don't know what's happening, but I feel as though my heart is coming out of my body." She checked my heart rate and we were both shocked. It was hammering at 169 beats per minute, more than double my normal rate. She called Liz who was still in the cafeteria, and as soon as she told Jake and Bruce, she said she thought Jake was going to have a heart attack. It seems he had put rum into the eggnog, unaware I was on a temporary medication that did not mix with alcohol.

He asked her to run an electrocardiogram, which confirmed the PAT (paroxysmal atrial tachycardia). Though not as serious as ventricular tachycardia, that can stop the heart's beating by sending the patient into fibrillation, it's nonetheless frightening because of the rapid hammering beat. Knowing the EKG was normal except for that, he told me, "I know you're all right, Peg, but please do us all a favor and call your personal physician to let him know what happened." By then, my heart rate slowed enough I could go back on duty. I promised I would and left the room.

I did call and explained the situation to my doctor. After he stopped laughing, he said, "Peggy, it would be a good idea not to take the medication for 24 hours if you're going to drink something other than a virgin egg nog." He then assured me I would be all right.

I told him, "If I'd known I was going to be drinking the real thing, I wouldn't have done it." He laughed again, as did I. It all turned out all right and, to my knowledge, no one else learned Jake had taken such a risk to bring a little holiday cheer to us that Christmas weekend.

Dr. I. Petjovik, tall and slender, a nice looking man with silver hair and glasses, was now Medical Director. Dr. Petjovik was an astute leader, as Dr. Adil had been. He was a physician who knew tuberculosis and placed the patients first just as his predecessor had done. All of us admired and respected him. Just as most of the other doctors on staff were usually called by their first names, as were doctors at the health department because they believed they were partners with the nurses and did not want to be addressed formally, he was called Petjovik by many on staff. Even though it was easy to call most of the others by their first names, most of the other nurses and I never could call Dr. Petjovik by any other name except Dr. Petjovik, just as we always called Dr. Adil, Dr. Adil.

Many on staff, including other physicians, pressured Dr. Petjovik to dismiss Charlotte Fitzsimmons and place Marge Thompson, officially, in the position she was filling. But, ever the diplomat, he said, "My hands are tied. I can't do anything about it because, like the rest of us, she's a career employee for the State of Florida," and he was correct about that. It took drastic misconduct on duty or disastrous mistakes before such an employee could be dismissed. So she remained in the position for several more years, continuing to depend upon Marge and Liz to run the nursing department.

With the great medical staff, the patients were flourishing. Most of them had come into the hospital so underweight they looked emaciated. Under the good care of Drs. Manas, White, Cominole and Cutler, they gained weight and most felt they'd gained a new life because they felt so well after just a few months.

I was happy being back on the day shift, despite wishing Marge were the director of nursing, officially. Charlotte's priorities were not always mine, as much as I tried to respect her as my director.

Once, for some strange reason, since I still never weighed more than 100 to 105, I took a Dexedrine. Maybe I'd not slept well and took it to be more alert, but I can't remember if that was the reason. I had never taken a stimulating medication before and hated how it made me feel, wired as tightly as the strings on a violin. I told Carol that morning I felt as jumpy as a cat on a hot tin roof. She laughed and said, "Well, just don't go near the roof."

At one point, after the morning routine was finished, I said, "Oh my gosh, Carol, I just had the craziest urge to jump out the window. I'll be glad when this thing wears off." Of course, we both knew that's what was causing all the strange feelings. I had a cup of herb tea to try to settle down, but even it didn't help.

Another problem with my having taken it was that Charlotte had chosen that afternoon to call a nurses meeting. Of course, that was the last thing I wanted to do that afternoon, but I had no choice. We all had to go. I don't remember what the meeting was about, but at one point as Charlotte was speaking to us, I said, aloud, "This is nonsense. I'm not staying here and listening to this," and walked out of the meeting! I'd never done anything like that in all my years as a nurse.

Fortunately, Liz knew I'd taken the Dexedrine and explained that to Charlotte. To have one of her nurses walk out of a meeting she was leading, after insulting her, to boot, must have represented the height of insubordination to this military chief nurse. Carol followed me out of the meeting to be sure I was all right and wasn't going to carry through with my urge to jump out the nearest window. It took the whole day for the effects of that drug to wear off and I never took anything like it again.

When I was myself again, I went to Charlotte and apologized for leaving her meeting like that and for saying what I did. To my surprise, she said she understood since Liz explained it was the effect of a new medication. "You probably shouldn't take anything like that again, Peggy." She need not have worried. I'd already come to that conclusion the day before.

I thanked her and went back to my ward. I think Liz and Carol expected me to come back to say I'd been fired as did I, when I went to the director's office, instead of hearing her say she understood what had happened and seemed concerned for me. I doubt I would have been retained if that had happened anywhere else but Lantana, where we, the family, looked after each other and genuinely cared about each other.

Karen was involved with many activities at John I. Leonard High School and as much as my time allowed, I tried to support her in them. One of these was the making of tissue flowers for their homecoming float. They had flower parties at different houses, so I volunteered our apartment foolishly, I'd sold the house a few years before and never bought another for a flower party on one of my day's off.

Besides Karen, Suzy and I, there were forty other students sitting on the sectional sofas, chairs, piano bench and floor of our small living room and around the table in the kitchen. I kept the refreshments coming, and we made tissue flowers for several hours that night. It was one of the nicest times we'd had as a family, even with the forty other students present, since my divorce from their dad.

Because I worked the day shift, now, there were more things I could do with the girls than when I'd worked evenings. Karen and her future husband, Steve, were both with Jil Jive, the jazz vocal ensemble of John I. Leonard High School. As vice-president of the parents' support group, I went on a few competitions with them and really enjoyed that time in our lives. Of course, Suzy came with me when she wasn't at her dad's, and we cheered the ensemble on. I loved their music since so much of it consisted of the standards of days gone by, the days I'd lived as a young girl still in high school.

Karen had a wonderful music teacher at the school and he was the director for JIL Jive. I marveled at her knowledge of music and envied her at the same time, since that was what I knew I'd lacked as a piano player. There was nothing they did not learn about the rudiments of music and I think she could have had a great career in it, had she wanted to pursue it, but that wasn't the direction she headed when she finished school.

Suzy was growing up, too, but had another year before she got into what was known then as Jr. High School, the 7th and 8th grades. She had one more year at Kirklane Elementary School, and I was in no hurry for her to graduate from there. I wanted one of them to stay a little girl for a while longer. Suzy never enjoyed school very much after she left the ELC at the college, until her last two years at Kirklane. I think it was because she enjoyed being one of the upper classmen more than she'd enjoyed being in the lower grades, as all of us did when we were kids.

I was so happy I was on the day shift, as I'd missed so much with them when I worked evenings and nights. It was a more normal home life when I came home from work in the late afternoon and we could have dinner together in the evening. It made me feel like a better parent than a lot of the time in our recent past, when I was working in the evening and night hours, especially after the divorce.

Ron, Karen, Suzy, Peg, all smiles after Karen's graduation from John I. Leonard HS, Greenacres FL, 1981

Above: Karen at family graduation party.
Below: Suzy before elementary school graduation, 1980.

Suzy, wearing a happy smile, with favorite principal, Clifford O. Taylor, Kirklane Elementary School graduation, Palm Springs, FL, 1980

TWENTY
Haitian Influx

After my day position became available, I worked as 4A head nurse on this men's ward, at first, because it was the only one open. Dr. Cutler was the ward physician. This was a confusing and often perplexing time for me, as Dr. Cutler had the habit of giving me verbal orders and then shouting at me or the LPN for carrying them out, because he'd forget he had given the orders. Sometimes he'd apologize afterward, telling us he just had a lot on his mind. This was understandable, but none of us enjoyed being yelled at as though we were children who'd done something wrong instead of carrying out his orders.

Exasperated by this, one day I went to him and said, "Dr. Cutler, I'm sorry but I can't accept any more verbal orders." I had first cleared this with Liz. I expected an argument from him on this, as he did not appreciate nurses telling him how things were to be done on his ward. I knew it was to the benefit of all the nurses on each shift for me to stand firm.

As expected, he asked, "Why can't you? If I give orders to you, verbal or otherwise, you have to carry them out, Peggy. You're not the doctor; I am."

I reminded him how he sometimes forgot he'd given verbal orders to us and then yelled at the medication nurse or me for carrying them out. Then I informed him I'd been advised by the supervisor to accept only written orders.

With reluctance, he agreed to write all his orders from that day on. After that, things became more tolerable for both of us. And, underneath all the harshness and resistance, he was a good, caring man and we all knew that.

As on all the other wards in the hospital, the nursing assistants and nurses were excellent and caring. Our ward secretary, Lulu Sippio, a sweet young woman with a warm smile, was invaluable to us. As with the other ward secretaries in the hospital, the ward could not have managed without her making it all run smoothly.

Besides the others, there were two special people working on 4A at that time. One was Ralph Gervasio, our orderly. Ralph was a big Italian New Yorker who could be as loud and obnoxious, in a good-natured way, as it was possible for anyone to be.

Ralph never meant any harm to anyone; he loved the patients and was loyal and protective of the staff. When anyone was going though a difficult time, he would be the one to get the person aside and make him or her take a deep breath to stop the mind from accepting any more clutter. Then, he would replace that clutter with how he saw that individual. He was a true diamond-in-the rough, if ever there was one.

He and his wife, Emma Lou, who worked in Housekeeping, could bake homemade pizza, New York Italian style, like nobody else could. Emma Lou, a sweet, cherub-faced and five foot tall woman we all adored, and Ralph had my daughters and me over for a special family dinner one night, and the homemade pizza was delicious.

Ralph could bring levity to just about any situation. There was only one problem with this. He enjoyed practical jokes and on at least one occasion, the joke had an unexpected effect upon one of the other staff members.

On that day, he and Jesse Allen, one of our other orderlies, took a patient to the morgue. On the way back, Jesse climbed up on the stretcher they had just cleaned, pulled the clean sheet over his head and Ralph pushed him back onto the ward, 3A.

One of the unsuspecting nurses asked, "Ralph, why are you bringing the patient back to the ward? You were supposed to take him to the morgue."

With a solemn face, he explained, "I'm sorry, the morgue was full."

The morgue at A. G. Holley was never full since we seldom had a death, so I don't know why she even believed him. But, she seemed to accept his reason for bringing the patient back to the ward.

At that moment, Jesse, still covered by the sheet, sat up and it was such a shock to her, the poor nurse fell back against the wall and almost fainted. Both of the orderlies felt badly about this and never pulled that prank again on anyone.

The other special person on 4A was Maggie Bunner, LPN, the medication nurse and relief charge nurse. Maggie was "Edith Bunker," personified, with a thick Massachusetts accent. She saw the good in everyone and was everyone's mother, including the patients'.

And Then There Was One

We all adored Maggie. Just as she was "Edith," her husband, Luck, a retired policeman, was "Archie." There was always a good laugh from their stories, which she told in abundance. Even their purchase of a Winnebago became a story because something was always going on with it. Luck filled it too full of things she thought they didn't need on their trips, it would break down always something that had us laughing when she related the tale.

What a treasure Maggie was to all of us. She has been deceased for some time now, and I still find myself wanting to hear her voice and special laughter every now and then. And, just as with my own mother, I have longed more than once for one of her special warm hugs again.

Eventually, after his head nurse, Helen Carter, RN, retired, I asked for and was given a transfer to 3A, where Dr. Cominole was the ward physician. With that transfer I stepped back into 1961.

Bruce Cominole was a dream to work with, just as Dr. Adil had been then. He was quiet, nice to everyone and we functioned as a real team. The orders he gave were clear and concise to both the patients and us nurses. He would take so much time with the patients; sometimes it took twice as long to finish rounds as with another physician. We never minded because we knew how caring he was and how important each patient's recovery was to him.

Bruce had the most infectious laugh; a giggle, actually, and he loved to listen to amusing stories. Unlike some physicians whose interests seldom went beyond the realm of medicine and golf, he had many interests. He loved music, all kinds of music, but especially Beethoven. He would listen to it for hours and sometimes tears would come to his eyes because of the beauty of it. His favorite singer of standards was Rosemary Clooney, whom he believed had the purest voice in the world. I told him, even though I loved Rosemary Clooney's voice, also, she couldn't have the purest voice in the world, since that honor belonged to my favorite, Patsy Cline. He'd laugh and say I could believe that if I wanted to, but he'd stick with Rosemary.

War heroes had a special place in Bruce's heart. He admired them all, ally or enemy, especially WWII's German General Erwin Rommel, the Desert Fox, and American General George Patton. He would read every book he could find on them. He also loved football and never missed a game on TV, if he could avoid it. He loved to talk and could discuss anything, even with young people, without being condescending or critical. He loved working and being around people at work, but he was a private man, as well, and enjoyed his quiet home on the hospital grounds when his workday was finished.

Shortly after I went to 3A, he went into the hospital for a serious condition requiring surgery. He had a difficult time recovering from it. He was hospitalized for several months and I was again working with Dr. Cutler, though still on 3A. I will give Herman Cutler his due. He worked like a trooper on both 4A and 3A to make certain Bruce came back to a clean slate of work. He was fond of his co-worker and did not want him to work so hard when he returned. This was not lost on Bruce who thanked him many times for all he'd done to make his return smoother.

During that year, we started seeing the influx of Haitian immigrants as tuberculosis patients, and I accepted the additional duties of patient education director and instructor. I spoke only a handful of Creole words, but most of the Haitian patients understood what I was trying to tell them.

This job was rewarding to me, seeing how the patients responded to what they were learning about the disease and complied, most of the time, with all they were taught, including the ever-important sputum precautions.

It is important to emphasize tuberculosis is still a communicable disease, spread from one person to another through the person with TB of the lung or larynx (voice box) coughing, sneezing, speaking or even singing. This is because the tubercle bacilli are contained in airborne droplets.

If another person, who does not have tuberculosis shares the same airspace with the diseased person for long periods of time day after day, the smaller droplet nuclei can be inhaled. If this person without TB is susceptible, he can be infected by the one with the disease, as shown by a positive PPD skin test. If he is positive, but then is not given preventative INH treatment for the prescribed period, he might develop TB disease.

Approximately ¼ of all close contacts to persons with active tuberculosis disease become infected, and about $1/20$ of these individuals will develop the disease within the first year, if not discovered early and placed on preventive treatment.

It is important to understand that no person infected

with the tubercle bacillus can transmit tuberculosis to someone else. Only a person with pulmonary tuberculosis disease can transmit it.

It was disconcerting when public school administrations created a media circus because a student had a positive tuberculin skin test, which did not mean he had TB. Health department officials got involved as soon as it was called to their attention. They tried to downplay it in a calm rational manner, but between the public and the media, it could get out of hand in a hurry before the student could be examined by his physician or chest clinic to learn whether he just had the infection or was a case of tuberculosis.

Because TB is transmitted through the air, it is important for hospitals to keep the air circulating to the outside through open windows or reverse circulation systems.

Even more important, as it always has been, is to keep the tuberculosis bacilli from getting into the indoor air in the first place. The patients taking sputum precautions and habitually covering their mouths and noses with tissues when coughing or sneezing and disposing of these tissues properly in the paper bags, as they have been taught, accomplish this.

After at least two weeks of tuberculosis chemotherapy, their risk of transmission is reduced or non-existent, because the TB chemotherapy has rendered their positive acid-fast sputum to be negative or non-infectious.

However, because there are treatment failures in which some individuals fail to respond to the tuberculosis medications, it is still essential each patient continue the habit of protecting others through good sputum precautions. Most patients did understand the need for this and did comply with it.

Sometimes, it was difficult to get through to the Haitian patients what I needed them to learn. And, when that happened I had to dig deep within myself to try to find a better way of saying what I was trying to say to them. Once in a while, one of them would turn to the others and explain in Creole what it was I believed they needed to know. I appreciated those patients for their assistance.

The Haitian Creole interpreter informed me all Haitians learn to read and write English in grammar school, so perhaps they did understand it and were reluctant to admit it for one reason or another. Regardless of the reason, the rest of the staff and I continued to reinforce what they needed to learn.

TWENTY-ONE

A Deadly New Virus

After a while, Bruce and I started noticing something strange happening with the Haitian patients throughout the hospital. Instead of getting better on the TB medications, we noticed many of them were getting sicker, some even dying. Their fatigue worsened, their coughs did not lessen, and their chest x-rays did not show the improvement we expected after so long on TB chemotherapy.

One day, Bruce said, "There has to be some kind of virus or bacteria in addition to TB in these patients, zapping their immune systems."

I agreed with him, because they were wasting away before our eyes, and yet nothing conclusive was showing up in the labs he ordered. Whatever was wrong with them was making their tuberculosis worse, not better.

It continued to be a puzzle to us until 1981 when the CDC announced the discovery of the HTLV3 virus (later re-named HIV), which was causing an autoimmune deficiency syndrome AIDS.

We looked at each other and said in unison, "That's it!" Now, understand, it has never been documented by CDC that the first cases of AIDS came into the United States in 1978 or 1979. It is on record as 1981.

But, Bruce and I never doubted it. We believed there could be no other explanation for why this group of people did not respond to the same tuberculosis drugs others were getting cured by taking. It would have been different if this population of patients drank instead of taking their medications, but this was not the case. They wanted to get well and always took their meds. They seldom left the wards and enjoyed playing dominos or just sitting together laughing and talking or watching TV.

It would be interesting, provided their serum samples were still banked in the State Lab, if technicians would go back and run HIV tests on each of their samples. It might prove us wrong, but, then again, those investigators might discover HIV was in this country before 1981.

(NOTE: When I was visiting A. G. Holley State Lab Director Dr. Roberta Lopez a few months before this book was released, she told me the samples were still banked in the Jacksonville State Lab and HIV testing had been run on them. In some of the samples, the blood was positive for HIV, so Dr. Cominole and I were right in our assumption HIV was present in the United States before 1981. I'm sorry he wasn't around to hear that from her.)

Of course, not knowing there was such a virus, Dr. Cominole and the other ward physicians would not have known to order such a blood test on those patients. And, since the virus was not known, there was no such blood test in existence before its discovery, anyway.

With the advent of AIDS, tuberculosis morbidity in the United States started to increase by 1986, despite a great decrease since the 1950s when multiple drug therapy was first initiated. This was because of the loss of immunity within the patients' bodies from the human immunodeficiency virus (HIV), especially in those who were PPD positive before they contracted HIV. By 1988, when this author left the field, this increase remained level.

This might be a good time to mention HIV is not the only risk factor that might make a person more susceptible to having a tuberculosis infection develop into tuberculosis disease. Some other risk factors include diabetes, end stage renal (kidney) disease and gastrectomy (removal of all or part of the stomach). Other factors can be severe loss of body weight (10% or more below the ideal), silicosis and prolonged corticosteroid therapy.

1980 was a sad year for all of us on the hospital staff because right after Dr. Cominole had another serious surgical procedure, Dr. Jake White had a massive CVA on duty. Jake was as beloved as Bruce by all the staff and patients. Everyone was devastated over both of them. Jake was taken home to Tampa to be with his family after the stroke. He was never able to return to Lantana. Bruce left for the VAMC in Miami.

On Memorial Day of that year, the Haitians decided to riot on my ward. I was the only RN on duty besides Charlotte who, in the absence of a supervisor, was in charge of the house. Supervisors were more often than not on the house on holidays, so it was rare the director was on duty.

I was talking to a patient in a four-bed ward when the fighting broke out, so foolishly I was trying to separate them. Of course, I called for help. When my aide came running down the hall and saw what was going on, she would not come into the room. I asked her to call the nursing director. She called, but Charlotte refused to come to the ward. I told her to tell her that I needed her now.

When the nursing director finally came, she would not come into the room, either, or try to do anything to help me diffuse the situation. She could see I was in trouble. The patients were not fighting me but I did get shoved across a bed when one, who had taken a punch, landed backwards onto me. I was unhurt but concerned one or more of the patients might be if it continued unabated.

Despite the chaos, I managed to tell her to call Charlie. Charlie Willingham had been the hospital administrator since the hospital opened its doors. A tall handsome man who'd always reminded me of William Holden, the actor, he had a commanding presence. He was a calm man with great common sense, sized up a situation immediately, and we always could count on him to act with prudence and haste. I knew he would come with the Lantana police and he did not disappointment me. No one was seriously hurt and it seemed the presence of the police officers frightened the patients into submission, so no one needed to be arrested. Subdued, they went back to their rooms.

I later learned from an interpreter, who never arrived until it was over, the riot started as a protest over the meals the hospital dietary department served. As happens in many riots, why they, then, ended up fighting each other was a mystery. He said the Haitians could not eat our food and wanted chicken and rice at every meal just as they'd had in Haiti. Our dietician was able to get a compromise from them and they settled for rice at every meal and chicken often. By their accepting this concession, there was no further cause for rioting.

In 1981, after a year in the VAMC in Miami, Dr. Cominole returned. He looked well and rested. Needless to say, everyone was happy to see him back at the hospital, where he began to work four to five hours a day.

By then, since the nutritional needs of the Haitian patients were being met, the ward was peaceful. He wanted to know everything that had gone on in his absence and was grateful, once again, to Herman Cutler for having helped to keep things running smoothly. He had expected to come back to a huge backlog of charts to go through, x-rays to look at and dictation to do, but to his delight, Dr. Cutler had taken care of all of it and there was no backlog.

The only change with Bruce's way of managing the medical end of the ward was having the patients brought to him separately for rounds rather than walking to every room as before. This, of course, was more time consuming, but we understood and worked with him on it.

The patients seemed to enjoy going into the office and speaking with him in private, rather than discussing everything in the presence of three or four other patients and staff members. As my time allowed, I stayed in there with them to answer any questions he or the patient might have of the nursing staff.

There was always another way of doing things at Lantana, if the need arose. We were a flexible group and no one seemed to mind change if there was a good reason for it. That's not to say I wasn't still a bit of a rebel, but when I was, it was usually from frustration with a situation and I came around if there was no other way.

Every now and then, one sees a humorous bumper sticker that says something like the worst day of fishing is better than the best day of working. The same could be said of working at A. G. Holley State Hospital. The worst day at Lantana was still better than the best days I'd had in the general hospitals, so it remained the best working environment for me.

Life was different for me, personally, as my daughters were growing up and many changes were taking place. That year, 1981, Karen married Steve Arner, who'd been in JIL Jive with her in high school at John I. Leonard. I had truly enjoyed my time as vice-president of our parent support group for the vocal jazz ensemble, and joining the other parents on the bus or van, to go to the jazz competitions with the students when I had the time off. It was sad to me when Karen graduated earlier that year. I was proud of her for all she'd accomplished while in school, but it meant she would be leaving for Warren Wilson College in North Carolina. She returned the same year and they were married in the summer. Suzy and I were happy Karen was back in West Palm Beach.

With Karen gone, Suzy was lonely, because we'd moved into a house at the end of Hampton Road in West Palm so they could each have a bedroom of their own again. They'd not had separate bedrooms since I sold the house west of town in 1978. It was a pretty little brick home in an older neighborhood and I really liked it. I could understand how Suzy felt, though, since we knew no one in the neighborhood.

Financially, because the house rented for more than the apartment, I had to work at a nursing home on the 4-12 shift, several nights a week. After my shift ended at A. G. Holley, I would drive straight to the nursing home. This left Suzy, now 13, alone in the house in West Palm where she had no neighbors she'd known for years, as in the old neighborhood.

On one of those nights, she called me multiple times at the nursing home because she was frightened. Apparently, drug dealing was going on not too far away and she was afraid someone would break in. She knew the rules: don't call my workplace, unless it is an emergency. She never violated this, so I knew it was serious for her. I resigned that night and never went back. I always had given at least a two-week notice, except when I learned my mother might have cancer and I left Ohio the following morning. That didn't matter; my daughter was my priority, not the second job I was leaving.

After that was resolved, and I came home every evening by four, things seemed to be better for her, until I needed to fly back to Ohio for a family funeral, and she wanted to be with her dad until I returned. I told her she could, since she never knew the family member who died. However, I didn't expect what she was soon to ask me.

The day before I was to leave, she asked if she could try living with her dad and just visiting me during holidays and when school was out in the summer. She'd already called Ron and spoken with him about it. He'd remarried and was living in Brooksville at that time. Brooksville was a nice small town and there seemed to be none of the drug problems there, as in West Palm. Suzy's dad was happy she wanted to come live with them. He and his wife both worked at the health department and were home after five every night.

Even though I'd quit my second job so I'd also be home by late afternoon for Suzy, I knew she wasn't happy living in that part of West Palm Beach. I couldn't afford to move again right away, so ignoring my feeling of disappointment, I agreed to let her go to Brooksville to live with Ron.

Suzy was happy there and enjoyed school more than she had in West Palm. Her grades improved and I thought she might want to attend high school in Brooksville when that time came. I missed her, as did Karen, but if she was happier in the school there and wanted to be with her dad, I did not believe it would be right for me to coerce her into returning to West Palm.

I was surprised, therefore, when she called several months after that, to say she wanted to come home. Of course, I was happy to have her back with me, and Karen was glad she was so close to Steve and her, again.

Suzy and I were thrilled two years later when Karen made me a grandmother of a beautiful baby girl, Lindsey, and Suzy became an aunt, a role she took seriously. I adored being that precious little girl's grandma and loved it when, without my asking her to do it, she called me Grandma Peggy when she started talking.

TWENTY-TWO

TB Control

Later, the year Suzy returned, I took a promotion within IIRS to become the D & E Nurse for District IX. I had been working on my degree in social work at FAU for a year, so it was an easy transition into the Developmental Services position. My only experience working with the developmentally disabled up until then had been a volunteer project.

The work was interesting and my office was still on the A.G. Holley State Hospital grounds. In fact, I worked directly below the room in the former nurses' residence where I had lived in 1961 before Ron and I were married. Since I sometimes took coffee and lunch breaks in the cafeteria, my contact with the hospital and its staff was never broken.

Because my work involved not only the initial evaluation of clients who came to the D & E offices, but their annual reassessments, as well, I traveled throughout the five counties of the district to do reassessments at least one day every week.

I would meet with all the disciplines involved in each client's case, re-write the habilitation plan (for each member of the D&E team) according to what the reassessment team decided, and go to the next client's home, workplace or school.

After doing a few of these, I became familiar with the language of the psychologist, social worker and education specialist, who with me, made up the D&E team. Each evaluated and wrote his and her own assessment, as did I, after we did the initial evaluation to determine eligibility, but only one member of the team attended the reassessment meetings and wrote the new habilitation plan each year, after the client was deemed eligible for developmental services. Each of us represented the entire team when we did reassessments.

That sometimes meant driving over a two hundred mile round-trip in one day, so it could be time-consuming as well as tiring, even though I was still only in my late 40s at the time. As much as I enjoyed the job and working with the team, I was ready for the next opportunity to rise further up the HRS ladder.

This opportunity presented itself in 1983, when the Palm Beach County Health Department created a new position, Nursing Supervisor of TB Control, and I was appointed to that position.

Ron had worked at the health department all his adult life after he graduated from FSU, until he retired thirty years later from his position as Director of Hernando County Health Department in Brooksville.

I knew many of the people in the Palm Beach County Health Department because he'd worked there until two years after we divorced in 1975, but this was going to be my first experience working in a health department. I have to admit I had no idea what to expect, except I'd be working in TB again, which was a positive.

I was responsible for TB Control throughout the county, so I was located at the main offices on Evernia Street in downtown West Palm Beach. The health unit acquired the present structure at 3701 Broadway in 1986 for TB and STD Control, in addition to Epidemiology, which was over both departments. The epidemiologist allowed each department to operate independently under its supervisor, without interference. STD (sexually-transmitted diseases) was under CDC and TB was under the State of Florida.

How totally different working in tuberculosis at the health department was from working at A. G. Holley. It shocked me the pace usually was as hectic as that of a general hospital. My phone never stopped ringing and it was always a call I had to take, since I was responsible for TB Control at several clinics around the county as well as our own. Capable nurses worked at each clinic and had been working chest clinic for quite a while. However, it was my responsibility to assure everything functioned well, especially in the area of compliance and sputum conversion. However, I did not supervise the out of town clinic nurse. That was the responsibility of the senior supervisor (nurse manager) at that particular health unit, whether in Belle Glade, Lake Worth or Riviera Beach.

In those early days, despite enjoying the challenge of working with patients immediately after they contracted TB, I often longed for the relaxing pace of the TB hospital and the predictable routine of my days there. Although the clinics were for the most part, routine, the rest of my week was unpredictable. I had no idea what lay ahead for me every morning when I walked through the door. The problems always seem to be there to greet me, instead of waiting until I'd shared my first cup of coffee with the TB Control nurse as we went over the day's proposed schedule. To say it was a different work experience than I'd enjoyed at the TB hospital, was a true statement.

The director of nursing, Betty Kilgore, R.N., advised me, before I accepted it, they'd created the supervisor position because the department had been disorganized for a long time. I accepted the challenge of trying to bring it all together. The state of the department wasn't the fault of the TB Control nurse, because she had more work than she could deal with, nor was it the fault of the field rep because he was only one person, too, and the territory for which he was responsible was too large.

Betty gave me carte blanche to re-organize TB Control, with her final approval on all changes, and the talented staff helped to make my job easier.

Betty had a favorite and wise saying, "If it ain't broke, don't fix it." I kept that in mind as I went through every aspect of the procedures the TB Control staff was working with and changed only those things that would make the job easier for one or more members of the staff, as well as improve patient compliance.

With these changes, it did not take us long to see a considerable increase in treatment compliance throughout the county. Other reasons for this change were CDC's assigning more field positions to us, plus the continued diligence of Pearl Kaufman, RN, now that she was free to be in the field as much as she wanted and needed to be out there. This beloved TB Control Nurse for the West Palm Beach office was superb at doing contact investigation and getting those families into TB Control for PPD testing as soon as we learned of a new case.

Besides all the responsibility I had in the office, I let her know from the beginning she could count on me to pick up the slack if she had an unusually large clinic and to help in the field with contact investigation at busy times. That's how we managed and it took the burden off her for everything entailed in working the clinic and field. I had asked that her desk be placed in my office when we moved to the Broadway facility. It made it easier for me to keep her apprised of all that was going on and vice-versa.

Tom Privett, one of the field workers (health service reps) we'd gained through the grant and assignment of the new field positions by CDC, became a godsend to us almost overnight, especially in the area of recalcitrance. His direct supervisor, Jim Cobb, who had carried the ball alone for too many years, was especially happy to have Tom in the field.

Pearl, ten or so years older than I, like me, was five feet tall and attractive with a pleasant smile for everyone. Her short, curly brown hair was never mussed, even in the wind, and she was immaculate in her Navy suit, white blouse and low Navy pumps (which served as our uniform). She always wore a scarf or tie with the white blouse.

Pearl loved to shop, especially at the high-end stores, like Lord and Taylor, and suffered no end of teasing over it. Goodnatured, she took it in stride and laughed with everyone else. Married for many decades to Bill Kaufman, a lovely man she adored, she'd held a responsible position at Massachusetts General Hospital for years before they moved to Florida. Like Herman Cutler was over Harvard, she was quite proud of that distinction, as she should have been.

At first, my coming aboard as supervisor was difficult for Pearl. I expected this; after all, for years, she'd been the only TB Control nurse in the main office. In fact, all of us at A. G. Holley, who knew her from all the years she came to the hospital to check on Palm Beach County patients, thought of her as Miss TB Control. No other nurse came to the hospital from the health departments and we had much respect for her.

After she realized how much she still was needed, the two of us enjoyed working together. We learned a great deal from each other during those years; she, about the inpatient end of tuberculosis nursing and I, the outpatient end of it.

When I was on vacation in Jamaica one year, she had a major heart attack, which frightened all of us, but she came back a few months later, almost as energetic as ever and worked another year before retiring in 1987.

Tom was just a few inches taller than Pearl and I and overweight when he first started working with us. He had dark brown, neatly groomed hair, mustache and a short, well-trimmed beard. The things that drew a person to Tom, besides his great intelligence, were his twinkly eyes and his ability to laugh and find humor in just about every situation. He was a great defuser for the stress that could pop up at any moment in the busy atmosphere of TB Control.

Within a year of his employment, Tom decided he was going to lose weight, went on a diet and trimmed to an amazingly slim figure he maintains to this day. I have never known anyone with the steely will power of Tom Privett when he makes up his mind to do something. The youngest of our staff at twenty-five, he absorbed tuberculosis knowledge rapidly. He applied this knowledge in every way possible to help us achieve better tuberculosis control.

Tom had the analytical mind of a mathematician or chemist and was a treasure to the TB clerk, Mary Melvin, and me when it came time to prepare our intermittent statistical reports, a giant headache for each of us.

The reports had to be precise and accurate because the rate of conversions from positive to negative culture status was what told Palm Beach County Health Department administration, State TB Control and CDC whether we were doing our jobs as we should be doing them. If that rate decreased rather than increased, my head was on the chopping block and we had to do better.

Fortunately, that was a rare occurrence and it was Tom who could explain the reason for it after he went back and reprocessed all the figures. And, with his diligent work in bringing recalcitrant patients back into compliance, we were able to bring the conversions to an above average or outstanding rate once again within the next six-month reporting period.

We averaged around 100 new cases of TB every year in Palm Beach County, always a surprise to people who did not work in TB. They thought the disease had been eradicated decades ago, which of course, was never true. There is always going to be tuberculosis in the United States, to some extent, unless a true vaccine, superior to the current BCG, is developed and used on a widespread basis.

Tom was promoted to field supervisor within a short period of employment, after Jim became the manager in the HIV/AIDS program. In 1988, CDC recruited Tom to head TB Control in Los Angeles; no mean feat for a thirty-year-old man who had no idea what TB Control was just four and a half years earlier. In 1990, he was assigned to head TB Control for the State of Virginia in Richmond, where he served for several years before being reassigned to LA. He has been Director of TB Control for the State of New Jersey for the past several years and is doing a superb job there, as well.

Soon after I was promoted to the TB Control Supervisor position, I revamped the medication system in such a way there was no longer any question of whether the patients picked up their medication from the pharmacy after they were seen in chest clinic. That helped with recalcitrance, as well, because it permitted the field staff to contact the patients right away, if they were non-compliant with obtaining their medication and work with them to correct their recalcitrance.

There was no reason for them not to get the medication, which was provided at no cost to them by the health unit. The health department pharmacy was close to TB Control so they had easy access to it.

None of my changes would have made a dent in the recalcitrance had it not been for Pearl Kaufman and Tom Privett. We had other capable staff members but those two were the hub of TB Control, as far as I was concerned, and I let everyone else know it. The two of them made me look good to Administration, but I was always aware I would be nothing without their work behind the scenes. They were truly the wind beneath my wings.

TWENTY-THREE

A New Epidemiologist for Palm Beach County

In 1984, the health unit appointed a new epidemiologist, Dale Tavris, MD, formerly in public health at the Medical College of Wisconsin. He also served as an epidemiologist in the U.S. Air Force. He was dedicated, organized and supportive of all our efforts in TB Control, as well as Epidemiology. Dale, unlike Tom, was tall and slender, clean-shaven, with short, dark brown hair. He had a flair for dressing well, usually in dark or medium brown suits, white short sleeved shirts and conservative ties.

He was in his early forties and highly intelligent, but he had this shy grin, which made him look as though he were embarrassed much of the time. He could be the only person in the room to know the answer to a technical question, yet if someone challenged him, that grin appeared as if that person had proven him wrong rather than the other way around.

Dale liked to start his work day, as did Pearl and I, with a cup of decaf coffee, since we'd all had our quota of caffeine before coming to work, so he usually came to our office as soon as he smelled the coffee. We all enjoyed these brief interludes before everything got too hectic, which they often did even before I could make the coffee.

All of us in TB Control, Epidemiology and STD enjoyed Dale and learned a great deal from him. His lectures, because they dealt so much in statistics, were far from exciting as he'd say often, but nonetheless, because he always furnished an abundance of handouts to all of us to supplement the lectures, we did learn the material.

A few weeks after Dale came to the health department, I had another heartbreaking death to deal with; Bruce died the end of January 1984. He'd been in the hospital for a month and I knew to expect his death, but just as with Curt eight years earlier, it made it no less difficult to experience. And, as before, my work got me through it because it was so rapidly paced. At the same time, I was taking my finals at FAU, so my stress level could not have been higher. Tom helped me a great deal during this time and I'll always be grateful to him for that.

Dale and one of our other excellent physicians, Ron Wiewora, MD, were responsible for initiating HIV/AIDS education for the health department and the community. Their joint efforts led to the development of HIV/AIDS clinics within the county health department. Ron became the director of the clinics and HIV/AIDS soon had their own building south of us on Broadway.

The last year I was at the health department, early in 1988, the year Suzy married the love of her life, Brian, whom she'd dated for seven years, I was asked to write a TB Control manual. Nursing Administration wanted it finished as soon as possible since none existed. There was no opportunity to write it between eight and five because my phone never stopped ringing, I was on the road to other TB clinics in the county or in one meeting or another. So, even though I was not paid to be at my desk after the building was locked at five and working after five was not permitted, I had no other choice.

Our office was in the part of West Palm Beach known for its prostitutes and drug dealers. More than once, I came out of the building after nine or ten at night and found the parking lot full. Not so much with cars but with men. Many drug deals went down there after hours, I'd been told, and when I saw this, it was obvious. But, no one bothered me, probably because I went straight to my car and did not bother them. By doing so, I never saw what they were doing, which was the way I wanted it.

Moreover, most of this population respected public health workers, knowing we went into the worst areas as well as the better ones, not to turn them into law enforcement, but to do contact investigation to help them and their families stay free from TB, if they'd been contacts to a TB case. Consequently, they left us alone.

Tom once walked up onto a porch in Belle Glade, forty miles west of West Palm Beach, and right into the midst of an obvious cocaine deal. They knew why he was there, so no one stopped him from going into the house to conduct his business with the patient and family. And, being the diplomatic, calm person he was, he never alluded to what was going down on the porch. They had no reason to fear he'd report them to law enforcement. Unless we saw someone being hurt, in which case we were obligated to report it, it was not our function as public health caregivers to involve ourselves with reporting to law enforcement such crimes as drug dealing without violence.

Dale was always working at his desk down the hall after five, as well, and often one or more of the STD supervisors was across from my office, but many times I was the last one left to set the alarm and leave the building.

Despite this and the fact I had to write the manual by hand, as Administration did not furnish me with a typewriter or word processor, in those days before computers occupied every desk in every office, I managed to finish the manual after several months and Dale's secretary typed it in the word processor for me.

It was a huge burden off my shoulders. Personally, I thought it was too detailed, but my nurse manager, Judy Cobb, R.N. wrote on the cover that it was "wonderful; exactly what" they "wanted," so it was worth all the nights of working after hours.

Of course, since it was work I had to do in conjunction with my job, my name never appeared anywhere in the manual. I did not mind not getting credit for it when it was published; I simply was happy to have it completed. Dale had been so supportive of the venture and never failed to offer input when I asked.

It was detailed because, before I'd started writing it, I was told they wanted it in case I ever left TB Control (Pearl had already retired). They wanted the nurse taking my place to pick up the manual and know exactly what to do and what to teach her staff to do, by following the steps I outlined in the manual.

So, it was two-fold; teaching the TB Control staff everything they needed to know about tuberculosis, plus defining the procedures to follow in Chest Clinic and TB Control. I have no idea whether it is still used today since as in everything else, especially since the advent of computers on every desk, things have changed at the health department, also.

Dale Tavris reminded me of the stereotypical absent-minded professor; always thinking so hard about something, he neglected himself. Once he, Tom and I went to a CDC and State TB Control meeting for a few days, one of many we had to attend out of Palm Beach County every year.

After our day was over, we agreed to meet in the lounge with some of the other participants in the meetings for a drink and discussion of the day's sessions after dinner.

Tom and I arrived at the appointed time but Dale was nowhere to be found. We waited a half hour or so and Tom was on the verge of going to look for him when Dale walked in. He was bleeding badly from a forehead wound. We were alarmed but I initiated first aid right away. He refused to let us call the hotel doctor or 911. After what seemed an hour of maintaining pressure on the wound with a clean white cloth napkin, it stopped bleeding, so I was able to dress it with sterile bandages someone found for us.

When Tom asked him what happened, he grinned in his coy way and said, "I was walking through the open glass double doors leading out to the lounge area, but the side I started to walk through was closed."

Tom, in his usual humorous manner, asked him, "How did the door fare, Dale?"

"I didn't make it through so I guess the glass didn't break," he answered.

Dale's wound was not serious but, like all head wounds, it bled for a long time. We suspected he had a concussion from the impact of the accident, but he flatly denied any other symptoms except a "very mild headache."

Of course, we didn't believe him, but he swore he was all right so we let the matter drop and he had no further problem. I would have preferred a physician in the ER look at it and possibly suture the wound, since I'd only applied a butterfly suture with tape, but he wanted no part of that. He was as bad as I was about going to a hospital.

In 1990, two years after I left TB Control, Dale took a position as State Epidemiologist for the state of Pennsylvania.
When I was visiting his wife, Carol, and him the next New Year's Eve, he told me another amusing story, not funny at the time, which happened right before he interviewed for the position.

He had flown to Harrisburg the night before and gotten settled into a hotel to have time to relax before the next day's interview. The next morning, bright and early, he awakened and got into the shower.

"I picked up the small bottle of hotel shampoo and when I pressed on the part of the lid that released the shampoo, a large quantity squirted directly into my eye," he told me, grinning like that was the silliest thing he could have done.

Dale wore thick-lensed glasses at the time and could barely see without them. His eye was so irritated and painful he could not even wear the glasses, so he had a difficult time driving through Harrisburg to the state offices. He could not see to read a map without his glasses, so he had to guess at the directions he'd written down earlier. Even with all that, he ended up where he needed to be at the State Building. He was embarrassed because his eye was blood red and tearing so badly that he had to keep pressing it dry with a tissue throughout the interview.

Then he was in for another harrowing ride after the interview, because even though the interviewer had been kind enough to call an ophthalmologist and gave him good directions, he still could not read the street signs. But, he made it there and was treated. It took several weeks before his eye healed.

The interviewer must have been impressed with him, despite his visual disaster, because he was hired shortly after the trip to Pennsylvania. He and his family lived in Mechanicsburg, Pennsylvania near the capitol city for several years.

He left that position to become epidemiologist and Director of Medical Products for the Federal Drug Administration in Washington, D. C. He and Carol bought a home in Silver Spring, Maryland where they've lived since leaving Pennsylvania and where Carol coordinates a large undertaking for refugees. Her organization supplies clothing to the refugees and she even prepares large dinners for them in her home. It is not unusual for Dale and her to invite refugees, singles or couples, to live with them for a time while they are seeking employment. They act as though this is something everyone else does, never taking credit for the generous people they are. Dale is still with the FDA.

TWENTY-FOUR

Intermittent Drug Therapy

While I was still at the health unit, I saw the advent of what was known as intermittent drug therapy, also known as directly observed therapy or DOT. This was placed under the supervision of our supervisor of the health service reps, Tom Privett, right after his promotion to the position.

DOT was particularly useful on those outpatients who for one reason or another could not or would not take their own medication. It proved to be quite a successful tool for all of us, but in particular for the field service rep whose responsibility it was to see that these patients came back into compliance.

As its name indicated, the medication was given on intermittent days under the watchful eyes of Tom and his staff in the field. It was first given on a daily basis so it could be determined who needed the program. After Tom determined him to be eligible, the patient was placed in the DOT program. It increased compliance among those who were recalcitrant; another insurance against drug resistance.

This was brand new to all of us, so no one, including Tom, knew how well it was going to work, if it worked at all. We were both excited and anxious as he and his rep set out the first morning to see whether the patients we had chosen were going to measure up to being in the program.

After speaking with them and determining whether they would make themselves available for him to give them the meds each day they were scheduled and extracting a promise from them that during the time they were participants in the program, they would not deviate from cooperating with his staff and him, he began the program.

To our collective relief, almost all of them stuck to the guidelines and it worked to give them medication a few days a week rather than every day. All the patients who cooperated in the effort enjoyed being in the program and it gave them the freedom to do whatever they wanted on the days Tom did not come with their medication. It prepared them for the day when they could go off it, altogether, when they were discharged from TB Control.

There were times, of course, when a few patients were not home to take the meds, but Tom was as relentless as a bloodhound. I remember one patient who hung out around the tree in the small town of Jupiter, just south of the Martin County line. This was a big banyan tree with massive roots to lean against or sit upon, where a group of men would sit and talk, smoke and drink, in its shade.

Tom called me from the field one day, not in exasperation but resignation. "I think I'll just have to start observing him at the tree because that's the only place I know I can always find him."

I laughed and said, "Hey, whatever works, Tom."

From that day forward, on the days Tom observed the patient taking the medication, the tree was the only place he could always find him. And, everyone in Jupiter did call the location the tree. Improvisation was the name of the game when you worked the field, as Tom learned early in his career about TB Control.

I continued to teach in my position as TB Control Supervisor.

Now, it was limited to educating new Palm Beach County public health nurses about tuberculosis as part of their orientation to the health department.

The health department, like A. G. Holley, did not have a high employee turnover. Most of the staff had worked there for several years and had no desire to leave until they retired from State employment. They'd found their niche long ago and were content to stay for the duration. Consequently, I was not needed to teach very often.

Tuberculosis control is a dry subject if one is not working in it and interested in it, as I suppose any subject can be in which one does not have direct involvement, knowledge or interest.

I attempted, and believe I met with some success, to make the classes enjoyable as well as informative. Without naming the patients involved, I told the small class of nurses several anecdotes about my experiences with different patient situations, both in the health department and the hospital. Some were amusing; others, not so much, but it made it real for the new nurses who were being bombarded by nurses and other personnel from each department in the large health unit.

As a tool to help them retain the material about TB Control and tuberculosis disease, I created a simple flip chart. I used it as a guide because if I got off on a story-telling venture, I could easily get off-track. In those instances, I only had to glance back at the chart to remember what I was telling them before my story took hold, and since it highlighted the most important aspects of TB Control and care of the patients, many of them wrote it down in their notebooks for future reference.

I never stood up there with a baton and pointed to every word on the chart. That would have made for an extremely boring class, but it did keep me on track and was a good visual aid for the new public health nurses who were assigned to work other areas of the health department than TB. They were not tested on any of the material in orientation, but several did jot down notes, I noticed, during my talk.

Not long after I made the chart, I was asked by my supervisor to tape a tuberculosis course for all public school employees at a public television station in West Palm Beach. The purpose of the course was to make the teachers and other employees aware of the symptoms of TB, so they could be skin tested if they or any of the students had any of these symptoms. In the past, schools did mass PPD skin testing, but it did not turn up enough positive results to be cost-effective, so the screening was stopped.

Another purpose of the course was to teach them to be aware of the procedure the health department followed if a student became a case of active TB. Those of us who worked TB Control simply called it a case. If they knew what to expect, they wouldn't panic when the health department started skin testing the school's close contacts of that student.

Those were worthy reasons for doing the course for them, and I was happy to do it since panic in the schools was an ongoing problem for both TB Control and Epidemiology when a student was found to have contracted the contagious disease.

However, against my protestations, instead of allowing me to present the material in my usual spontaneous manner, the producer insisted upon my taking a pointer and pointing to each word on my flip chart as I read to the camera.

That presented a problem for me. The thought of doing it like that was embarrassing and I resisted it. I explained that I spoke extemporaneously because I knew the material so well, but all the material on each page of the flip chart would be covered. I contended it would be less stilted if I simply spoke to the camera, as I did when teaching students in my classes. I lost that argument. Although the producer did not know anything about the subject matter, she believed she knew what was best and my supervisor who'd gone with me, agreed. (She, too, knew very little about TB, since school immunization was her area of expertise, not tuberculosis.)

Granted it was the producer's studio and she was the boss. I had done two TV shows before, one an hour interview when I was acting coordinator of the sexual assault assistance program and the other when I was on a panel with other nurses speaking to the difficulties nurses faced in the general hospital setting. However, there was no problem with the producers of either of these programs.

Exasperated, but trying not to show it, I suggested having the flip chart in front of me but hidden by the camera would make it look more spontaneous to the employees who were trying to learn from watching it, but I did not win that argument, either.

At one point, I thought I was winning her over, but by then, my supervisor was becoming irritated with my delaying the start of the taping, and asked me to do it as the producer wished. So, there I stood, pointer in hand, reading verbatim from my words on the flip chart, as I pointed to them. I felt like I was a five year old in kindergarten, standing up there saying everything I was told to say.

I hoped those who had to attend the course in the schools derived some benefit from it, regardless of how foolish and stilted I believed it made me appear on camera, not that I wanted to see the video afterward. I just wanted out of the studio and away from the embarrassing situation. I was told several years later it was still used in the public school system.

It was not all work and no play at the health department, but fun times were few and far between because of the fast-paced nature of the job and the never-ceasing telephone calls into the office.

At A. G. Holley, each year, every employee of every ward in the hospital would prepare a dish to bring to the Christmas party, held at the lunch hour. All the large ward kitchens would be brimming to over-flowing with delicious hot and cold entrees, vegetable dishes, desserts, coffee and other drinks.

Every department in the hospital participated. It was a day of relaxation for each employee, so we did not feel rushed as we visited around the hospital, sampling each other's delectable dishes on the different wards and enjoying the day, which seemed like a bonus day off to us.

Since most of the patients, who were able, went home for the week, there was very little work to do, so it was a nice social occasion for staff and administration to commingle and enjoy themselves and each other. Those patients who never left the hospital were given plates of the homemade food and enjoyed being a part of the party.

Missing that, I talked to some of the other nurses and other staff at the health unit and we decided to have the same thing in the large auditorium where pediatric and TB clinics were held when TB Control was still on Evernia Street.

As at the hospital, everyone brought a dish or two and we had loads of food. After the fast pace of the health department on any given day, that was one of the most relaxing days we ever had while I was working there. Even the phones were quieter than usual, so all the supervisors were able to enjoy the day with everyone else, without having to rush back to their desks right after filling their plates.

Another Christmas, while we were still in the Evernia office, they could not get anyone to dress as Santa, ride on the fire truck and then be dropped off at the Evernia Street lobby where the children of the pediatric clinics waited to sit on Santa's lap.

Not wanting the children to be disappointed, I said I would do it. The men thought that was ridiculous because I was so short and slender, but like I told them, I would not have to do it if one of them volunteered. This did not faze them and none volunteered.

Now, remember, I was five feet tall and weighed one hundred and four pounds, so even in a Santa costume, padding, and beard, I'm afraid I did not make the best Santa the world has ever seen. I slipped out of the building and climbed up into the front seat of the fire engine while the pediatric staff members were gathering the children in the lobby to wait for Santa.

At first, when we drove up with the alarms sounding and the bells ringing, the children were all excited to see Santa step down from the fire truck well, helped down from the it so 'he' wouldn't break his neck when 'he' fell to the sidewalk.

That accomplished, I walked in with a big "Ho, Ho, Ho" and took my seat in Santa's large chair in the lobby. The children were lined up and quiet as mice while each waited his turn to sit on Santa's lap.

While I was sitting there, trying to make my voice as deep as possible with the Ho, Ho, Hos, the first little girl came up and sat on my lap. I asked her if she'd been a good little girl and she said, "Yes." I assured her Santa would come to see her the next night on Christmas Eve and asked what she'd like Santa to bring her.

All of a sudden, after I asked this, her lips puckered up and she turned around to locate her mother. When she saw her, she said, in a loud but tearful voice everyone on the first floor could hear, "He's not Santa. He's a girl!" and started to cry.

Oh dear, I was busted. She ran from my lap and I signaled for the next child to come up, but nothing doing. The first little girl had set the tone for the rest of the disappointed children as well.

The little boy I was motioning to shook his head. Another behind him did the same. Finally, I asked, "Would anyone like to come up to talk with Santa?"

Like robots in synchronized motion, each child looked at his or her mother and with a shake of the head, said a resounding "No!" The mothers looked at me with helpless expressions. I shrugged and smiled at them since there wasn't anything anyone could do about it.

None of them wanted any part of that girl Santa, so my reign was short-lived. I must say, though, I enjoyed the ride on the fire truck immensely, so thank you, West Palm Beach Fire Department.

And Then There Was One

Peg's graduation from FAU, 1985.
From left: Karen, with Peg's first grandchild Lindsey;
mother Norma; Peg; Suzy.

A. G. Holley State Hospital

TWENTY-FIVE

From 500 to 50 Bed Hospital

As TB Control Supervisor, it was also my responsibility to admit Palm Beach County patients to A.G. Holley State TB Hospital, if they were court-committed. When the clinic physician gave the order, I initiated the proceedings with the judge's secretary to have the non-compliant or combative patient court-committed to the hospital's locked unit. She, in turn, got the judge's signature on the commitment papers.

Then, as today, if TB patients were not compliant with their treatment, they could not remain out in the community.

One of two things is going to happen to TB patients if they don't comply with treatment: they are going to become a public health threat because their sputum status will become positive again, or they are going to become resistant to the TB medications and that will make it more difficult for them to get well. Since the general hospitals cannot accommodate these patients, it is essential there is a place to put them while they are noncompliant or combative, for the sake of the public health.Fortunately, that place still exists: A. G. Holley TB Hospital.

The locked unit of the hospital, which is the east end of A. G. Holley, used to be the east solarium for all the patients in the ward east of the elevator on the 4th floor. It was the logical place to put the committed patients; otherwise, the ward would have had to be divided in two to accommodate them.

I came back often to attend Conference and make rounds on our Palm Beach County committed patients and the patients who were sicker and voluntarily agreed to hospitalization.

During those intervening years, in addition to Dr. Cominole, Dr. Petjovik and Personnel Director Cecil Teague had died, leaving tremendous gaps to fill. Dr. Jorge` Manas stepped in to fill Dr. Petjovik's position as Medical Director. Drs. Susan Sekely and Jean Tabuteau came on staff and Dr. Cutler retired.

Jean was a godsend because, being Haitian, he could communicate with the ever-growing Haitian population in the hospital. He was a thoughtful, quiet and caring doctor and well liked by all his patients, not just the Haitians.

Susan, petite and energetic, was a sweet and caring physician, as well. The patients liked her, too, although with her thick European accent, many had difficulty understanding her. Realizing this, she would slow down and try to speak as distinctly as possible when she realized they were having difficulty. She was never impatient toward them because of this, from what I observed when I was there.

By 1987, Karen was a single mom to Lindsey. (Two years later, she married an old friend, Stephen Pain, bringing two more daughters, Samantha and Elizabeth, into the family for all of us to love. In 1992, they became the parents of my fourth granddaughter, Emily, with whom all three big sisters, and the rest of us, were thrilled.)

That same year, 1987, A. G. Holley's director of nursing services, as the position was called then, retired after ten years, and as required by HRS, the position was advertised outside the hospital, as well as within.

Dr. Espino, Pearl, who had retired by that time, and Tom, who was hoping to have a permanent CDC position out of Florida in the near future, and therefore, would be leaving our health unit, persuaded me to apply for the position.

Marge Thompson, who formally applied even though she was the acting director, also called to encourage me to apply. With their urging, I did apply and waited a couple weeks before I got the call to interview.

I had a very good interview with Dr. Manas. We discussed ideas I had thought about for years, some as long as when I last worked there. I told him about the flex hours I had worked when JFK first opened. He was familiar with that concept since he'd worked the ER at JFK at times. I told him how relaxed that made me, both at home and work, knowing I could choose when to work as long as there was enough coverage on the unit. I thought flex hours for the TB nursing staff would be nice for those with children, even if they worked full time, since they could split their shift to be home when the children came home from school, get their dinner and come back to finish their other four hours of the shift. He said he liked that idea, also.

Another thing I mentioned I'd like to do if I were chosen for the position, would be to sit down with the nursing assistants to see which of them would be interested in special work projects that would be their own, that they could do at their leisure to make working more stimulating during those times when the patients were resting. I told him it would be their choice if they wanted to do such a thing, since many of them enjoyed the idle periods in the afternoons and did not like change. And, they all worked hard, so there was nothing wrong with that.

For instance, I was thinking, one of them could have the exclusive job of making sure all the nurses had their care plans up to date, so the director of nursing would not have to be concerned about that when JACHO came to inspect. That nursing assistant could have a book where she checked each nurse off when she updated her care plan, since sometimes the nurses got busy and forgot to update them. I know I did more than once and had to be reminded. There were several little jobs like that a nursing assistant, if she were ambitious and wanted more responsibility, could do for the director of nursing or anyone else if she chose to do it. It could also be an incentive for merit raises, if the hospital ever went back to giving them.

I told him, with a smile, that having worked there for so long over the years and understanding the nursing staff, if I were given the position, "I wouldn't be interested in rocking the boat just for the sake of saying here I am, now watch what I can do." He laughed, but said it was nice I was interested in giving the staff choices, not in mandating change. He said he appreciated that because he knew from hearing the nurses and aides talk when he was a ward doctor, how a staff could get roiled up when someone came in and just started changing things without any input from them.

I said, "That's right." And, I meant it. There was nothing worse for the morale of a nursing staff, including the nursing assistants and orderlies, than for a new director of nursing to come in and change everything around just because she could. Like Marge, I'd had the lower positions before I was put into supervision as a young nurse, so I knew how that felt. I also knew how it felt to be asked my opinion and to be offered a different way, if I chose to take it, rather than having to make changes for the sake of making them.

Had it not been for my feelings for Marge and my knowledge she had been doing the job so well for ten years, nothing would have made me happier than to be applying for and possibly coming back as the director of the nursing staff I still considered family.

However, a few days later, after giving much thought to the matter, and even losing sleep over it, I called Dr. Manas and asked him to remove my name from the list of candidates. I told him what he already knew, had he been at liberty to admit it to me then; no one deserved that position as much as Marge Thompson did, and I believed he would be well served to appoint her to the position so she could continue the work she started. After all, as I pointed out, she'd been doing the job for ten years so who was better qualified? Certainly not I, even if I did have a few positive ideas.

He, of course had first-hand knowledge of that, because it was Marge to whom he'd turned for assistance after he, without advance preparation upon Dr. Petjovik's death, was thrust into the position of Medical Director.

As was the only correct and logical action to take, Marge Thompson, finally and officially, was appointed to the position of Director of Nursing Services and Liz Phillips was given the post of Assistant Director.

No two nurses ever worked harder to assure a hospital ran smoothly and by the book. They seldom, if ever, worked an eight-hour shift. If they left the hospital within ten hours, it was rare. As regular as clockwork, they updated all the nursing manuals, assured themselves all the nurses' care plans were up to date and all the nurses were current with their in-service education course requirement. Nurses still had to earn 24 CEUs within a two-year period. They were prompt to correct any JACHO deficiencies and assured they would never recur as long as they were Nursing Administration.

By then the State had made more drastic cuts in staff positions, and Marge made numerous trips to Tallahassee to persuade the legislature to allocate more funds for the hospital so she could provide more adequate staffing. Most of her pleas fell on deaf ears but once in a while she won a slight concession and could hire another nurse or two.

One day as I made rounds on our Palm Beach County patients throughout the hospital, Marge called me in for a talk, which was not unusual since we always tried to catch up while I was making rounds. This time she had something definite on her mind. She said, "You know, Peg, Liz is talking about retiring in two years and I hope you'll apply for her position."

"I appreciate your asking, Marge," I told her, "and I'd love to work with you again, but I have to be honest with you about this. I'm thinking of leaving HRS within the next year or two to do self-contracting, so I don't think you should count on me."

I had been with the State of Florida in tuberculosis work and other positions for over two decades throughout the past thirty years and there were other things I wanted to do, like work for another cruiseship once in a while.

I was thinking, also, of contracting with several home health agencies; anything that would allow me to be in control, for once, of when and how often I worked before I was old enough to retire from nursing, which wouldn't be for twelve more years, at the earliest. Most, likely, I'd be working until I was sixty-five which was fourteen more years.

Before I got my social work degree at the age of fifty, I was asked to come in with two therapist friends in Deerfield Beach, handling all their new clients. They told me that until I sat for my boards, I could work under one of their licenses and make the same $80 an hour they did. Of course, this was contingent upon my going to school for eleven more months to earn the master's in social work. What a wonderful opportunity this presented. Eighty dollars an hour was a substantial increase over the twenty-something I made as a nurse, so I told them I would do it after I got the master's, since my ultimate goal when I began the social work program was to go into private practice. They told me I could fulfill my internship during the master's program in the office, as well. I appreciated being offered something like that, plus a ready-made internship without having to search for a facility in which to do it.

Unfortunately, by the time graduation rolled around I was too burnt-out from the past several years of full-time work and school, plus the death of a loved one during my senior year, and made the decision to stop with the bachelor's degree. As a result I never formally worked as a social worker, because, as with the opportunity to enter law enforcement nine years before, the salary simply was too low for bachelor degree social workers compared to what I could make in any field of nursing. Social workers with just bachelor degrees are not legally qualified to have a private practice as a therapist.

For a few years, I regretted my decision to stop with the BSW, especially since it would have meant just eleven more months of school, and I had five years in which to commence the program from the time I earned the bachelor degree in 1985. Even if I had waited until 1990 to begin the program and went into practice with my friends a year later, I could have built a nice practice for ten to twelve years, earning a sizable nest egg to add to my state pension and Social Security benefits.

To stop short of the MSW seemed foolish to everyone at the time, and no more so than to me after it was too late, since I'd sacrificed so much to earn the BSW for the sole purpose of qualifying for the master's program.

I never was able to earn, as a seasoned RN, even half the pay per hour as I could have as a private therapist, something I know I would have enjoyed doing. My friends, Ed and Dick, had a large practice, so I knew I would have had enough clients by taking all the new ones who came for help, to sustain a better lifestyle for myself than I had as a nurse with the smaller pay. It wouldn't have helped Karen, as she had been married for several years by then, but Suzy might have had a better life with me for a year or two before she married. I would have had a less stressful one with more income, and no doubt would not have worked until I was almost 66.

However, I have always had a personal philosophy that told me I had to walk the road I walked in order to get to where I was supposed to be at different times in my life, although at the time I walked some of those roads, I could not understand why.

As the years went by, I reconciled with my decision to stop with the BSW, since that road took me in so many positive directions in the ensuing years. I now have many wonderful friends I'd have missed, otherwise, and began a personally rewarding career in writing, in which I'd only dabbled prior to retiring from nursing. At this late date, I don't expect to make nor have I made a great deal of money from my writing, but it is rewarding to me, so from that aspect, it is worth it. The stories in my heart waited a very long time to come out, so it was time.

Knowing I was thinking of leaving state employment, a former health department quality control nurse, Donna Lyken, who had her own home health agency, had already approached me about doing some contracting at the beautiful new Hospice of Palm Beach County inpatient center, opening within the next several months.

This, cruiseship nursing and home health nursing were just a few of several options I would be free to pursue (and did) if I didn't tie myself down to another full-time position with the State of Florida, as Marge was suggesting I do.

She asked me to please consider it, before I made the decision to leave state service. She said, "I'm so worn out. I don't know why, but I'm just so tired all the time, I can hardly keep going. And, I don't want to work more than five more years. I know you love this place as much as I do, and I'd really like to leave, knowing you were already on board to step into my shoes."

This was alarming to me because Marge was several years younger than I. Granted, she'd been working terribly hard but we all worked hard. No, it seemed to me at that moment, the amount of work she was doing could not be the entire reason for her fatigue.

"Okay, I promise I'll give it some thought, but I doubt I'll change my mind. Will you do something for me, also?"

"If I can, Peg. What is it?"

"Will you see a doctor to find out if it's anything more than fatigue?"

Marge just smiled at me. After a few anxious moments in which I wondered whether she knew something she was not telling me, she said, "Okay, I'll see the doctor if things ever slow down enough for me to make an appointment."

"I get the feeling you already know something's wrong."

"No, honestly, I don't. I'm sure I'm just over-doing too often and just need a real good rest," she said with the smile still on her lips.

It was easy to see she was being dismissive about it, but it frightened me to think she had reason to believe there was something seriously wrong with her. I let it go and asked no more questions. The conversation with her left me with an ominous feeling as I left the hospital that afternoon; a feeling I couldn't shake for weeks to come.

As planned, I left HRS the following year, in November 1988. Liz retired in January 1991 and Marge died of leukemia in October 1992, exactly five years after our conversation. Liz told me the diagnosis had been a shock to Marge; she really had not believed she was ill.

Marge Thompson's coming to work there as a young nurses aide all those years before was, without a doubt, the best thing that ever happened to Southeast Florida State Tuberculosis Hospital. Those of us who knew her for over three decades loved her and still miss her. Sometimes, as with Maggie Bunner and my mother, Norma Gardner, I would love to see Marge's face, again, and hear her infectious laughter.

My brother Larry died in January 2009, on his 75th birthday. He'd had cardiac problems and emphysema for a very long time and told me during our last phone conversation, "Sis, I'm just plain worn out. This is no way to live." His was my first sibling death, and it left me shaken, despite knowing his suffering was over. Since I'm now the oldest in the family, I hope it will be my last.

Death cannot be avoided. It comes to all of us. It seems the older I become, though, the less I seem able to accept loss, recent or past. Perhaps I'm feeling my own mortality creeping up on me already at 74? I really don't know the answer to that. I do know I'm going into this old age kicking and screaming, because I'm not ready to be in it, yet. I like to believe I'll be around for at least three more decades, as I still have much to do. However, to paraphrase something said by one of my all-time favorite television news anchors, John Chancellor, after he learned he had terminal cancer: "If you want to make God laugh, tell him your plans." So, we'll see whether I'll be around to finish all those other things I've planned or already started or if God's already laughing.

Today, few of the original hospital family are still there and A.G. Holley State Tuberculosis Hospital, although it is relegated to 50 beds instead of the original 500, is the last remaining freestanding tuberculosis hospital in the United States.

Dr. David Ashkin, M.D. has been the Medical Director of A.G. Holley State Tuberculosis Hospital for the past eighteen years.

Pearl and I were taken aback when we first saw Dave at a TB meeting right after he became the Medical Director. We'd both left TB Control by then and still enjoyed coming back to take courses from our CDC friends, an easy way to earn continuing education credits since we already knew the material.

David Ashkin, from New York, was young, had long curly black hair and seemed perfectly suited to a big city hospital in New York City. In fact, we thought he could have played one on television with his extraordinary good looks. But, a tuberculosis hospital in Palm Beach County? We truly wondered what this man was doing here in such a position.

It did not take long to learn the answer to that question. From the beginning of his tenure, Dr. Ashkin demonstrated that same dedicated, caring devotion that drove his predecessors. He did, and still does, everything in his power to see his hospitalized patients cured and discharged from tuberculosis treatment, so they might have the opportunity to live the rest of their lives in a productive way and in optimal health.

He has said that the miracles he and his staff see happening to their patients, every day, give them the courage to go on despite all obstacles, just as it gave us the courage to do so all those years ago.

In memoriam
Marjorie Knowles Thompson, RN

Postscript

It is with sadness and dismay that I must add this post script: On July 2, 2012, six months prior to its scheduled closing, which we hoped would not occur, because of an order by Florida Governor Rick Scott that A. G. Holley be shuttered and its patients, except for those with multi-drug resistant strains of tuberculosis, be transported back to their home counties to be treated as outpatients by their private doctors and the local health department chest clinics, this grand old hospital closed its doors, and its 138 dedicated employees were suddenly without jobs. Shands Medical Center in Jacksonville and Jackson Memorial Hospital in Miami were the recipients of the patients who could not be released to outpatient care. Let us hope that these facilities have the proper negative pressure rooms and staff to adequately care for these patients who are a serious danger to the public health, otherwise.

What makes this sudden closing more perplexing is that it comes on the heels of what CDC in Jacksonville calls the worst tuberculosis outbreak in 20 years. The outbreak is linked to 100 new illnesses and 13 deaths within the past two years involving patients from Jacksonville's homeless shelters and food banks, an outpatient mental health clinic and area jails, and over 2000 contacts, some of whom might be close contacts who might yet become ill with tuberculosis disease.

Acknowledgements

Bill Belisle, Bert Russell and Mac Anders, CDC tuberculosis control specialists, for traveling throughout the state of Florida, every year, to share their expertise with the rest of us in TB Control, and update our knowledge base with advancements in the field, and whose historical perspectives and other course materials were invaluable and provided much of the material in the historical perspective of this book.

Margaret Swinford, Bethesda Hospital Alumni Association, in Cincinnati, for her timely updates on the status of our training school hospital and student nurses residence, for sending material on the history of the original Bethesda Hospital, and for contacting just the right person to find my graduation class portrait.

Sister Patricia McQuinn, of the order of Sisters of Charity, in Cincinnati, who searched the archives until she found the portrait of my class of 1958, when my original could not be used.

Esteemed SeaStory Press Publisher Sheri Lohr, who works so hard, every day, to assure her authors' books excel in quality.

Fellow Key West expatriate and writer, Professor Dan DiStasio, never too busy to answer my SOS e-mails and phone calls, to share his expertise, when I question my grammar or word choices.

Key West writer and author Joanna Schmida, my voice of reason and unwavering cheerleader throughout this lengthy project.

A.G. Holley State TB Hospital's Medical Director David Ashkin, M.D., for writing the Foreword and encouraging me to write the book, and Tim Smart, IT, for sending the perfect photograph of the hospital for the book cover.

I am indebted to all of you.

Peggy Butler

There are so many more people who deserve to be recognized as having been a part of the history of A. G. Holley State Tuberculosis Hospital in Lantana, Florida, from the time its doors first opened in 1950, than just the few mentioned in this brief portrait of the hospital. Some of these, living and deceased, are listed below and no one is intentionally omitted from this listing, which spans sixty years.

Please forgive the lapse of memory in those instances of omission, as each and every one who worked there contributed to making the hospital the unique institution it has always been.

I realize some of those listed below might have been promoted to other positions since I was affiliated with the hospital. And others might have been hired of whom I have no knowledge. They are no less important, as tuberculosis control is still not at the top of the list as far as today's nurses, other professionals and lay medical workers are concerned. Just to be in the field of tuberculosis control remains commendable.

The names of the following are listed in no particular order nor are the years of their service noted, for that was not what was important. Whether they are living or deceased is not noted here. Their service and dedication were unique. Most of them who are deceased, died while still employed by the hospital, or shortly after leaving the hospital, after serving it for decades.

Just reading the completed list brings back a wealth of memories and tears to this writer's eyes, for with every name, I can retrieve a memory. Some bring smiles while others bring sadness. I can recall where I was when each memory or memories occurred:

Martha Neebe, respiratory therapist
Mary Bean, RN
Jim Bean, maintenance
Midge Tietbohl, LPN
Glenda Rich, LPN
Ora Sokel, PBX operator
Carol Wavrick, PBX operator
Ginny Wimer, PBX operator
Irene Mariz, admitting clerk
Susan (Cricket) Calkins, LPN
Ila Moore, lab secretary
Martha Chick, lab technician
Estelle Brown, lab technician
Cody Allen, administrative secretary
Judy Mitchell, ward secretary
Lulu Scippio, ward secretary
Diane Trotter, LPN
Juanita Hickock, LPN
Marian Best, LPN
June Best, nursing assistant
Susie Brannon, nursing assistant
Elizabeth Jones, nursing assistant

And Then There Was One

Wilber Jean Sims, O.R. technician
John Bowery, maintenance
Jim McBride, maintenance
Lily Mae Wright, nursing assistant
Mazell Young, housekeeping
Ella Karginian, RN supervisor
Josephine Baniewicz, RN
Tina Dirazio, LPN
Brina Susie Lovelace, nursing assistant
Lee LaFramboise, RN
Virginia Edlebeck, RN
Sonja Benson, respiratory therapist
Thelma Bemis, administrative secretary
Daisy Morgan, nursing assistant
Lou O'Donnell, RN supervisor
Carolyn Jorgensen Weir, medical records
Mary Cook, microbiologist
Cynthia Albritton, admission clerk
Carrie Waters, nursing assistant
Ethel White, nursing assistant
Evelyn Smith, RN supervisor
Flo Gregor, LPN
Andrea Sweek, medical records
Velma Tee Miller, nursing assistant
Mary Madeiros, nursing assistant
Bertha Burch, nursing assistant
Bernice Berkenfield, administrative secretary
Amy Cray, RN
Gabrielle DeVries, administrative secretary
Joyce Westfall, x-ray technician
Agnes Naughton, RN nursing director
Annette Jenson, RN assistant nursing director
Annie Ruth Ellis, nursing assistant

Lynn Shurger, admitting office
Marie Scott, ward secretary
Caroline Furness, RN nursing director
Mary Nessein, LPN
Mary Shurger, RN
Eloise Hofstra, LPN
Diane Glinton, nursing assistant
MaeDee Bennett, RN
Florida Weaver, RN
Mel Foley, RN supervisor
Bob Gifford, x-ray department director
Efram Gottlieb, x-ray technician
Lillian Merrill, x-ray technician
Mary Wells, LPN
Dorothy Thompson, RN
Lillian Christiansen, RN Eleanor Oneta, LPN
Margaret Whidden, RN supervisor
Michael Holland, security
Doe Ballard, nursing assistant
Catherine Jackson, nursing assistant
Leona Staires, RN
Mary Phillips, nursing assistant
Sherry Teague, housekeeping
Mary Colson, nursing assistant
Fay Hillberry, PBX operator
Stan Gramail, pharmacist
Carol Brown, nursing assistant
Moira Mitchell, RN
Shirley Bennett, social services director
Betty Jaseicki, nursing assistant
Ross Coles, social services director
Leona Voytek, social services Secretary
Larry Hulme, pharmacist
Ginny Quelette, RN
Stacia Egbert, RN
Lorrice Adolphson, RN
Stan Blockowicz, maintenance
Janet Cotton, nursing assistant
Robert Augenfeld, MD
Roscoe Thorne, MD

And Then There Was One

Sandy Santiago, personnel director
Clyde Jordan, nursing assistant
George Reis, MD
Charlotte DeLiso, nursing assistant
Elizabeth Jenkins, nursing assistant
Will Ande, MD
Frank O'Bare, maintenance
Mary DuPuis, nursing assistant
Charlie Bloom, plumber
Mike Holland, food service
Carl Neubronner, stores
Harry Vandren, carpenter
Dorothy Shrimp, business office
Tom Lindros, business office
Elijah and Eleanor Lipschutz, volunteers
Kitty Oltar, volunteer
Dave Oscarson, purchasing
Robert Bugbee, purchasing
Beverly Brinson, purchasing
Dolores Bradley, purchasing
Wendy Kesty, RD dietary department director
Alberta Benton, food service
Craig Marshall, business office
David Hall, property administrator
Herb Comnick, housekeeping director
Janet Ballard, ward secretary
Dorothy Lobel, purchasing
Ernestine Washington, nursing assistant
Jacqueline Rhodes, RN
Marie Kaiser, RN
Janice McDonald, housekeeping
B. J. Hollis, nursing assistant
Conner Conners, administrative secretary
Ruth Behrman, administrator

Terry Mehan, administrative secretary
Ella Watkins, nursing assistant
Dolores Washington, nursing assistant
Gerald Dalton, storeroom
Susanne Hardy, RN
Tom Atkinson, business office
Gail Johnson, RN
Phyllis Woodley, nursing assistant
Sandra Murphy, LPN
Barbara and Ronnie Rowell, storeroom
Rosa Cobb, lab technician
Dr. Lorraine Carson, lab director
Helen Millines, nursing assistant
Doris Haynes, LPN
Irene Johns, RN supervisor
Beatrice Johns, RN
Karen Harris, RN supervisor
Velma Hamilton, RN
Annie Ruth Ellis, nursing assistant
Marie Scott, ward secretary
Emily Bennett, RN
Catherine Jackson, nursing assistant
Moira Mitchell, RN
Eileen Violette, RN
Anna Rodocker, LPN
Clyde Jordan, nursing assistant
Corinne Green, social services director
Ken Buscemi, food service
Doris Haynes, LPN
Anne Gould, special services secretary
Dottie O'Keefe, occupational therapist
Tim Smart, IT
Maria Gomez, Medical Services Coordinator

Special thanks to: (posthumously) Lee Perry, (posthumously) Cricket Caulkins, Maurine Butler, and (posthumously) Ron Butler for their willing assistance in helping me to recall those very important persons.

Lee, Tom Privett and Dale Tavris read the manuscript in one of its earliest drafts in order to help me assure its accurate content, and Lee generously re-waded through the final draft for the same reason. For that, they have my utmost gratitude.

Dale's editing style added to the depth of the writing and I know it made it an easier book to read than had I not followed his advice. Thank you for that, Dale.

Another big thanks to Andy (Andrews) Knepper for helping to jog my memory about some of the things I'd forgotten about our days in nursing school.

I hope, with our collective recollections, the story is as accurate as is possible after decades of history and memories.

Also I want to express my heartfelt gratitude to my publisher, Shirrel Rhoades, Chuck Newman, associate publisher, and the members of their team at New Atlantean Library and www.absolutelyamazingebooks, for all their efforts in producing the 2nd edition of *And There Was One*.

Glossary

Appendectomy – The surgical removal of the appendix, a small saclike appendage of the large intestine, for which there is no known purpose.

[To] bag – To place an object or objects into a special bag for disposal in a certain manner; i.e. to bag an amputated body part, bloody dressings, etc.

Blalock operation – This surgical procedure repairs Tetrology of Fallot.

Bleeding-out – hemorrhaging profusely, this almost always culminates in death.

Bronchoscopy – A procedure performed by inserting a tube (bronchoscope) down the throat passage and into the bronchial tubes (which connect to the lungs) to determine the presence of disease by visualizing it and/or withdrawing a sample of fluid or tissue upon which laboratory tests are performed to diagnose the presence of disease.

Catatonic – A condition, marked by stupor and rigid muscles, in which the person is unresponsive to his surroundings.

Cavity – A hole. In TB, if the disease isn't detected and treated very early, it can advance to the extent that it causes a tear or hole to develop in the affected lung.

CDC – Centers for Disease Control in Atlanta, Georgia

Cholecystectomy – The surgical removal of the gallbladder, a membranous sac attached to the liver in which excess gall (bile) is stored.

Circulating nurse – nurse responsible for running errands for scrub nurse and/or surgeon, who brings extra supplies, instruments, etc. to the sterile field as needed but is not, herself, sterile. She always wears a mask when in the OR. She is as critical to the success of the surgery as is the rest of the surgical team, because time is of the essence for her to get these items to the operating table.

Dendritic cells – Blood cells that function in small numbers and are like law enforcement detectives in the blood stream. They ID foreign substances like cancer or tuberculosis, process this information about the substance and then activate the swat team, or immune response, by bringing it to the attention of the rest of the immune system (mostly T-lymphocyte cells, which are a type of white blood cell). This is demonstrated most commonly by high fever in one who is ill with this substance or disease.

District IX – A section of the state of Florida consisting of five counties: Palm Beach, Martin, St. Lucie, Indian River and Okeechobee, located on the east coast of Florida. 1964-1991.

Droplet nuclei – Microscopic airborne particles of sputum coughed by the TB patient, which can carry the tubercle bacilli (TB germs/MTB) to the alveoli (air sacs of the lungs) of other persons who are susceptible to tuberculosis.

EST – electroshock therapy or electroshock treatment given to patients in an attempt to erase or dim those memories from their minds which were responsible for their mental illness, by the use of electricity. Its use is limited today with the advent of modern drug therapy.

Extrapulmonary tuberculosis – This term refers to any tuberculosis outside the lungs, i.e., tuberculosis of the kidneys, lymph nodes and pleural sacs. Only about fifteen percent of reported cases of TB in the United States each year are extrapulmonary.

Gastric washings – A procedure used if a sputum specimen cannot be otherwise obtained, or what was obtained was inadequate to culture. This involves inserting a tube into the stomach to recover bacilli that have been coughed up, but swallowed.

Hepatitis – inflammation of the liver

Herniorraphy – The surgical repair of a hernia or

protrusion (bulging) of all or part of an organ through a tear in the wall of the surrounding structure.

Induration – Swelling which surrounds the site of injection of old tuberculin.

Lobe – Sections. Each lung has upper and lower lobes

Lobectomy – Removal of a lobe of the lung.

Mayo – Lightweight metal table used in the operating room and examination room to place sterile field; i.e. sterile towel on which sterile instruments, sutures, sponges, etc. are placed for use during surgical procedures. There is also an unsterile field (for used instruments and supplies) on another Mayo.

Miliary tuberculosis – In this type of TB, great numbers of the tubercle bacilli are disseminated by means of the bloodstream to several areas of the body.

Nightingale Pledge – Florence Nightingale was regarded as the founder of modern nursing. The pledge bearing her name engenders all the qualities a nurse aspires to as she begins her nursing career.

Pneumonectomy – The surgical removal of a lung.

Pneumothoracotomy – The surgical removal of a lung and ribs.

Positive PPD – A specific measurement of induration (swelling); 5mm or more in a close contact to a TB patient, those who are immunosuppressed and those with abnormal chest x-ray indicative of TB, or 10mm or more in others. The swelling remains 48-72 hours after having received the PPD skin test and indicates that the person has been exposed to the TB germ and was infected recently or at some other time in his life. A diagnosis of TB disease cannot be made on the basis of a positive PPD, alone.

Positive TB sputum culture – A smear from a sputum sample, which when grown in a media is identified as mycobacterium tuberculosis.

Positive TB sputum smear – A sample of sputum which when washed with an acid solution, shows bacteria, which have retained dyes. These acid-fast bacteria (AFB) are usually mycobacteria. Although a presumptive diagnosis of mycobacterium TB is frequently made on the basis of this positive smear, the definitive diagnosis cannot be made without a positive culture.

PPD test – A test administered by injecting 0.1 ml of 5 tuberculin units of purified protein derivative (old tuberculin) just under the skin (intradermally) usually on the inner forearm to determine the presence of TB infection. Also known as Mantoux test. It is not a vaccine.

Psychotic – Suffering from psychosis, a mental disorder in which the personality is seriously disorganized and contact with reality is impaired.

Recalcitrant – Refusing to comply with treatment.

Receiving – Admission ward; the ward where newly admitted patients were brought for initial processing, assessment and treatment.

Resuscitate – Bring back to life by a process that forces air (oxygen) into the lungs and compression or shock to the heart to cause it to re-start to pump and circulate the oxygenated blood. The most recent approved method of resuscitation is to skip mouth to mouth breathing (forcing air into the lungs) and immediately begin chest compression until the patient's breathing and heartbeat return, or one is relieved by medical personnel such as paramedics, nurses or physicians.

Scrub nurse – nurse responsible for anticipating the surgeon's needs, who hands the surgeon the correct instruments used to perform the operation, who maintains a sterile field on the Mayo, who assists with whatever the surgeon needs him or her to do such as holding a retractor, who maintains accurate sponge count, etc. This nurse is sterile; that is, she scrubs her arms and hands prior to surgery and wears sterile gloves, cap, mask and gown throughout the surgery.

Service— departments or units in a hospital, i.e. medical, surgical, urology, surgery, orthopedics, obstetrics, emergency room, etc.

Sutures – Various sizes of surgical thread, used in closing (stitching up) a wound.

Symptomatology – Specific conditions which indicate the presence of disease, i.e. in pulmonary tuberculosis, this could be a cough, with or without the presence of blood, lasting longer than two weeks, loss of weight, loss of appetite, fever, fatigue and night sweats.

Tetralogy of Fallot – The simplest definition is a condition where there is a congenital 'hole' in the heart; an unnatural opening between one part of the heart and another, which prevents normal cardiac function and could lead to death if not corrected. Tetralogy of Fallot is classically understood to involve four anatomical abnormalities, although only three of them are always present. For further explanation of this, see: http://en.wikipedia.org/wiki/Tetralogy_of_Fallot

Tracheotomy – (Also called tracheostomy) The surgical incision performed to make a hole in the trachea (windpipe) to facilitate breathing. A tracheostomy tube is then inserted into the hole to keep the trachea open. If need be, a respirator can be connected to the tracheostomy tube to mechanically breathe for the patient.

Tuberculosis – A disease, usually of the lungs, caused

by the mycobacterium tuberculosis bacillus, commonly referred to as the TB germ. The individual has had a tuberculosis infection, which has progressed to active disease with signs and symptoms of the illness, an abnormal chest x-ray, and positive bacteriological sputum smear and culture. This individual can be infectious to others, and statistically is considered to be a case of tuberculosis.

Tuberculosis Infection – Tubercle bacilli are present in an individual but they have not progressed to tuberculosis disease. The individual has a positive PPD reaction but has no symptoms, a normal chest x-ray, a negative bacteriological smear and culture and is not considered a case of tuberculosis nor is he infectious to others.

SUGGESTED READING:

Time Bomb, by Lee B. Reichman, MD

Clinician's Guide to Tuberculosis, by Michael D. Iseman, MD MMWR Recommendations and Reports, June 20, 2003/52

(RR11); 1-77 MMWR Recommendations and Reports, November 4, 2005/54 (RR12); 1-81

Thank you for reading.
Please review this book. Reviews help others find Absolutely Amazing eBooks and inspire us to keep providing these marvelous tales.

If you would like to be put on our email list to receive updates on new releases, contests, and promotions, please go to AbsolutelyAmazingEbooks.com and sign up.

About the Author

Peggy Butler retired from hospice nursing in 2002, after 47 years in several diverse fields of nursing, including tuberculosis control. A community and political activist, the author lived on the island of Key West for several years where she reported on the Key West City Commission meetings for a local publication and multiple websites, including her own, and coordinated a food pantry for her church, among other volunteer endeavors. Her debut novel, *Starfish* (SeaStory Press, 2003), was written under her pseudonym, Peg Gregory. Her short stories and professional articles have appeared in national and local publications and won numerous awards. She has two daughters, four granddaughters, and a great-granddaughter in Florida and Kansas. The author recently moved to mainland Florida.

Peggy enjoys hearing from her readers and may be contacted by e-mail at Pegb.gregory@yahoo.com, or through her website, http://www.peggregory.com.

And Then There Was One

photo: Crystal Guerra Photography

Peggy Butler

(left)
Sam, 10, Peg, Lindsey, 10
Emily, 2, Elizabeth 8
Christmas 1994

(below)
Sam, 26, Lindsey, 26
(standing), Emily, 18
Elizabeth, 24, holding her
daughter and Peg's first
great-granddaughter,
Kadence, 1 mo
Thanksgiving 2010

photo: Crystal Guerra Photography

Karen and Stephen
Thanksgiving 2010

Brian and Suzy
Thanksgiving 2010

The New Atlantian Library

NewAtlantianLibrary.com
or AbsolutelyAmazingeBooks.com
or AA-eBooks.com

www.ingramcontent.com/pod-product-compliance
Lightning Source LLC
Chambersburg PA
CBHW071647160426
43195CB00012B/1386